The World of Ceramics

MASTERPIECES FROM THE CLEVELAND MUSEUM OF ART

Edited by
Jenifer Neils

With an introductory essay by
Sherman E. Lee

PUBLISHED BY THE CLEVELAND MUSEUM OF ART

In cooperation with
Indiana University Press

Front Cover:

34 Mosque Lamp. Turkey, Isnik. Ottoman Period, mid-16th century.

Back Cover:

99 Harpist. China (northern). T'ang Dynasty, second quarter 8th century.

Manuscript editing by Jo Zuppan
Photography by Nicholas Hlobeczy
Design by Merald E. Wrolstad
Typesetting by Square Composition, Cleveland, Ohio
Printing by McNaughton and Gunn Lithographers, Ann Arbor, Michigan
Color lithography by Modern Impressions Inc., Eastlake, Ohio

A special exhibition held at The Cleveland Museum of Art
June 30 through September 5, 1982.

Library of Congress Cataloging in Publication Data

Cleveland Museum of Art.
The world of ceramics.
Bibliography: p. 164.
1. Pottery — Exhibitions. 2. Porcelain —
Exhibition. 3. Cleveland Museum of Art —
Exhibition. I. Neils, Jenifer, 1950–
II. Title.
NK3712.C53C52 1982 738'.074'017132 82-1308
ISBN 0-910386-68-4 AACR2

Contents

Color Plates

Following page 22

Following page 54

Following page 86

Following page 150

Contributors

VC	Virginia Crawford
MRC	Michael R. Cunningham
SC	Stanislaw Czuma
HH	Henry Hawley
WCH	Wai-ching Ho
WKH	Wai-kam Ho
HJK	Henry J. Kleinhenz
APK	Arielle P. Kozloff
SEL	Sherman E. Lee
EM	Elizabeth McDevitt
JN	Jenifer Neils
EP	Elinor Pearlstein
MW	Marjorie Williams
PdeW	Patrick de Winter

Preface

Clay — more than any other medium — is universal. Whether modeled into sculpture or thrown into vessels, it constitutes a basic artistic ingredient used by nearly all cultures of the world from prehistoric times to the present. The aesthetic range of ceramics (earthenware, stoneware, and porcelain) is equally broad, from humble cooking pots and mass-produced molded figurines to luxuriously glazed and decorated vases and statuettes. The objects in this exhibition represent the latter end of the spectrum. Drawn from the Museum's collection of over two thousand ceramics, they have been selected for their good condition, high quality, and rarity. Although The World of Ceramics is not intended as a historical survey, it is noteworthy that a general art museum can display such an extensive sampling of master pottery and porcelain from both the Orient and the West.

Even before its doors opened in 1916, The Cleveland Museum of Art had already amassed a number of ceramics, many the gifts or bequests of its founders. The Egyptian collection, including clay vessels and faience *shawabtis* [4–6, 8], was inaugurated in 1914 by the John Huntington Art and Polytechnic Trust. A year later the Hinman B. Hurlbut estate came to the Museum. It included an important Greek drinking cup by the fifth-century BC painter Douris [18], which lay in fragments until rescued and restored in 1953 by the then Curator of Ancient Art, Sherman E. Lee. That same year Ralph King, a Trustee and friend of Charles L. Freer, gave some very fine early Chinese pieces (e.g., [95]). This budding but somewhat erratic assortment was substantially augmented by later gifts and bequests of prominent Cleveland collectors: Worcester R. Warner from 1915 on, J. H. Wade from 1916 on, John L. Severance in 1942, and Elisabeth S. Prentiss in 1944. These four bequests were particularly rich in later Chinese decorative porcelains, collected so avidly in the first two decades of this century as adjuncts to old master paintings and European furniture.

In later years the most significant ceramic objects have been acquired by purchase, either singly or in groups. The most notable instance of a group acquisition was the purchase in 1948 of twenty-five Chinese vessels (e.g., [89, 104, 112, 115]). Formerly in the Henri Riviere collection, these pieces had been on loan to the Museum since 1929 courtesy of Dikran G. Kelekian. This famous dealer was also responsible for the Museum's purchase in 1944 of many important Islamic vases (e.g., [26, 33]). The European ceramics collection was launched by a gift in 1919 from the Reverend Alfred Duane Pell, a benefactor of many American museums. Since then the Museum has added many major pieces, a number of which were bought at the auctions of renowned collections, such as the Damiron Italian maiolica, the Rothschild St. Porchaire ware [52, 53], and the porcelains of J. P. Morgan [63, 67]. During the 1960s the collection of French faience and porcelain was enriched by gifts from R. Henry Norweb [59, 72]. A small number of outstanding pieces have also been donated by private collectors in New York [69, 70, 74]. Although Pre-Columbian objects have been in the Museum since its inception, serious collecting began in the 1930s. Also at that time the American Indian collection was given a boost by a large gift that included twenty-eight pieces of pottery [86]. The donor was Amelia Elizabeth White, the New York gallery owner who was so instrumental in the early appreciation of native American art.

The ceramics collection of The Cleveland Museum of Art has been formed not only by the chance of gifts and the marketplace, but also by the tastes of individuals — directors and curators. Former Director William M. Milliken, for example, was particularly fond of Italian maiolica and European porcelain. Sherman E. Lee is best known for his connoisseurship in the field of Oriental art. Early in his term as Director, he purchased a major group of Chinese imperial porcelains, formerly in the possession of Edward Chow. This eminent collector had obtained these Sung and Ming ceramics [101, 106, 110, 111, 126, 127] from the Salt Bank of Shanghai — a source also used by Sir Percival David — where they were held as loan collateral. Since then the Chinese collection of ceramics has grown steadily so that it now contains nearly all the major classic wares and types. Perhaps less widely known is the Director's acumen in the area of classical vase-painting. Since 1965 the Greek vase collection has grown steadily and has improved immeasurably in quality. The last sixteen years have also seen the purchase of many of the Museum's most important and rare pieces: the white-ground lekythos by Douris [16] and the highly prized Japanese tea ceremony wares [143–147, 149, 150], for example.

In addition to the Museum collection, this exhibition has also drawn on that of Severance A. and Greta Millikin. While their collection is rich in all areas of Oriental ceramics, it is especially the later Japanese porcelains which have so admirably served to fill gaps in the Museum collection. These eighteen objects are gifts with life interest retained, and we are grateful to the Millikins for allowing them to be exhibited.

The World of Ceramics, both exhibition and catalog, has been a collaborative effort on the part of nearly all the departments of the Museum. The following members of the curatorial staff have been responsible for the choice and publication of objects in their particular fields: Arielle P. Kozloff (Ancient Near Eastern and Egyptian), Jenifer Neils (Classical), Patrick de Winter (Medieval and Renaissance), Henry Hawley (Later European and Pre-Columbian), Virginia Crawford (American Indian), Sherman E. Lee (Chinese, Japanese, and Korean), Wai-Kam Ho and Elinor Pearlstein (Chinese), Marjorie Williams (Korean), Michael Cunningham (Japanese), and Stanislaw Czuma (Indian). Miss Pearlstein was especially helpful in coordinating the Oriental sections of the catalog. We are also grateful to Henry Kleinhenz, former assistant to the Chief Curator of Oriental Art, Wai-Ching Ho, and Elizabeth McDevitt for contributing a number of the catalog entries. Special thanks go to those without whose expertise the exhibition and catalog would not have been possible: Nicholas C. Holbeczy (Photographer), William E. Ward (Chief Designer), Merald E. Wrolstad (Chief Editor), and Jo Zuppan (Associate Editor).

Jenifer Neils

Introduction

Poor Johann Friedrich Böttger, torn from his alchemical efforts to produce gold from baser elements, was the "inventor" of porcelain in the West. In 1708 he created, at Albrechtsburg near Dresden, what had already been made in China for at least six centuries — a high-fired ware whose vitreous glaze and body had coalesced to produce a homogeneous unity, embodying whiteness and translucency. Porcelain technically surpasses both the low-fired (1100° C.) earthenware common to most early cultures, and the stonewares, fired at slightly higher temperatures (1200–1300° C.), found in some developed societies in both the East and West. That Böttger was an alchemist is no coincidence, for the perfection of ceramic techniques in both China and Europe depended on the philosophy inherent in the pre-modern science of alchemy. Its technical mysteries transformed the raw materials of ceramic art, first by trial-and-error and progressively by calculated formulas, in ways that often seemed divinely inspired.

Earth, Fire, Water, and Air were the traditional elements of alchemy, both East and West, whatever the esoteric goals desired — ranging from the manufacture of gold to elixirs of longevity and potency. The Four Elements are certainly the essential ingredients of ceramic art. Earth, from lowly clay to nature's already vitreous china clay (kaolin or petuntse), is the basic substance of pots. Fire, from that in the simple open hearth to those in "beehive" or hillside "dragon" kilns, was the means by which earth became useful and permanent. Water was the medium through which earth became plastic and capable of assuming an infinite number of useful and decorative shapes. Air, the atmosphere within the firing enclosure, provided the changing environment — whether full of oxygen (an oxidizing atmosphere) or deprived of it (a reducing atmosphere) — in which the heated earth could be changed in color and texture to become seemingly magically transmuted into ceramic objects, a new class of material totally unlike the raw matter of its origin.

There was a fifth essential ingredient required to produce a pot, an ingredient crucial to its success or failure as a work of art — human hands. The earth has to be shaped, a process requiring both thought and manipulative skill. Man began with simple shapes, mud-pies pinched into elementary receptacles. The clay could also be pressed into or around wood, stone, or other vessels like gourds and baskets and then, by a leap of the imagination, into molds made solely as a means of mass-producing clay forms. The construction of vessels by shaping coils or ropes of hand-rolled clay into jars or cups produced some of the most monumental and sculptural of early ceramics. In turning the pot during this process of coil-building lay the idea of the slow turntable, a flat disc rotated on a pivot. From this followed the most important of all ceramic equipment, the potter's wheel. Fast or slow, the wheel allowed both hands to manipulate and guide the plastic clay into perfectly symmetrical shapes, encouraging the imagination of the potter to infinite possibilities still not exhausted.

Mixes of clay and water varied with the differing speeds of the turning wheel and the thinnest, "soupiest" mixes were found useful not only for decoration applied to already shaped bodies, but also for making vessels, especially plates, by "slip-molds." Instead of pressing stiff clay into a mold, the liquid clay or slip was poured on or into baked but porous clay molds. When the coatings of slip dried, they produced relatively thin, flat wares. The mass-production possibilities of the casting process are as endless as are the shapes made possible by the potter's wheel.

The glazing of ceramics is equally varied and complex. The glazes range from soft, low-fired, and often colorful coatings, with lead or tin as the metallic ingredient, through the various ash-flux, salt-flux coverings on stoneware, to the more difficult varieties of iron-based glazes (and the high-fired, sober-colored iron family), the brilliant copper reduction types, and clear glassy coatings — these last three being commonly used in the porcelain tradition. Decoration can be incised, carved, or applied onto the body of a pot before glazing. Colored slips provide a painterly dimension under transparent or colored glazes; while underglaze copper-reds, iron-browns, and cobalt-blues provide a technically difficult but sophisticated extension of painted decoration. Overglaze enamels allow great varieties of color and require an additional firing process to fix the enamels on the previously fired glaze.

Pre-modern ceramics can be divided into three basic types with some uncertain boundaries among them. The vast majority are utilitarian works — pots, bowls, cups, jugs, platters, and many others. A second group can be described as decorative. These usually occur later in ceramic and social development when luxury items become popular — for instance, tiles, highly decorated vases with no functional intent, ornamental centerpieces, decorative elements in chandeliers and candelabra. The third category is that of ceramic sculpture; these range from crude images of fertility or animal deities to elaborately developed funerary or decorative figurines. Terracotta sculpture was important in societies with strongly developed sculptural traditions such as those of India or Renaissance Italy.

It is both dangerous and difficult to generalize about historical or cultural distinctions in the development and production of ceramics throughout the world. Nevertheless certain broad and general but by no means universal propositions can be defended. First, there is a whole class of ceramics that is studied in its Neolithic beginning, but not in its continuance almost into the twentieth century. These are the ordinary earthenwares or, less commonly, stonewares, made in the billions as everyday household pots in primitive or folk cultures and traditions. They survive in mountains of sherds and thousands of wares usually found in ethnological or anthropological collections. In certain specific social contexts where the folk tradition became a major factor in a later and more sophisticated environment — most notably in Japan — these "folkish" wares became major inspirations for ceramic art.

Secondly, one can discern certain general preferences in the ceramic traditions of high cultures. In the great Chinese tradition one can say that its major theme is the development and refinement of monochrome stoneware and porcelain, whether the green glazed celadons or the white wares of Ting and *ch'ing-pai*. This is not to underestimate Chinese decorated wares, whether the earliest painted tomb potteries of the fourth and third centuries BC, the glaze decorated wares of the fifth to the ninth centuries AD, or the extraordinary development — after the aesthetic revolution of the fourteenth century — in Blue-and-White porcelain and the enameled wares. But even in the Ming and Ch'ing dynasties, equal attention was given to monochrome reds and yellows, while the fabled peach-bloom, ox-blood, and clair-de-lune monochromes of the Ch'ing Dynasty have always commanded the utmost respect. By contrast the Islamic and Western traditions of ceramic art have tended to emphasize decorated wares at the expense of monochrome color. Whether the brilliant and bold designs of Persia and Mesopotamia, the passionate rationality of the pictorial vases of the Greeks, the florid picture painting of the Spanish and Italian maiolica makers, or the elegant and cheerful decorative style of eighteenth-century European porcelain — decoration rather than color or form has dominated the Western tradition.

Thirdly, priority in ceramic art must be assigned to the Far East and particularly to China. There, porcelaneous stoneware goes back to 1500 BC, and true porcelain antedates its European counterpart by at least six hundred years. Chinese porcelain was first imported into the West at places like Samarra (Iran) or Fustat (Egypt) in the ninth and tenth–twelfth centuries respectively. The great Chinese Blue-and-White collections at the Topkapi Serai and at the mosque of Ardebil were formed in the fifteenth and sixteenth centuries. The envy and admiration of Europe for Chinese porcelain is embodied in the use of our word "china."

As a corollary to China's predominance, one increasingly recognizes the importance of the Korean and Japanese ceramic traditions in the Far East. We are only now beginning to understand the informal sobriety of Korean celadons and the white porcelains of the Li Dynasty. The particular and unique contribution of the Japanese potter in his emphasis on roughness and naturalness, especially in the folk and tea taste wares, has been increasingly important to Western ceramics. It has been particularly influential in the Arts and Crafts movement in late nineteenth-century Europe and the vigorous artist-potter movement in the United States and England today. Still the majority of wares we use every day for dining whether at home or out — however much they may owe in ultimate origins to the Orient — are direct inheritances from the European ceramic industry of the eighteenth and nineteenth centuries.

The use of tableware does not normally include more than a cursory examination of what the food is served on. We may note the subject of a stenciled decoration; we may clandestinely examine the bottom of a plate for its factory of origin. But there is a ritual of examination used by all ceramic enthusiasts that, by extension, can become an effective means of aesthetic education. This involves the holding and close study of a single ceramic in an effort to extract as much information and pleasure as is possible from the inanimate but expressive object. The most famous and systematic of these examination systems is the Japanese tea ceremony *(cha-no-yu)*, wherein the ceremony prescribes a time for the study and appreciation of the implements one has just used in the communal experience of drinking powdered green tea. The range of ceramics is restricted and prescribed — tea bowls, cold water jars, serving plates for sweets, and perhaps some non-ceramic objects, to say nothing of the hanging scroll of painting or calligraphy displayed in the appropriate niche. Examining a collection of ceramics, whether Oriental or Western, makes use of the same methods in a less structured and more informal manner. One looks carefully at the glaze and decoration enmeshed within it. One feels the weight and mass of the piece and judges its appropriateness to its form and function. One turns the bowl over to see how the foot rim is finished and how the interior of the foot relates to the general flavor, tone, or feel of the bowl. In this careful scrutiny the serious and purposeful study of ceramics is a prime means of aesthetic education, whether pursued in a potter's workshop, a teahouse, or a museum study room. The problem with the museum display of choice ceramics in glass cases stems from the conflict between the absolute need to protect the objects and the equally absolute need to handle, even fondle, the works so frustratingly removed from the realm of touch. A museum exhibition requires an even more demanding and subtle means of study — the translation of what one sees into an inkling of how it feels. This method of appreciation is comparable to that required in looking at pictorial or sculptural art — where the realization of the values suggested by a material and technique makes an image comprehensible to the mind in both its intellectual and sensuous capacities.

At this level of appreciation, we can imagine collecting ceramics to be not only a gratifying but an important endeavor, and so it can be. But the ever-present Western tendency to classify and specialize can be counter-productive. Unfortunately we have all been subjected to large collections of Chinese export wares mass-produced for "barbarian" consumption, or to the collection based on a rigid theme — whether all-white porcelains or those decorated with a selected motif, from roses to fish — or to the collection of miniatures, or to a compendium of the folk wares from a given Japanese province. The Greek vase galleries of the Louvre or the systematic collections of European porcelains at the Victoria and Albert Museum (however useful they may be for the student of the history, iconography, or technology of ceramics) do not attract even the interested non-specialist to the sheer delight inherent in the miraculously thrown or daringly decorated vessel. Art is as rare in ceramics as it is in any other artistic medium. To discover it requires not only aesthetic discrimination but also an understanding of its history and technology. Ideally both approaches are required, but the beginning is in delectation. And this is how the ceramics shown here have been selected and displayed.

Sherman E. Lee

Ancient Near Eastern

1 The Bear Lady 67.35

Earthenware, fired brick-red. H. 21.5 cm., W. 17 cm. Iran, Marlik. Early Gray Ware, ca. 1200–1000 BC. Purchase, James Albert and Mary Gardiner Ford Memorial Fund.

Our knowledge of early Iranian civilizations is very sketchy. Most of our information has come to us only in the last three decades through scientific excavations. However, commercial "digs" at those same sites, as well as a flood of forgeries, have only served to confuse the issue.

The civilization that existed in northern Iran from the end of the second millennium BC into the first few centuries of the first millenium BC had a number of distinctive characteristics, but one of them, a peculiar type of gray pottery, has given it a name: the "Gray Ware Culture." The name itself is more misleading than helpful because it identifies a group of people who owned not only long-spouted gray ware vessels, but also red burnished wares like the one discussed here [2], as well as wonderful silver and gold vessels and bronze figurines.

Characteristic of early Iranian ceramics are vessels in animal form. This whimsical example is a version of a favorite type with its mouth open and lower lip pinched forward to act as a spout. The "Bear Lady" duplicates a vessel found by Dr. Ezat Negahban, the excavator of Marlik. The creature displays human female genitalia as she reaches forward with bestial paws (to embrace a lover in a bear hug?). Her ears are in the form of two small, pierced lugs which may have acted as suspension loops or perhaps were simply decorated with earrings. APK

LITERATURE Edith Porada et al., *7000 Years of Iranian Art* (Washington: Smithsonian Institution, 1964) pp. 58, 122, no. 46. Dr. Ezat O. Negahban, "The Wonderful Gold Treasures of Marlik: A First Report from a Newly Discovered First Millennium BC Mound in Northern Iran," *Illustrated London News*, 28 April 1962, p. 663. "Further Finds from Marlik," *Illustrated London News*, 5 May 1962, p. 699.

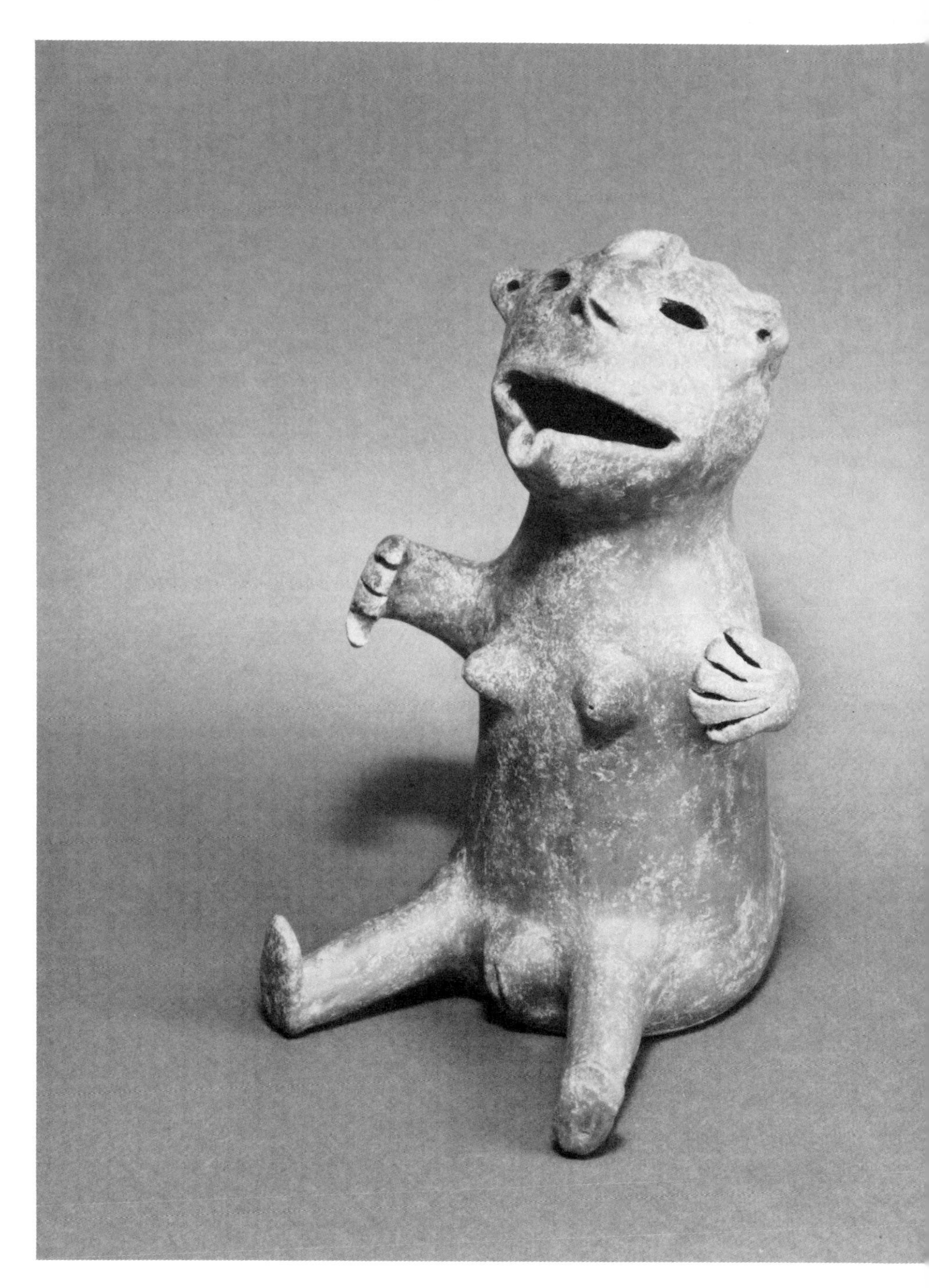

2 Massive Jug 77.180

Earthenware, burnished brick-red. H. 44.2 cm., Diam. 38.8 cm., Diam. of mouth 10.3 cm. Iran, Marlik. Early Gray Ware, Iron Age II, ca. 1200–1000 BC. Gift of Osborne and Gratia Hauge.

Although this type of earthenware was produced over several centuries in Iran, the elegance and technical perfection of this voluptuous vessel impel one toward assigning it to the Marlik culture of northern Iran. Discovered in 1961, the royal cemetery at Marlik has surrendered a wealth of objects in gold, silver, bronze, glass, and clay to its excavators. The generally high technical quality of the Marlik finds is very much in keeping with the perfectly balanced, thin-walled construction of this huge vase.

The pomegranate — which still grows wild in Iran — was a symbol of fertility and therefore a favorite shape at Marlik. Perhaps this jug is a stylized version of that shape. Pomegranate-shaped pendants and beads were made for gold necklaces and earrings; bronze pomegranate bells might have had some ritual use. While the purpose of this massive jug is no longer known, one senses here the work of a fine craftsman and a product surely destined for ritual or royal use. APK

LITERATURE See [1].

3 Four-Legged Ewer 42.1081

Buff earthenware with small inclusions, reddish-brown slip decoration. H. 19.3 cm., W. 18 cm., L. 23.2 cm. Iran, Luristan. Iron Age II, ca. 1000–800 BC. Purchase from the J. H. Wade Fund.

Nearly contemporary with the Gray Ware Iron Age II culture of Northern Iran (see [1, 2]), was a group of people who settled in southwest Iran, in the Luristan region. It is quite possible that both of these cultures derived from the same source west of Tehran, but that their cultures diverged after settling in different regions. Some of the painted decorations on this vessel, such as the striated "kite" and the simplified "Kassite cross," are considered Bronze Age motifs and suggest an overlapping of the Luristan and northern cultures.

The buff fabric and reddish-brown decoration of this ewer fit well into what is called the "genre Luristan" ware. Teapot-shaped vessels, mostly in sherds, with beaked spouts and twisted basket handles adorned with animal heads are ubiquitous among the finds in Iron Age II cemeteries in this region. The Cleveland example has all of these features attached to a very amusing shape. Its body is formed of three simple jugs joined at their midsections like Siamese triplets. The forward jug — determined by the spout and the animal head — is supported by two stocky legs. Another stout limb supports each of the rear jugs, which, by their position, are turned into very rounded, well-fed animal haunches. APK

LITERATURE Clare Goff, "Excavations at Baba Jan: The Pottery and Metals from Levels III and II," *Iran (Journal of Persian Studies)* XVI (1978) 29-38. Clare Goff Meade, "Luristan in the First Half of the First Millennium B.C.," *Iran (Journal of Persian Studies)* VI (1968) 115-126.

Egyptian

4 Jar with Nautical Scene 14.639

Buff-colored earthenware with brownish-red slip decoration. H. 31.4 cm., Diam. 28.27 cm. Egypt, possibly Naqada or Ballas. Predynastic Period (Naqada II or Gerzean) 3200–3000 BC. Gift of the John Huntington Art and Polytechnic Trust.

The cemeteries of Naqada and nearby Ballas comprised more than three thousand graves, which yielded, among other funerary goods, buff-colored pottery decorated in reddish-brown pigment with many-oared boats, antelopes, flamingos, trees, and human beings. These figures were often placed among solid-colored triangles, set side by side like rows of sharks' teeth, probably representing a mountainous landscape.

The stylized mountain ranges have been used by some scholars to strengthen the identification of a foreign landscape, though they could represent Egypt's own desert ridges. Topping each of the boats' masts is a different sign which, judging from similar examples, are province or tribal insignias. Many-oared, tall-masted ships like the two on the Cleveland vase imply long-range travel. The flattened crescent shape of these ships, as contrasted to the high-bow and high-stern pleasure boats of the period, seem in keeping with cargo vessels. The boxy, two-handled devices amidships — which have often been called cabins — are probably better identified as wooden or even basketry cargo containers. Three similar containers remain on shore, one of them holding a flowering plant. Such containers pictured in a few other Gerzean paintings have carry poles drawn through their handles.

This type of vessel would have been made for funerary purposes as a storage container full of grain for use in the afterlife. APK

PUBLICATION Caroline Ransom Williams, "The Egyptian Collection in the Museum of Art at Cleveland, Ohio," *Journal of Egyptian Archaeology* V (1918) 166.

LITERATURE Sir W. M. Flinders Petrie, *Prehistoric Egypt: Corpus of Prehistoric Pottery and Palettes* (Warminster, England: Aris and Phillips, Ltd., 1974) pp. 16-22, pls. XIX-XXIII, XXXXIII-XXXV. Björn Landström, *Ships of the Pharaohs* (Garden City: Doubleday, 1970) pp. 12-13.

5 Honey Pot 14.609

Green-blue faience with manganese decoration. H. 10.5 cm., Diam. 7.3 cm. Egypt. Late Dynasty XII, ca. 1700 BC. Gift of the John Huntington Art and Polytechnic Trust.

The term "faience" is applied to two entirely different ceramic compositions, one produced in the ancient Near East (most characteristically in Egypt) and the other in seventeenth- to nineteenth-century Europe (see [59]). We do not know exactly how ancient Egyptian faience was made, but the result is a porous body consisting largely of quartz held together by a glass-like binder and covered with a colored glaze. The glaze itself is a glass-like coating that adheres well to the faience body because of its high quartz content. Ordinary pottery requires that lead-oxide be added to the glaze in order for it to adhere.

Faience appeared on a modest scale as early as the late Predynastic Period. For the remainder of this lengthy civilization it became a favored luxury fabric for everything from small amulets, like the frog [7],to jewelry, to vessels and sculptures both large and small. In quality this material reached its apex in late Dynasty XVIII under the reign of Amenhotep III and his immediate followers. The astonishing colors — not just blue, green, and turquoise, but also brilliant white, yellows and reds — that were achieved at this time required perfect control over temperatures in kilns.

This type of container is rare, and its date and use have always been uncertain. However, in an unpublished discussion, John Cooney compared these pots to jars in painted and sculpted offering scenes where similar conical-roofed vessels filled with honey (according to the hieroglyphic legend) were presented to gods, kings, and noblemen.

The jar itself is a thick-walled cylinder with six holes piercing its lip. Cooney felt that a piece of fine linen was stretched across the top and sewn onto the lip in order to keep out insects. The conical lid is pierced once to allow a slim but even flow of honey to trickle onto the waiting piece of bread or fruit.

Both cover and box are decorated with standard Egyptian marsh fauna and flora: a register of lotuses on the box, above which dances a chorus line of wing-flapping ducks, and on top are two more ducks with papyri and lotuses. The drawing all over is crude, which seems at variance with the proposed luxurious nature of the object. APK

LITERATURE On faience see Sidney M. Goldstein, *Pre-Roman and Early Roman Glass in the Corning Museum of Glass* (Corning, N.Y., 1979) pp. 12-13.

6 Flask in the Shape of a Seed Bag 14.726

Earthenware, fired reddish brown with brown slip details; sealed with clay. H. 13.5 cm., W. 4.7 cm. Egypt. Dynasty XVIII, ca. reign of Tuthmosis III, 1479–1425 BC. Gift of the John Huntington Art and Polytechnic Trust.

During the reign of Tuthmosis III, highly burnished reddish-brown ware was transformed into a variety of sculptured shapes, from obese or pregnant women to a magnificent ibex with its fawn in the Louvre, to heads and figures of the domestic god Bes. Despite the vast predynastic production of clay vessels, Egypt was never artistically strong in earthenware during historic times. The far more colorful materials of glass and faience easily usurped the position of clay in the garish taste of the times. Burnished ware similar to this example was something of an anomaly in a land of thick-walled, coarsely decorated vases. The workmanship seems more compatible with that of Cyprus and Anatolia, although the motifs produced in this ware are purely Egyptian.

The subject is the farmer's seed bag, illustrated in countless agricultural scenes on tomb walls and carried by *shawabtis* [8]. The exact use of these clay containers is unknown. Similarly dated alabaster vessels in the shape of over-large women are now thought to have been filled with an ointment used during pregnancy. Most of the red burnished ware vases known seem to carry some sort of reproductive connotation. APK

PUBLICATION C. R. Williams, *Journal of Egyptian Archaeology*, V (1918) 166.

LITERATURE W. M. F. Petrie, *Sedment II* (London, 1924) pl. LVII (33), p. 24 (41). Emma Brunner-Traut, "Gravidenflasche," *Archäologie und altes Testament: Festschrift für Kurt Galling* (Tübingen, 1970) pp. 35-48. Christiane Desroches-Noblecourt, "Pots Anthropomorphes et recettes magico-médicales dans l'Égypte ancienne," *Revue d'égyptologie*, IX (1952) 49-67.

7 Frog Amulet 80.123

Blue and red faience. H. 0.9 cm., W 1.1 cm. Egypt, El Amarna (?). Dynasty XVIII, late 15th–14th centuries BC. Gift of Cyril and Jessica Aldred.

Frog amulets were commonly worn by both the living and the dead in antiquity as a charm that provided fertility for the former and rejuvenation and everlasting life for the latter. These items were especially popular during the New Kingdom, when they were made in a variety of materials, from gold to faience to semiprecious stones. This particular example, pierced longitudinally for attachment, is inscribed on its underside with the hieroglyphic *nefer* sign, meaning "beautiful" or "good."

Naturalism was the hallmark of late Dynasty XVIII art. To have achieved this marvelously detailed imitation of nature on such small scale as this little frog required the hand of a master craftsman. APK

LITERATURE Arielle P. Kozloff, ed., *Animals in Ancient Art from the Leo Mildenberg Collection* (Cleveland: The Cleveland Museum of Art, 1981) pp. 60-61, no. 47.

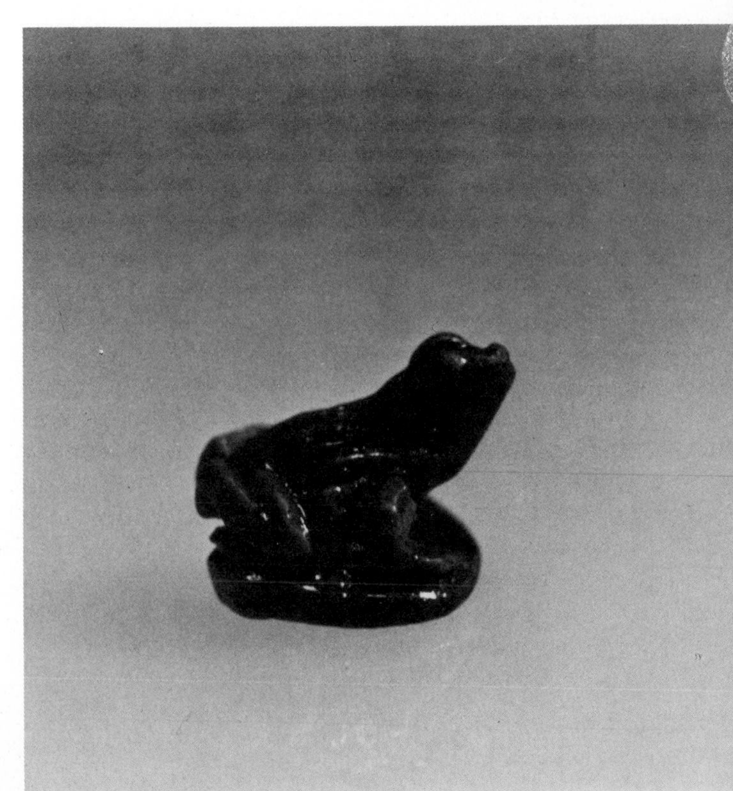

8 *Shawabti* of King Nectanebo II 20.1989

Light blue faience, mat finish. H. 19 cm., W. 5.8 cm. Egypt. Dynasty XXX, 360–343 BC. Gift of the John Huntington Art and Polytechnic Trust.

The ancient Egyptian view of the afterlife was carried to such an extent that in earliest dynastic times, servants were actually sacrificed after their master's death and buried with him. In the Old Kingdom, these living retainers were humanely replaced by limestone statuettes. Then, in the Middle Kingdom, perhaps in response to a somewhat more democratic philosophy, new funerary figurines appeared. These were not statues of lowly, second-class individuals, but figures of the deceased himself. As time went on, virtually every individual of high or low status was buried with at least a few *shawabtis*. At first, it was not clear exactly what function this new figurine was to perform, but by early Dynasty XIII the ritual was set. The spell that involves the *shawabti*'s duties says that if the deceased is called on (by the gods) to do any work in the fields, the *shawabti*, as the deceased's surrogate, is to say, "Here am I" and shoulder the work for him. In fact, the *shawabti*'s name, later *ushabti*, is ancient Egyptian for "I will answer." In keeping with their duties in the next world each *shawabti* carries the tools of his trade such as hoes, seed bags (see [6]), and baskets.

This *shawabti* is inscribed with the name of Nectanebo II, who was the second and last significant king of Dynasty XXX. His *shawabti* is mold-made and exhibits a clarity and precision of detail rarely achieved in molded ceramics. APK

LITERATURE Jacques Aubert, *Statuettes égyptiennes: chaouabtis, ouchebtis* (Paris: Adrien Maisonneuve, 1974).

9 Openwork Spacer Bead 16.661

Blue faience. L. 5.4 cm., W. 2.5 cm. Egypt, possibly Tuna el-Gebel. Probably Dynasty XXII (ca. 945–712 BC). Gift of Mr. and Mrs. J. H. Wade.

Delicate, double-sided openwork was a hallmark of Dynasty XXII faience. Although this rare piece is called a "bead," it seems too fragile to have been worn as jewelry. Its long sides are pierced ten times each for the insertion of wires or threads to add it to a more complex design. Perhaps it was attached to either a ritual object or a gift to the king.

One side is a symmetrical design centering on a head of the goddess Hathor resting on the hieroglyph for "gold." This is flanked by Double Crowned *uraei* (cobras), each facing a winged cobra which hovers above an illegible cartouche. The design terminates on the viewer's right with the *ma'at* feather of truth and on the left with what may be the ribbed palm frond which stands for "year." (A spacer bead in the British Museum is inscribed with good wishes for the New Year.) The other side bears two scenes of rather indistinct figures: on the left the king appears to grasp a foreigner by the hair and salute a god who faces him from behind an offering table; on the right the king, wearing the Double Crown, faces two deities who stand on the other side of a double cartouche. APK

10 Lion Head 74.87

Blue-green faience. H. 2.9 cm., W. 3 cm. Egypt. Dynasty XXVII, Persian Period, 525–404 BC. Purchase, A. W. Ellenberger, Sr. Memorial Endowment Fund.

The lion, symbol of Egyptian royalty, was rarely disturbed from his benevolent close-mouthed pose during the many centuries of Egyptian history. The Persian Period was one of two times (the other being the reign of Tutankhamen) when lion sculptures opened their mouths to roar. In both cases, this aggressive expression is certainly influenced by leonine representations from the Near East. During the Persian Period, as in this example, other features, such as the exaggerated canthus of the eye, bulging brow muscles and eyeballs, also attest to the influence of Eastern styles.

The piece is finished flat in back and pierced vertically in back of the head, through the animal's mane. A similar-sized lion head, made of "Egyptian blue," in the Norbert Schimmel collection, holds an African's head in its jaws and is pierced horizontally through its neck. The subject matter is so close to the stem terminal on one of Ramesses III's boats in a relief at Medinet Habu, that one wonders if the Schimmel and Cleveland heads once decorated the stems of model boats or miniature ceremonial boats. APK

LITERATURE Oscar Muscarella, ed. *Ancient Art: The Norbert Schimmel Collection* (Mainz: Philipp von Zabern, 1974) no. 202 (entry by J. D. Cooney, there discussed as a furniture ornament). Landström, *Ships of the Pharaohs*, pp. 111-112.

Classical

11 Funerary Neck-Amphora 27.6

Earthenware with slip decoration. H. 59 cm., Diam. of body 29.5 cm. Greece, Athens, attributed to the Workshop of Athens 894. Late Geometric II, ca. 720 BC. Purchase from the J. H. Wade Fund.

The earliest phase of Greek pottery is termed Geometric because of the vase painters' penchant for decorating the surface of their pots with abstract, linear ornament. Gradually animal and then human figures are admitted to the reper-

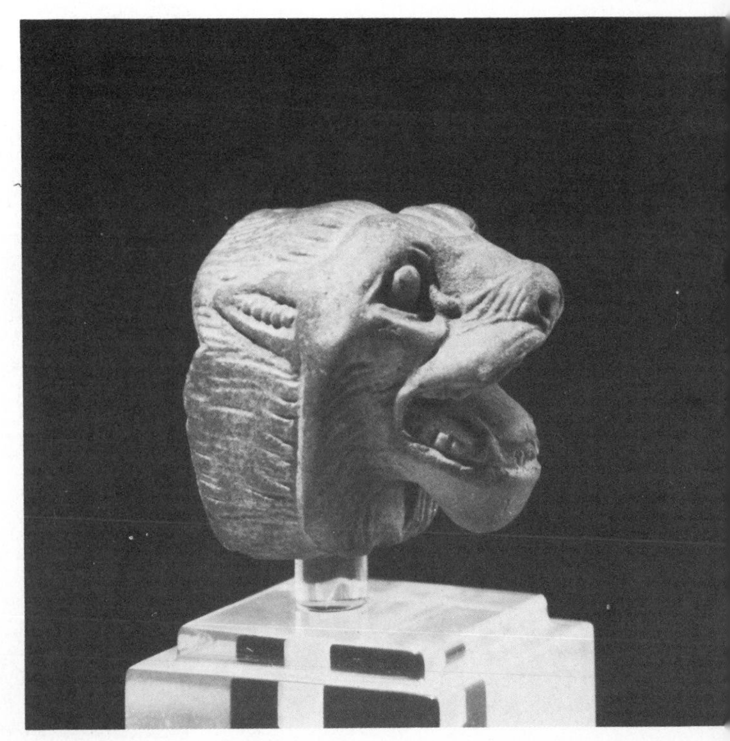

toire of motifs, but in style and repetitive treatment they conform to the rectilinear decoration. The first narrative scenes in Greek art appear on vases at the very end of the Geometric Period (900–700 BC). Their imagery is closely related to the function of these early vessels, as grave-markers or ossuaries. The two most common subjects are the *prothesis*, or laying out of the corpse, usually accompanied by mourning women, and the *ekphora*, or funeral cortège.

The Cleveland amphora displays both. The neck panels show the deceased lying on a bier over which hangs a checkered pall. Four mourners in trailing skirts flank the bier, while a fifth crouches beneath. A series of six more mourners moves solemnly to the right on the reverse panel. The continuous file of two-horse chariots around the belly of the vase represents a procession in honor of the dead. A lone foot soldier with a round shield and two spears accompanies the horsemen. The lowest figured register shows hounds chasing a hare. These narrative bands are firmly anchored on the vase by subsidiary bands of dense geometric design, the most distinctive being the large meander just below the lip. Zigzags and lozenges fill the empty spaces around the figures. In addition to the painted ornament, applied snakes — symbolic of the underworld — writhe along the shoulders, handles, and rim.

This amphora is assigned to a prolific Athenian workshop of the late eighth century whose products represent a decisive turning point in Greek vase painting. Growing restless under the rigid discipline of the ripe Geometric style, these painters are looser and more expressive, occasionally sloppy, and look forward to the full-bloom figurative compositions of the seventh century. JN

PUBLICATIONS Cedric Boulter, *Corpus Vasorum Antiquorum*, Cleveland Museum of Art, fasc. 1, U.S.A. fasc. 15 (Princeton: Princeton University Press, 1971) pp. 3-4 (with earlier bibliography), pls. 2 and 3.1 (hereafter cited as *CVA*). Elizabeth Finkenstaedt, "Mycenaean Mourning Customs in Greek Painting," CMA *Bulletin*, LX (February 1973) 39-43, figs. 1-4.

LITERATURE J. N. Coldstream, *Greek Geometric Pottery* (London: Methuen and Co., 1968) esp. pp. 58-64.

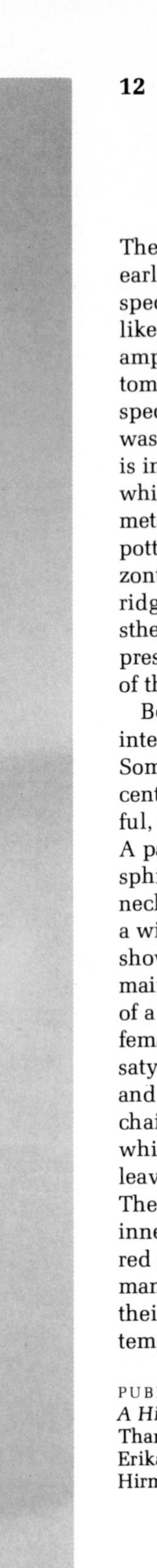

12 Nikosthenic Amphora 74.10

Earthenware with slip decoration. H. 31.1 cm., Diam. of body 16.9 cm. Greece, Athens, attributed to Painter N. Signed: Nikosthenes epoiesen. Ca. 530 BC. Purchase from the J. H. Wade Fund.

The Athenian potter Nikosthenes was an early Greek entrepreneur. His workshop specialized in vases of unusual shape, like this amphora. Since nearly every example has been found in an Etruscan tomb, it is certain that they were made specifically for export. That Nikosthenes was aiming his trade at the Italian market is indicated by the shapes of his vases which imitate Etruscan wares, either of metal or *bucchero*, the shiny black local pottery. Hence, amphoras with thin horizontal lips, broad strap handles, and ridges on the belly are called Nikosthenic. The Cleveland example even preserves the potter's signature under one of the handles.

Besides the shape, the decoration was intended to appeal to provincial taste. Somewhat old-fashioned for the late sixth century, but nonetheless lively and colorful, are the dancing figures and animals. A pair of lions flanks a white-faced sphinx on each shoulder. Each side of the neck displays two nude frolicking youths; a wine bowl, the source of their gaiety, is shown between them on the front. The main frieze, encircling the belly, consists of a procession of dancing maenads, or female revelers, alternating with pudgy satyrs, identifiable by their equine tails and ears. A double palmette-and-lotus chain decorates the handles (one of which is partially restored), while ivy leaves and dotted rosettes adorn the lip. The black slip is incised to mark the inner details and is enlivened with added red and white. The lively color and the mannered gestures of the dancers find their mural-sized counterparts in contemporary tomb paintings in Etruria. JN

PUBLICATIONS P. E. Arias and Max Hirmer, *A History of Greek Vase Painting* (London: Thames and Hudson, 1962) pl. XIII (color). Erika Simon, *Die griechischen Vasen* (Munich: Hirmer, 1976) pl. XIII.

13 Black-Figure *Dinos* 71.46

Earthenware with slip decoration. H. 33.6 cm., Diam. 50.8 cm. Greece, Athens, attributed to the Circle of the Antimenes Painter. Ca. 520 BC. Purchase, John L. Severance Fund.

Among the ancient Greeks large bowls had two major functions. They were dedicated to the gods and, depending on the largesse of the donor, were often of bronze. And they were used at drinking parties for serving the heavy wine which was diluted with water. The Cleveland example represents one of many bowl shapes known as the *dinos* because of its rounded bottom which necessitated a stand. Both its shape and its shiny black exterior reflect a metal prototype.

Painted decoration is restricted to the rim. On the top are six combats: three mythological (Theseus slaying the Minotaur, Herakles fighting the centaur Nessos, and Herakles wrestling the Nemean lion) and three military (fully armored warriors dueling with spears). Serving to separate the combats one from the next is a four-horse chariot driven by a man carrying a shield over his back and accompanied by a spectator, who acts as a filler in the space over the horses's rump. A look inside the bowl reveals another continuous figural frieze along the interior rim. Here plying the "wine-dark" sea are five ships, fully rigged and equipped with bands of oarsmen. Such ships commonly decorate the interior of *dinoi*, for when filled with wine they offer a picturesque setting for the sailing vessels. The restraint of the black-figure decoration, which relies on incision and added red for its details, gives a special elegance to the vase and accentuates the lustrous black slip which was the *sine qua non* of Attic vase painting. JN

PUBLICATIONS Barbara Kathman, "A Trio of Late Black-Figure Vase Painters," CMA *Bulletin* LXVI (February 1979) 54-57, figs. 8, 9, 11. Warren G. Moon and Louise Berge, *Greek Vase-Painting in Midwestern Collections*, exhib. cat. (Chicago: The Art Institute of Chicago, 1979) pp. 110-111, no. 63 (entry by B. Kathman).

14 Black-Figure *Hydria* 75.1

Earthenware with slip decoration. H. 42.2 cm., Diam. with handles 37.6 cm. Greece, Athens, attributed to the Antimenes Painter. Ca. 520 BC. Purchase from the J. H. Wade Fund.

Complete and in an excellent state of preservation, this ancient vase epitomizes the best of Attic black-figure vase painting and potting. The shape, a *hydria* or three-handled water jug, is both functional and aesthetically pleasing. The widely flaring rim nicely balances the broad flat shoulder. The two horizontal handles, which were used for lifting and carrying, are set at the widest part of the body, which tapers down to a disc foot. The vertical handle at the back connects lip and body and served for pouring. Likewise the decoration of the vase strikes a harmonious balance between the shiny black areas and the figured panels with their orange clay background.

The subject matter of the panels represents the three main concerns of black-figure artists: myth, genre, and animals. The shoulder shows the Cretan bull-man or Minotaur about to be slain by the Attic hero Theseus in the company of two maidens and two youths who represent the annual tribute to King Minos. Such a myth which featured their local hero naturally appealed to Athenian artists. The main panel displays a frontal war-chariot flanked by a pair of armed warriors. To the chariot are harnessed four elegant black horses: the inner two nuzzling each other, as the others look outward. Holding a goad and wearing a long white robe, the charioteer stands ready in the cart along with a third warrior. The narrow register, or predella, is devoted to animals: two lions attacking a doe in the center, while a stag grazes nonchalantly at either end. Although panels on vases such as this often have nothing in common, the scenes here display an interest

See also color plate following page 22.

in different modes of combat: heroic, mortal, and bestial.

The *hydria* is attributed to an anonymous artist called the Antimenes Painter. His style is distinguished by its great control and precision, here demonstrated not only in the figures but also in the careful palmette ornament. The Antimenes Painter decorated many large vases, but this is certainly among his finest. JN

EXHIBITION Zurich, 1974: Archäologisches Institut der Universität Zürich, Das Tier in der Antike, exhib. cat. by Hansjorg Bloesch et al., p. 39, no. 225, pl. 38.

PUBLICATIONS Barbara Kathman, "A Trio of Late Black-Figure Vase Painters," CMA *Bulletin*, LXVI (February 1979) 49-54, figs. 1, 2, 4. W. G. Moon and L. Berge, *Greek Vase-Painting in Midwestern Collections*, pp. 106-107, no. 61 (entry by B. Kathman).

15 Red-Figure Eye-Cup 76.89

Earthenware with slip decoration. H. 11.2 cm., W. 33.6 cm. Greece, Athens, attributed to Psiax. Ca. 520 BC. Purchase from the J. H. Wade Fund.

Psiax, to whom this unsigned cup is attributed, was a "bilingual" artist. He painted in two techniques: black-figure (see [13, 14]) and red-figure, which was invented in Athens ca. 530 BC. One of the reasons for the appearance of red-figure was the desire on the part of the more progressive Athenian vase painters to depict lifelike figures and convincing movement, forms which were not attainable in the stiff, silhouettelike black-figure. As a pioneer in the new technique, Psiax exerted a significant influence on the first generation of red-figure vase painters. The Cleveland kylix is called an eye-cup because of the pairs of eyes prominently featured between the handles. Such eyes appeared on Greek vases as early as the seventh century BC, and were believed by the ancients to have apotropaic qualities. Since the eyes would interrupt any narrative composition, Psiax simply placed three isolated figures on either side, linking them by pose and movement. The most important figures, the falling warrior and the cithara (lyre) player, are placed in the center between the eyes. From the edges of side A, two attendant warriors rush to the aid of their helpless comrade. On the other side, two young men are listening to the music. Psiax's interest in anatomy (note especially the abdominal muscles of the fallen warrior) and movement is most clearly demonstrated by the central characters. Although somewhat awkwardly posed, they are nevertheless bold for the period and convey a vitality new to Attic vase painting. JN

PUBLICATIONS Stella Patitucci Uggeri, "Kylix di Psiax in una collezione ticinese," *Quaderni Ticinesi*, I (1972) 33-60. J. R. Mertens, "Some New Vases by Psiax," *Antike Kunst*, XXII (1979) 31-33, pl. 13, 1, 2, 4, 6. W. G. Moon and L. Berge, *Greek Vase-Painting in Midwestern Collections*, pp. 104-105, no. 60 (entry by J. R. Mertens).

LITERATURE John Boardman, *Athenian Red-Figure Vases: The Archaic Period* (London: Thames and Hudson, 1975). Beth Cohen, *Attic Bilingual Vases and Their Painters* (New York: Garland Publishing, 1978).

16 White-Ground *Lekythos* 66.114

Earthenware with slip decoration. H. 32.5 cm., Diam. of body 12.2 cm. Greece, Athens, attributed to Douris. Ca. 500–490 BC. Purchase, Leonard C. Hanna Jr. Bequest.

Rarest and usually finest of Athenian vases are the so-called "white-ground." The decorated portion of the vase is covered with a creamy slip and the painting executed in diluted black slip which can vary in tone from pale tan to shiny black. Freed from the constraints imposed by the black- and red-figure techniques, the white-ground artist was able to draw his composition freehand, as if on paper. In fact, such vase paintings are the ancient counterpart of fine master drawings.

Among these already exceptional vases, the Cleveland *lekythos* (oil flask) stands out as an incomparable piece. It is one of only three white-ground vases attributed to Douris, an important artist of the early fifth century (cf. also [17, 18]); one is in a Swiss private collection, the other a mere fragment in the Palermo Museum. The subject is unique: Atalanta running with three Erotes in pursuit. The closest Eros is offering her the alternatives of love: a wreath representing the joys and a flail, the torments. Finally, the composition is cleverly adapted to the action as well as the shape. Most *lekythoi* are decorated only on the front (cf. [17]), but here Douris has spread the figures entirely around the cylindrical body. When the vase is rotated to the right, one's eye is led by diagonals from one figure to the next so that Atalanta's plight is unending. JN

PUBLICATIONS J. D. Cooney, "Atalanta in Cleveland," CMA *Bulletin*, LIII (October 1966) 318-325. *CVA*, pp. 21-23, pls. 32-34 and 35, 1. W. G. Moon and L. Berge, *Greek Vase Painting in Midwestern Collections*, no. 104, pp. 184-185 (entry by A. P. Kozloff).

LITERATURE For the *lekythos* in the Swiss collection, which is probably the work of the same potter as the Cleveland *lekythos*, see José Dörig, *Art Antique, Collections privées de Suisse romande* (Mainz: Philipp von Zabern, 1975) no. 205.

17 Red-Figure *Lekythos* 78.59

Earthenware with slip decoration. H. 38 cm., Diam. 14.1 cm. Greece, Athens, attributed to Douris. Ca. 480 BC. Purchase from the J. H. Wade Fund.

Another *lekythos* by Douris, this, however, is painted in the red-figure technique. The scheme of decoration is also more traditional with two figures placed at the front of the vase. They are the warrior goddess Athena engaged in combat with the giant Enkelados. She is moving in swiftly from the left, her spear poised overhead, and her round shield held forth for protection. Highly unusual is the profile view of the Medusa head on her aegis; the Gorgon is usually shown frontally. Before her and collapsing backwards is her opponent who resembles a Greek hoplite. His pirouetting pose is extremely complex and dynamic for the period. The three-quarter face, upturned eyes, loosening grip, and blood streaming from his side and thigh all convey his helplessness. There is no question of his fate, symbolized by his broken spear in the background. This scene is an excerpt from the larger theme of the Gigantomachy, a battle between the Olympian deities and the giants of Greek mythology. It was represented in marble on the east pediment of the old Temple of Athena on the Athenian Acropolis (dated ca. 520 BC). There Athena also figures prominently in the center, striding to the right — the traditional side of victory — with a dying giant underfoot.

The Cleveland Museum of Art now possesses three vases by Douris (see [16, 18]), a fortuitous happenstance that allows comparison of his changing style. At the transitional point in his career represented by this vase, Douris is striving for more ambitious compositions, complicated poses, and greater detail. JN

EXHIBITION Chicago, 1979–1980: The Art Institute of Chicago, Greek Vase-Painting in Midwestern Collections, cat. by Warren G. Moon and Louise Berge, pp. 186-187, no. 105, color pl. VI (entry by A. P. Kozloff).

18 Red-Figure Kylix 508.15

Earthenware with slip decoration. H. (with restored foot) 12 cm., Diam. 29.5 cm. Greece, Athens, attributed to Douris. Ca. 480–475 BC. The Hinman B. Hurlbut Collection.

Douris was a prolific artist; over three hundred of his vases are extant, the vast majority of which are kylixes, or wine cups. The themes he chose often related to the function of the vessel, as in this case. The interior shows Dionysos, the god of wine, recognizable by his large-handled drinking cup known as a *kantharos* (see [20]), ivy wreath, and grape-laden vine. He is accompanied by a dancing satyr. On the exterior are quintets of frolicking satyrs and Dionysos's female followers, maenads. Drunken revelers and the god of wine are apt decoration for a kylix, and Douris painted remarkably similar figures on other cups (e.g., Fogg Art Museum 1925.30.129 and Boston Museum of Art 00.499).

As compared to the Atalanta *lekythos* [16], there is much greater calm and dignity in this scene. Also characteristic of Douris's later style are the somewhat static poses and schematized drapery folds. Nonetheless, as Beazley, the great connoisseur of Attic vase painting, noted, "the red-figured cup is a very good and important piece." JN

EXHIBITION Chicago, 1979–1980: The Art Institute of Chicago, Greek Vase-Painting in Midwestern Collections, cat. by Warren G. Moon and Louise Berge, pp. 188-189, no. 106, repr. (entry by A. P. Kozloff).

PUBLICATIONS Sherman E. Lee, "A Cup by Douris," *American Journal of Archaeology*, LVIII (1954) 230. *CVA*, p. 24, pls. 37, 2 and 38.

19 Red-Figure *Lekythos* 28.660

Earthenware with slip decoration. H. 43.6 cm., Diam. of body 14.4 cm. Greece, Athens, attributed to the Oionokles Painter. Ca. 480–470 BC. Purchase, Charles W. Harkness Endowment Fund.

In contrast to the earlier *lekythoi* [16, 17], this vase depicts a quiet scene, the moment before battle. A warrior, having donned his protective armor (corselet and greaves), holds sword in hand and is concentrating on cutting off a lock of his hair. While the figure may be an anonymous Greek soldier making a propitiatory dedication before going into combat, comparison with an inscribed vase suggests that he is Parthenopaios, one of the Seven against Thebes. These warriors fastened locks of their hair onto the chariot of the commander Adrastos as mementos for their parents back in Argos in the event of their deaths (Aeschylus, *Seven Against Thebes*, 49). Although isolated from his comrades in arms, this lone warrior evokes in his ceremonious and fateful act the dire consequences of the encounter outside the gates of Thebes.

In terms of draftsmanship and composition the painting is masterful. Especially noteworthy are the details of the armor, such as the anatomical markings on the breastplate, the inner webbing of the large shield, and the rampant lion on the cheek-flap of the elaborate crested helmet. The sword and spear form the apex of a well-balanced triangular composition. A smaller, broader triangle is formed by the three crosses, on the neck-guard and at the two upper corners of the stool. JN

EXHIBITION Chicago, 1979–1980: The Art Institute of Chicago, Greek Vase-Painting in Midwestern Collections, cat. by Warren G. Moon and Louise Berge, pp. 164-165, no. 94, repr. (entry by L. Berge).

PUBLICATIONS *CVA*, pp. 20-21, pl. 31. Norbert Kunisch, "Parthenopaios," *Antike Kunst*, XVII (1974) 39, pl. 8, 1. John Boardman, *Athenian Red Figure Vases* (London: Thames and Hudson, 1975) pp. 194-195, fig. 361.

20 Janiform *Kantharos* 79.69

Molded earthenware with slip decoration. H. 19.6 cm., W. 17.2 cm. Greece, Athens, assigned to the Toronto Class. Ca. 470–460 BC. Purchase, John L. Severance Fund.

A two-headed, twin-handled drinking cup, this *kantharos* is less a masterwork of the potter's or painter's art than one of the modeler's. The two bearded heads — one a satyr, the other a Negro — were made in molds with certain features like the satyr's large equine ears added freehand. The lip with its lotus and palmette decoration was thrown on a wheel and attached to the conjoined heads. While the two faces have similar features like the pug nose and bared teeth, it is the painting and modeled additions that distinguish them. The Negro has black skin and woolly hair; the balding satyr wears a banqueting garland and has a broad black beard.

Although Negro and satyr heads are common on such vases, they are usually paired with a white female head. The Cleveland combination is thus far unique but is eminently logical on the grounds that both were exotic types, well known for their addiction to wine. Head vases, like their modern counterparts, Toby jugs, were no doubt as amusing in antiquity as they are today. JN

PUBLICATION Arielle P. Kozloff, "Companions of Dionysus," CMA *Bulletin*, LXVII (September 1980) 206-211, covers (color), figs. 2-3.

21 Apulian Red-Figure *Situla* 77.179

Earthenware with slip decoration. H. at rim 28 cm., Diam. 23.5 cm. Italy, Apulia, attributed to the Group of the Dublin *Situlae*. Ca. 360–350 BC. Purchase, Leonard C. Hanna Jr. Bequest.

Greek colonists living in southern Italy and Sicily began to produce their own pottery in the late fifth century, when Attic imports were curtailed due to the Peloponnesian War. One of the most prolific areas was Apulia on the southeast coast of the Italian peninsula. In the fourth century there were two distinct schools here: the "Plain" and the "Ornate." The Cleveland vase is a fine example of the latter.

Characteristic of the ornate style are mythological scenes, ambitious compositions, and profuse use of added color. The myth depicted here is Bellerophon fighting the Chimera, a fantastic beast with three heads (lion, goat, and snake). The Greek hero on his winged horse Pegasos is surrounded by abettors: Hermes, Athena, two Pans, and a satyr who assists by throwing rocks at the monster. The figures are ranged at different levels with their own dotted groundlines suggestive of monumental wall painting. The sober Attic color scheme of red and black is enlivened with much white, yellow, and brown. JN

PUBLICATIONS Margaret Mayo, ed., *The Art of South Italy: Vases from Magna Graecia* (Richmond: The Virginia Museum, 1982) no. 32 (entry by K. Hamma). A. D. Trendall and Alexander Cambitoglou, *The Red-Figured Vases of Apulia*, vol. II (in press), Appendix, p. 1065, Chap. 15, no. 44b.

LITERATURE Konrad Schauenburg, "Bellerophon in der unteritalischen Vasenmalerei," *Jahrbuch des deutschen archäologischen Instituts*, LXXI (1956) 59-96.

22 Duck *Askos* 75.23

Earthenware with slip decoration. H. 15.3 cm., L. 25 cm. Italy, possibly Chiusi, assigned to the "Clusium Group." Etruscan red-figure, ca. 350 BC. Purchase from the J. H. Wade Fund.

Vases in the shape of animals were popular throughout the ancient Mediterranean. A type which is fairly common in central Italy in the fourth century is the duck *askos*, a medium-sized pouring vessel whose body takes the form of a bird. It is equipped with a filling spout and strap handle on the back, and its bill is pierced with a hole, small enough to control the flow of precious scented oils.

In most Etruscan vase painting the techniques and styles are borrowed from Greece. However, by the fourth century, the supply of Athenian vases was dwindling and local schools were established in Etruria to meet the ever-present demand. One such workshop produced a number of duck-*askoi*, but none of the extant vases is as finely decorated as the Cleveland example. The body of the bird is covered with a net of richly patterned plumage, before which floats on either side a nude winged female. Her spread wings and extended body ending in a flutter kick are neatly adapted to the tapering vase. Known as a Lasa, she is a minor Etruscan goddess associated with Turan (Venus). Each Lasa is heavily bejeweled and carries attributes: perfume flask and dipstick, plumed helmet, and shield. Other duck-*askoi* are just as ornately decorated, but our artist displays an elegance and fondness for feathers not found on the others. JN

PUBLICATION Mario del Chiaro, "An Etruscan Red-Figured Duck-Askos," CMA *Bulletin*, LXIII (April 1976) 108-115, figs. 1-3.

LITERATURE J. D. Beazley, *Etruscan Vase-Painting* (Oxford: Oxford University Press, 1947). Maurizio Harari, *Il "Gruppo Clusium" della Ceramografia Etrusca*, Bibliotheca Archaeologica, I (Rome: L'Erma di Bretschneider, 1980).

See also color plate following page 22.

Islamic

23 Polychrome Bowl with Human Figures 59.249

Earthenware, lead-glazed with underglaze slip decoration. H. 8 cm., Diam. 35.6 cm. Iran, Nishapur. Samanid Period, 10th century AD. Purchase from the J. H. Wade Fund.

A dynamic design painted in deep purplish black slip against a bright yellow background fills the inner surface of this low, widely flaring bowl. Four figures, alternately male and female, are seated around the walls of the vessel, holding in their hands cups and flowering branches, details which suggest a connection with Dionysiac rites. Small birds, long-horned animals, tiny flowers, and highly stylized Kufic inscriptions (repeating the Arabic word *baraka* ["blessing"] written retrograde) appear to float in the field around the principal figures. In the central tondo stands a horse with a spotted panther above its back. An elaborate geometric ornament arranged in concentric bands covers the exterior. Splashes of green and yellow highlight details of both interior and exterior designs, and the whole bowl, including the foot, is covered with a colorless lead glaze.

The Museum's bowl is an outstanding example of a style produced in Nishapur, a once prosperous provincial capital in eastern Iran, situated on the caravan route connecting the Far East with the provinces and countries to the west. Its style and iconographical content constitute an important document for the study of an as yet little known style of painting incorporating Chinese, Indian, Sasanian, and Classical influences. EM

EXHIBITION New York, 1963: Asia House, Iranian Ceramics, cat. by Charles K. Wilkinson, no. 26, p. 123, repr. in color.

PUBLICATIONS Dorothy G. Shepherd, "Bacchantes in Islam," CMA *Bulletin*, XLVII (March 1960) 42-49. Ernst J. Grube, *The World of Islam* (London: Paul Hamlyn, 1966) p. 21, fig. 6. Johanna Zick-Nessen, "Figuren Mittelalterlich-Orientaleschen Keramikschalen un die "Sphaera Barbareca,"' *Archäologische Mitteillungen aus Iran*, N. F. VIII (1975) pl. 50, no. 3.

24 Polychrome Bowl with Bird 56.225

Earthenware, lead-glazed with underglaze slip decoration. H. 11.5 cm., Diam. 28 cm. Iran, Nishapur. Samanid Period, 10th century AD. Purchase from the J. H. Wade Fund.

A variant of the more elaborate "buff" ware described above ([23]), this deep bowl is typical of the more common, red-bodied Nishapur wares. The single motif filling its curved interior is a primitive stylized bird with elaborate flowing crest. Two ornamental motifs derived from the Arabic word *baraka*, similar to those found on [23], are randomly placed on either side of the bird.

The bowl is richly polychromed. Pigments are applied over a pinkish-white slip. Outlines are drawn in dark purplish brown. The bird is predominantly dull brick-red; splashes of yellow and green brighten the patterned wing. The circles on the rim which form the border of the design are also splashed with yellow and green. The entire background between the principal motifs is filled in with bright yellow. A band of freely designed vertical strokes in brown with occasional green and yellow splashes covers the vertical rim of the bowl; a slight indentation formed at the lower edge of the band is emphasized in deep brown. Just below on the sloping sides is a broad band of red slip.

The combined use of red pigment and the red clay body characteristic of the usual Nishapur wares and a drawing style similar to that found on the more elaborate buff figural wares suggest that this bowl provides a developmental link between the two. EM

PUBLICATION Dorothy G. Shepherd, CMA *Bulletin*, XLVII (March 1960) fig. 3.

14 Black-Figure *Hydria*. Greece, Athens, attributed to the Antimenes Painter. Ca. 520 BC.

29 *Lạkabi* Plate with Falcon and Duck.
Iran, possibly Rayy. Seljuk Period, 11–12th centuries.

22 Duck Askos. Italy, Etruria. Ca. 350 BC.

25 Lustreware Bowl with Man and Two Birds 59.331

Earthenware, tin-glazed with golden lustre decoration. H. 7.3 cm., Diam. 14.2 cm. Iraq, probably Baghdad. Abbasid Period, 10th century AD. Purchase, J. L. Severance Fund.

Enclosed within a festooned border, the entire inner surface of this bowl is covered with a richly varied, golden lustre-painted scene. The stylized head and torso of a bearded man appear in the center; his hands support a banner surmounted by a knob and crescent from which flutters a long streamer. Flanking him on either side are two long-tailed birds; the one on the right holds a palmette in his beak. The "peacock eye" motif fills details of the birds' wings and parts of the background. Remaining areas are filled with simple hatching or stippling. On the exterior, five large circles against a background of "raindrop" hatching surround the foot, on which there is an Arabic inscription. Contour panels surround the main design elements on both interior and exterior. Both figure style and background details are characteristic of tenth-century Mesopotamian lustreware. The lustre technique may have been developed by the glassmakers of Syria and Egypt in the late eighth century. Its use on tin-glazed ceramics, however, apparently originated among the potters of Samarra, the Abbasid capital near Baghdad, in the ninth century. Early pieces, such as this bowl, were widely exported throughout the Islamic world, from Transoxiana and India to southern Spain. EM

48 Plate with the Prodigal Son.
Italy, Gubbio and Faenza. Maestro Giorgio Andreoli, 1528.

26 Lustreware Bowl with Antelope 44.476

Earthenware, tin-glazed with golden lustre decoration. H. 6.7 cm., Diam. 25.4 cm. Egypt, Fustat. Fatimid Period, 11th century AD. Purchase from the J. H. Wade Fund.

By the end of the tenth century, with the decline in Abbasid power, the Samarra and Baghdad potters apparently emigrated to the prosperous court of the Fatimid caliphs in Fustat (Old Cairo). There, judging from vast finds of pottery fragments, the lustreware industry flourished for two centuries. Although the Fustat lustreware preserved some of the Abbasid "Samarra style" conventions, such as contour panels and details of background decoration, the painting style and themes followed a local tradition. Fatimid lustreware was generally decorated with floral, geometric, or animal motifs, and more rarely, human themes.

Here, in this shallow bowl, an unusually elegant and vivacious antelope is skillfully adapted to the shape of the vessel. Holding a branch in his mouth, the animal appears to be prancing against a background of simple whirl motifs in isolated fields, interspersed with branches and leaves. The entire design is painted in golden lustre on a white slip ground; the exterior is plain. EM

EX COLLECTION D. G. Kelekian.

EXHIBITIONS Cleveland, 1944: The Cleveland Museum of Art, Loan Exhibition of Islamic Art, cat. repr. p. 32. London, 1976: Hayward Gallery, The Arts of Islam, cat. no. 268, repr. p. 219.

PUBLICATIONS W. E. Cox, *The Book of Pottery and Porcelain* (New York: Crown Publishers, 1944) pl. 96. H. Hollis, "Two Fustat Bowls," CMA *Bulletin*, XXXII (June 1945) 94-95.

27 Lustreware Bowl with Polo Player 44.74

Earthenware, tin-glazed with golden lustre decoration. H. 7.2 cm., Diam. 35.5. Iran, Rayy. Seljuk Period, late 12th century AD. Purchase from the J. H. Wade Fund.

With the decline in Fatimid power in the last quarter of the twelfth century, potters migrated to the Seljuk court in Rayy (near present-day Teheran), where the industry flourished until the Mongol invasion in 1220. The potters of Rayy developed the lustre technique to its full maturity, combining elements of earlier lustreware styles with the fluid, calligraphic line and figural style which were characteristic of Seljuk art.

Set within a circular framework, a monumental, mounted polo player reserved against a yellow-brown lustre background decorates this low, flaring bowl. In the background, also in reserve, rhythmic foliate scrollwork with split-leaf arabesques is interspersed, emphasizing the circularity of the design. Surrounding the central field, a contour panel and festooned border provide a link with the earlier Abbasid and Fatimid lustreware (cf. [25]). The exterior is thickly covered with cobalt blue glaze. As befits a vessel displaying a sport of noblemen, the decoration is dynamic and imposing, making this bowl one of the finest of its type. EM

EX COLLECTIONS V. Everit Macy; Parish-Watson.

EXHIBITIONS New York, 1931: The Metropolitan Museum of Art, Loan Exhibition of Ceramic Art of the Near East, cat. by M. S. Dimand, no. 52, p. 13. New York, 1940: Iranian Institute, Persian Art, cat. by Phyllis Ackerman, p. 56. New York, 1963: Asia House, Iranian Ceramics, cat. by Charles K. Wilkinson, no. 56, p. 130.

PUBLICATIONS A. U. Pope and P. Ackerman, eds., *A Survey of Persian Art*, vol. X, *Pottery and Faience* (London and New York: Oxford University Press, 1964-1965) pl. 633B. H. Hollis, "Two Near Eastern Lustered Bowls," CMA *Bulletin*, XXXI (November 1944) 158–160.

28 Lustreware Bowl with Three Women 44.75

Earthenware, tin-glazed with brown lustre decoration. H. 10.2 cm., Diam. 36 cm. Syria, Rusapha. Ayyubid Period, late 12th century AD. Purchase from the J. H. Wade Fund.

Contemporary with the Seljuk schools of lustre painting in Rayy and Kashan (Iran), smaller and less important schools were established at Rakka (Iraq) and at Rusapha (Syria). Although their wares were generally more carelessly painted and less refined than their Persian counterparts, they retain the vigor of line common to both Egyptian and Persian lustre products. An elegant, fluid style of drawing is especially characteristic of the Syrian wares.

Such is the case with this deep bowl, the inside of which is divided into three triangles by a simple, yet graceful, foliate ornament ending in scrolls at the rim. Within a lobed medallion in the center of each triangle is a seated female figure holding a cup. The flat rim framing this trio is decorated with pseudo-Kufic letters interlaced with a running scroll. The design is painted in a rich, deep brown on a crackled, sea-green glazed background, which has decomposed in some areas to patches of iridescence. A similar glaze covers the exterior. The figures are reserved against the brown lustre, a convention linking Ayyubid lustreware to its Fatimid predecessors. In contrast to Fatimid ware, however, the figures are much smaller. Human figures are generally uncommon in Rusapha and Rakka ware. This and the fact that examples from Rusapha are quite scarce make our bowl outstanding. It has been suggested that such pieces were possibly made only for a few of the nobility. EM

EX COLLECTION V. Everit Macy.

PUBLICATIONS H. Hollis, CMA *Bulletin*, XXXI (November 1944) 158-160. Arthur Lane, *Early Islamic Pottery* (London: Faber and Faber, 1947) p. 39, fig. 59A.

29 *Lakabi* Plate with Falcon and Duck 38.7

Soft-paste porcelain with polychrome glazed and incised decoration H. 8.3 cm., Diam. 40 cm. Iran, perhaps Rayy. Seljuk Period, 11th–12th centuries AD. Purchase from the J. H. Wade Fund.

In the bold style typical of Seljuk art, a richly polychromed design of a falcon attacking a duck fills the inner surface of this deep, low-footed plate. It is an outstanding example of a technique in which designs were modeled and incised in the body of the vessel, thereby preventing the colored glazes which filled them from running. Against a background of ivory white, the luminous green, cobalt blue, and manganese purple glazes in this plate graduate in tone from areas of thin, almost transparent wash to rich, dark pools in the deeply incised areas.

Popularly called *lakabi* ("painted") ware, such vessels represent the third successive step in the development of a Seljuk tradition (inspired by Chinese porcelains) which began with plain, carved white wares and was followed by those with rich monochrome glazes. There are very few extant *lakabi* vessels and they are typically large, flat-rimmed plates with large-scale, polychromed designs of real or fantastic birds or animals, often arranged heraldically and composed with great fluidity. Considered to have been items of luxury, the finer examples (such as the Cleveland plate) may have belonged to a member of the court of the Great Seljuks. EM

EX COLLECTION V. Everit Macy.

EXHIBITIONS New York, 1931: The Metropolitan Museum of Art, Loan Exhibition of Ceramic Art of the Near East, cat. by M. S. Dimand, no. 34, p. 9. London, 1976: Hayward Gallery, The Arts of Islam, cat. no. 341, p. 243, repr. Ann Arbor, 1981: University of Michigan Museum of Art, The Meeting of Two Worlds: The Crusades and the Mediterranean Context, cat. by P. P. Soucek and C. V. Bornstein, pp. 32-33, no. 10.

PUBLICATIONS H. Hollis, "Two Iranian Pottery Bowls," CMA *Bulletin*, XXV (March 1938) 43, 44, 49. A. U. Pope and P. Ackerman, eds., *A Survey of Persian Art*, vol. X, *Pottery and Faience*, pl. 605. W. E. Cox, *The Book of Pottery and Porcelain*, pl. 92.

See also color plate following page 22.

30 "Gabri" Bowl with Rhinoceros 38.8

Earthenware, lead-glazed with carved slip decoration. H. 16.4 cm., Diam. 39 cm. North West Iran, Garrus District. Seljuk Period, 11th–12th centuries AD. Purchase from the J. H. Wade Fund.

An image of a fantastic rhinoceros set against large foliate scrolls fills the interior of this deep, high-footed bowl. The bold design was carved through the white slip which covers the reddish earthenware vessel. The background was filled in with a dark manganese brown and the whole then covered with a rich green glaze. Just below the exterior rim there is a band of white leaf ornament against manganese purplish brown.

An example of the *champlevé* technique, this bowl illustrates a development over the earlier sgraffito wares which were produced in Iran as early as the ninth century. This type belongs to a large group of Seljuk pottery consisting of plates, bowls, and ewers covered with monochrome glazes, which is often called "Gabri" ware. Birds and animals are the favored motifs; and as this bowl illustrates, the designs are always highly decorative. EM

EX COLLECTIONS Parish Watson; V. Everit Macy.

EXHIBITIONS New York, 1931: The Metropolitan Museum of Art, Loan Exhibition of Ceramic Art of the Near East, cat. no. 30, p. 8. New York, 1940: Iranian Institute, Persian Art, cat. by P. Ackerman, p. 54.

PUBLICATIONS H. L. Prangen, "An American Exhibition of Near Eastern Ceramics," *The Antiquarian,* August 1931, pp. 29-31. H. Hollis, CMA *Bulletin,* XXV (March 1938) 43, 48, 49.

31 "Silhouette Ware" Jug 47.495

Soft-paste porcelain with slip decoration, under alkaline glaze. H. 13 cm., Diam. 14 cm. Iran, Rayy (?). Seljuk Period, 12th century AD. Purchase, Edward L. Whittemore Endowment Fund.

This small jug exemplifies a group of twelfth-century Iranian pottery often described as "silhouette ware," a term derived from the dramatic contrast between the black, slip-painted decoration and the clear, ivory or turquoise glaze. In this case, the design is admirably adapted to the shape of the vessel. A narrow band of Kufic inscription adorns the narrow, straight lip, below which is a frieze of running animals. These exceptionally energetic creatures are surrounded by a continuous, scrolling foliate ornament. The lower band is divided into a series of trapezoidal panels gracefully tapering to a splayed, unglazed foot.

The problem of painted motifs smudging under the alkaline glaze was solved in "silhouette ware" by mixing the pigment with clay slip, in the same way this problem had been solved with ninth and tenth-century lead-glazed wares of Nishapur (eg. [23, 24]). The design in the lowest register of our jug was laid directly on the white paste body with a brush. In the inscription and animal friezes, the black slip was applied over the entire surface and the background and details were then cut away with a knife, sharply defining outlines and leaving portions in low, partly modeled relief. Finally, the entire vessel was covered with a rich turquoise glaze. EM

EXHIBITION New York, 1963: Asia House, Iranian Ceramics, cat. by Charles K. Wilkinson, no. 41, p. 126, repr.

32 *Minai* Bowl 39.214

Earthenware, tin-glazed with polychrome decoration. H. 9.2 cm., Diam. 20.9 cm. Iran, Rayy (?). Seljuk Period, Late 12th–early 13th century AD. Gift of Leonard C. Hanna, Jr. for the Coralie Walker Hanna Memorial Collection.

The late twelfth century saw a decline in the quality of lustreware in Rayy, owing in part to competition from that produced in Kashan. In addition, the development of a new, composite technique in ceramic decoration, commonly termed *minai* ("painted or enamel"), carried the ceramic art of the region to new heights. *Minai* vessels are generally smaller and more refined in shape than their predecessors, and are covered with an opaque cream-white or intense turquoise blue tin glaze. In a subsequent low-temperature firing, delicately painted, polychrome designs — most commonly consisting of human and animal figures and inscriptions — are fixed to the solid color background.

In this example — a deep, flat-bottomed bowl with outwardly flaring sides — the painted decoration was applied with a controlled, yet nimble brush, An enthroned king appears in the center, with a haloed attendant on either side, two peacocks at his feet, and two smaller birds above his head. Framing the scene, a band of foliated Kufic inscription bestows blessing on the owner of the bowl. Around the sides is a row of eight mounted horsemen galloping to the left, their dynamic counter-clockwise movement in contrast to the static, heraldic scene in the center. The colors of the conventional Seljuk costumes worn by the figures range from blue to red, white, black, and various shades of green; details are highlighted in gold leaf. Surrounding the horsemen, a second band of Kufic bears another benedictory inscription. The edge of the bowl is outlined by a scalloped border. The exterior decoration consists of a band of black *naskhi* script on the plain turquoise background which covers the entire surface, including the foot. It too conveys the stereotypical blessing of "Everlasting glory . . .

happiness . . . good luck . . . to its owner." The combination of finely painted decoration and brilliant color gives this bowl a jewel-like quality. And in this and other examples of *minai* ware, the figural style provides valuable information about the closely related contemporary school of miniature painting before the Mongol invasion. EM

PUBLICATION H. Hollis, "Oriental Art," CMA *Bulletin*, XXVI (June 1939) 107.

33 *Minai* Bowl 44.478

Earthenware, tin-glazed with polychrome decoration. H. 6.3 cm., Diam. 12.3 cm. Iran, Rayy (?). Early 13th century AD. Purchase from the J. H. Wade Fund.

In contrast to the more elaborate *minai* example [32], this small, hemispherical bowl is decorated with a simple design consisting of two seated figures against a turquoise background. They appear to be court entertainers, but probably can be more accurately interpreted as representing a scene of heavenly bliss — a subject common to the repertoire of *minai* painters. Here, the artist was a master of expressive gesture, which is further enhanced by the large scale of the figures in relation to surface area. The "entertainers" wear conventionally patterned, sumptuous costumes — one blue with a pattern of circular medallions, the other brown with a coiling split-leaf design. Details of the garments are highlighted in gold leaf, as are portions of the haloes surrounding their heads. In the free space surrounding them float a number of discs, some of them grouped in threes, an ancient pattern which was widely current in the pre-Islamic, Sasanian Period. Surrounding the scene is a band of blue Kufic inscription with black arabesques interspersed between the letters. Although it has not been translated, it presumably bears the conventional invocation for happiness and good fortune to the owner.

Like the previous example, a scalloped border decorates the rim and there is a band of black *naskhi* on a plain blue background on the exterior. The colors on this thinly potted bowl are particularly delicate and subtle, enhancing the graceful, fluid gestures of the figures which dominate its interior. EM

EX COLLECTION D. G. Kelekian.

See also Front Cover.

34 Mosque Lamp 44.236

Silacaceous paste, with underglaze painted decoration. H. 27.6 cm., Diam. 19.7 cm. Turkey, Isnik. Ottoman Period, mid-16th century AD. Purchase from the J. H. Wade Fund.

Garden images abound in Turkish pottery of the Ottoman Period, as seen in this magnificent mosque lamp, one of two such pieces in the Cleveland collection (44.287). The pear-shaped vessel has a high, slightly flaring mouth and three loop handles from which it was once suspended. Its graceful, rhythmic, and symmetrical design consists of six urns with carnations framed by undulating stems of hyacinths. A chain design separates the two portions of the vessel, and a rim of floral buds frames the design at the mouth. Against a flawless white ground, the flowers are colored in a deep cobalt blue, a light, thin turquoise which has run into the glaze, and a thickly applied tomato-red slip which stands out in relief. Portions of the design are outlined in black. The bottom of the vessel is white with a rosette in blue, red, and black painted around the air hole in the center. Adding to the brilliance of the colors is a bright, transparent glaze which yields a jewel-like quality to the vessel.

Initially inspired by Chinese Yuän and Ming porcelains, the potters of Isnik began using techniques brought to them from Iran, and continued to develop them during the sixteenth and seventeenth centuries. Their gradually changing style was divided into three different centers: Kutahya, Damascus, and Rhodes. This lamp represents the so-called "Rhodian" style (the third and latest Isnik phase), characterized by elegantly drawn, stylized arrangements of flowers and plants which were indigenous to Turkey. A bold color scheme including a newly discovered "Armenian bole" red and a deep copper green is found on these pieces, which were widely exported throughout Europe and the Near East. The Isnik potters combined their elegant designs and brilliant colors with the highest standards of technical excellence, making their work a virtuoso achievement in the history of ceramic art. EM

EX COLLECTION J. P. Morgan.

European

35 Sgraffito Plate 67.137

Earthenware, lead-glazed with incised decoration. Diam. 23.5 cm. Byzantium. Mid-12th century AD. Purchase from the J. H. Wade Fund.

The most widely known of the Byzantine wares are those whose decoration is achieved by thin, scratched lines or short pricks exposing the darker red body of the clay. The technique — probably borrowed from earlier Persian wares and referred to as sgraffito — appears in late eleventh-century Byzantium and becomes the favorite form of ceramic adornment for well over a century. Sgraffito earthenware was manufactured in Constantinople and in a variety of other centers including Salonica, Sparta, Athens, and Corinth.

The decoration of sgraffito ware includes a large number of themes. Among these is the geometrical, Kufic, and foliated design of which the present plate is a particularly appealing example. A spiral leafy motif is confined to a central medallion surrounded by alternating incised and plain bands. PdeW

LITERATURE David Talbot Rice, *Byzantine Glazed Pottery* (Oxford: Clarendon Press, 1930) pp. 31-45. Charles H. Morgan, II, *Corinth, Results of Excavations Conducted by the American School of Classical Studies at Athens*, vol. XI: *The Byzantine Pottery* (Cambridge, [Mass.]: Harvard University Press, 1942) pp. 115-140, pls. XXXIX-XLI,.

36 Sgraffito Plate with Hawk 67.139

Earthenware, lead-glazed with incised decoration. Diam. 22.1 cm. Greece, Corinth? Byzantine, mid-12th century AD. Purchase from the J. H. Wade Fund.

Among sgraffito ware, the bird is another common subject, sketched in vivid forms and generally quite freely rendered. In the present example, in which the glaze has a greenish cast, a large hawk, incisively drawn, occupies the center of the field. Its head is seen in profile as it twists back. The bird is surrounded by sparse but suggestive stylized foliage. A circular band of curvilinear design frames the central field. The decoration of this plate bears close relation to the work attributed to the "Interlace Master" who was active in Corinth in the twelfth century, though the drawing of the Cleveland plate is perhaps bolder and more assured. As is generally true of this type of ware, the undecorated rim of the plate is nearly vertical.

PdeW

LITERATURE C. H. Morgan, *Corinth, Results of Excavation*, XI, 118, 119, fig. 93, pl. XLII, figs. b, c. David Talbot Rice, "The Pottery of Byzantium and the Islamic World," in *Studies in Islamic Art and Architecture in Honour of Professor K. A. C. Creswell* (London: The American University in Cairo Press, 1965) pp. 218-219.

37 Albarello with Two Rabbits 43.276

Earthenware, tin-glazed. H. 22.2 cm., Diam. 9.8 cm. Spain, Paterna. Fourteenth century AD. In Memory of Mr. and Mrs. Henry Humphreys, Gift of their Daughter Helen.

This albarello — a cylindrical jar used to store dry medicinal herbs — exemplifies the mixed ornamental repertoire typical of Paterna ware with painting in brown and green. Its decoration is dominated by the crest of the Luna family, lords of Paterna, a locality close to Valencia. Under the shield, two rabbits drawn with skillful freedom are represented nibbling on a schematically rendered grapevine. Other areas of the jar show a stylized palmette, a pseudo-Kufic script, and segments of grapevine.

Both the basic shape and the decoration of this vessel reflect the diverse influences affecting fourteenth-century Aragon, especially that of the Spanish Islamic tradition. PdeW

EXHIBITION Ann Arbor, Michigan, 1981: The University of Michigan Museum of Art, The Meeting of Two Worlds: The Crusades and the Mediterranean Context, cat. by Christine V. Bornstein and Priscilla P. Soucek, p. 45, no. 22 (entry by P. P. Soucek).

PUBLICATIONS Helen S. Foote, "A Majolica Albarello from Paterna," CMA *Bulletin*, XXX (September 1943), 120-121. William M. Milliken, "Majolica Drug Jars," *Bulletin of the Medical Library Association*, XXXII, no. 3 (July 1944) 293-303, repr. 295.

38 Lustreware Albarello 53.287

Earthenware, tin-glazed with brown lustre decoration. H. 30.6 cm., Diam. of opening and base 11.4 cm. Spain, Manises. Early 15th century AD. Purchase from the J. H. Wade Fund.

For generations, the caliphs of Cordova and the Nasrid kings of Granada looked back nostalgically to Syria, endeavoring to recreate the surroundings of their former home. Lustred pottery from the East (cf. [25–28]) was among the rarities brought by Arab ships to Spanish soil. Eventually, difficulties in transport and rising demands led to the establishment of kilns in Spain, among which those of Malaga were particularly successful. Here were produced complex and graceful ovoid shapes with a diversity of rhythmic patterns adopting Andalucian motifs to the Near-Eastern vocabulary. These were painted in brown lustre with Kufic letters and chains of roundels with stylized "eye" of peacock feathers. Some of this ware was exported and profoundly inflenced ceramic decoration in the Valencian region, adapted, in fact, almost literally in the center of Manises in the fourteenth and early fifteenth centuries. A familiarity with the great vases of Malaga is suggested by our albarello which until now was in fact said to have come from the earlier center. Yet the shape of the piece, the handling of its decoration painted in a bronze-brown lustre with a band of knotted white cord rather than Kufic letters, the chain of roundels with small tracery, and the undulant blue and lustre scrolls on the collar are Manises simplifications of the designs of the Muhammadan-Andalucian style. The rosette or wheel mark on the bottom again points to the Valencia-Manises region. Similar pieces also attributed to Manises are in the Instituto de Valencia de Don Juan in Madrid and in the Victoria and Albert Museum in London. PdeW

LITERATURE Manuel González Marti, *Cerámica del Levante español* (Barcelona: Editorial Labor, 1944) p. 417, pl. XII, fig. 514. Alice Wilson Frothingham, *Lustreware of Spain* (New York: The Hispanic Society of America, 1951) p. 87, fig. 52, p. 133.

39 Lustreware Plate with the Name "Maria" 44.292

Earthenware, tin-glazed with golden lustre decoration. Diam. 46.2 cm. Spain, Valencia. Ca. AD 1437. Purchase from the J. H. Wade Fund.

In the second or third decade of the fifteenth century, potters of the Valencian region introduced into their gold lustred wares patterns based on flowers and leaves which recall those of textiles and which were enlivened with touches of blue. The same pattern was carried out on the reverse which in the present case frames a sun face. Large ornamental plates in this style became so renowned that personalized examples were ordered not only from the four corners of Spain but also from as far as Italy and France, with the prominent inclusion of the arms of the owner to be.

The present example has at center a shield charged with six fleurs-de-lis and with a superimposed band on which appears the name "Maria." The whole is surmounted by a royal crown. An albarello, now in Madrid, and a similar plate in an English collection in 1903 bear these arms, said to be those of René d'Anjou, but without the inscribed name. This suggests that our plate might be associated with Marie de Bourbon who

married John, Duke of Calabria, René's eldest son, in 1437. The arms of Bourbon were also fleur-de-lisé, lending weight to this possibility. The seven bold lozenge-shaped ornaments with mesh design which frame the shield might conceivably be a rebus element helpful in identifying still more precisely the original owner of the plate. PdeW

EX COLLECTION Colonel Baron du Feil, Paris.

PUBLICATIONS Helen S. Foote, "A Gold-Luster Dish," CMA *Bulletin,* XXXII (April 1945) 46-47. A. W. Frothingham, *Lustreware of Spain,* p. 130, fig. 90, p. 129.

LITERATURE Albert van de Put, *Hispano-Moresque Ware of the XV Century* (London: The Art Worker's Quarterly, 1904) pl. XI, pp. 65-67. M. G. Marti, *Cerámica del Levante español.*

40 Drug-Pot with Oak Leaf Design 43.54

Earthenware, tin-glazed. H. 20.3 cm., W. 21.4 cm. Italy, Florence. Mark: painted star (Giunta di Tugio). AD 1431. Purchase from the J. H. Wade Fund.

This two-handled drug container with bulbous body and short neck, intended for storing electuaries, belongs to a homogeneous group of wares known as oak leaf jars because of their decoration. Among oak leaves on branching stems, the present example includes two profile busts, that of a bearded man wearing a cap with a pointed visor, perhaps indicating a hunter, and that of a young woman sporting a feathered turban. Aroung the neck of the jar is a paneled border. This decoration is painted in heavy blue impasto while the drawing is in manganese purple. On each handle is a crutch, painted in green and manganese, badge of the Hospital of Santa Maria Nuova in Florence. Cora, on the basis of the paired star designs below each handle, attributes the Cleveland drug-pot to the kiln of the potter Giunta di Tugio and assigns to it the specific manufacturing date of 1431. PdeW

EX COLLECTIONS Sir Otto Beit; Sir Alfred Beit, Ireland.

EXHIBITIONS London, 1930: Royal Academy of Arts, Italian Art 1200–1900, p. 422, no. 948B. Cleveland, 1971: The Cleveland Museum of Art, Florence and the Arts, cat. by Edmund P. Pillsbury, no. 93 repr.

PUBLICATIONS William M. Milliken, "Italian Majolica," CMA *Bulletin,* XXXI (January 1944) 7-15. Idem, *Bulletin of the Medical Library Association,* XXXII (July 1944). Galeazzo Cora, *Storia della maiolica di Firenze e del contado, secoli XIV e XV* (Florence: G. C. Sansoni, 1973) p. 451, pls. 55a, 55b.

LITERATURE Henry Wallis, *Oak-Leaf Jars* (London: Bernard Quaritch, 1903). Wilhelm von Bode, *Die Anfänge der Majolikakunst in Toskana* (Berlin: J. Bard, 1911) p. 18. Bernard Rackham, *Catalogue of Italian Majolica:* Victoria and Albert Museum, 2 vols. (London: Her Majesty's Stationary Office, 1977) I, 10-11, nos. 38, 39; II, pl. 9, figs. 38, 39.

41 Maiolica Drug-Bottle 43.53

Earthenware, tin-glazed. H. 38.7 cm., Diam. 23.6 cm. Italy, Faenza. Ca. AD 1490. Purchase from the J. H. Wade Fund.

This large pharmacological bottle, one of a pair (with 43.52) in The Cleveland Museum of Art collection, is oviform with a gracefully flared tubular neck. It is painted in a rich palette of blue, yellow, brownish-orange, and copper-green. The main field is decorated with a running greyhound and large rhythmically swerving leaves. Below the panel, the bottle is inscribed with the name of its intended contents, *A. CAPILLU* (for *Aqua Capillorum Veneris* ["maiden hair water"] extract of fern). The neck is decorated with a double tier of overlapping leaves. Below the inscription is a course of stylized peacock feathers. Other examples of such vessels suggest that the present bottle may originally have included an earthenware lid in matching colors.

Towards the end of the fifteenth century Faenza, a town near Bologna, came to be the leading center of maiolica production. Its importance is emphasized by the fact that the term *faience* is coined after its name. Until shortly after 1500, the numerous factories of Faenza used a common repertory of designs and patterns of heavy leaves and peacock feathers in a powerful color scheme, as witnessed in the present example. Afterwards, the taste among Faenza potteries turned to a vocabulary of lighter floral designs and strapwork. PdeW

EX COLLECTIONS Sir Otto Beit, London; Sir Alfred Beit, Ireland.

EXHIBITIONS London, 1930: Royal Academy of Arts, Italian Art 1200–1900, p. 422, no. 948A. Bloomington, 1977: Indiana University Art Museum, Italian Maiolica from Midwestern Collections, exhib. cat. by Bruce Cole, pp. 36-37, no. 11.

PUBLICATIONS Alfred van de Put and Bernard Rackham, *Catalogue of the Collection of Pottery and Porcelain in the Possession of Mr. Otto Beit* (London: Chiswick Press, 1916) pp. 78-79, no. 742. W. M. Millikin, CMA *Bulletin*, XX (January 1944) 8-9, 13. Idem, *Bulletin of The Medical Library Association*, XXXII (July 1944) 297, fig. 3.

LITERATURE B. Rackham, *Catalogue of Italian Majolica:* Victoria and Albert Museum, I, 83, no. 264; II, pl. 42, no. 264.

42 Maiolica Albarello 40.12

Earthenware, tin-glazed. H. 29.8 cm., Diam. 18.9 cm. Italy, Faenza. Ca. AD 1507–1510. Purchase from the J. H. Wade Fund.

Faenza wares of the early years of the sixteenth century are characterized by a decoration in which the painting of narrative scenes is the principal element. Classical or pseudo-classical subjects had a particular appeal. On the present albarello, Venus, out of the sea, is shown drying her hair. The entire pictorial field, trees and seascape included, is a copy in reverse of an engraving of Marcantonio Raimondi (Bartsch XIV, 312), which is dated "1506 S[eptembris] 11" and was produced in Venice. On this vessel, likely to have been made very shortly after that date, the only addition is that of a face of a clock on the quiver of the goddess, an element which probably has a moralizing implication. The rest of the albarello's surface bears bands of vertical patterns with tendril ornaments. Lemon, ochre, and pale green dominate. This decoration relates to the work of a Faenza Master who signed himself F.L.R. (a fragment with Venus and Cupid in the Museo Nazionale, Florence, and a dish with Alexander and Thalestris in the Berney Collection). PdeW

EX COLLECTION Alfred Pringsheim, Munich.

EXHIBITION Cleveland, 1956–1957: The Cleveland Museum of Art, Venetian Tradition, cat. by Henry S. Francis, p. 43, no. 82.

PUBLICATIONS Otto von Falke, *Die Majolikasammlung Alfred Pringsheim in München* ([Leiden]: A. W. Sijthhoff's, 1914), I, pl. 50, fig. 85a, b. William M. Milliken, "Italian Majolica," CMA *Bulletin*, XXVII (March 1940) 33-34.

43 Maiolica Pilgrim Bottle 23.914

Earthenware, tin-glazed. H. 34.5 cm., W. 19.5 cm. Italy, Faenza. Ca. AD 1530. Purchase from the J. H. Wade Fund.

This type of Renaissance vessel is known as a pilgrim bottle because its pear shape with loops recalls the gourd in which pilgrims carried water in their travels by means of a shoulder strap (see also [57]). This example is decorated by courses of stylized acanthus patterns some of which end in dolphins. They are disposed in fluted oblique bands of yellow and orange on deep blue alternating with white and light blue on salmon-colored ground. The loop of the stopper and the two handles, which take the shape of bent branches, are chartreuse green.

A molded dish at the Victoria and Albert Museum (8897-1863), also adduced to originate from Faenza, is decorated with similar oblique bands of foliated designs in fluted grooves. PdeW

EX COLLECTION Spitzer, Paris.

PUBLICATION *La Collection Spitzer-Antiquité-Moyen Age-Renaissance* (Paris: Maison Quantin, Librairie centrale, 1892) IV, 38, no. 63, pl. IX.

LITERATURE Giuseppe Liverani, *La Maiolica italiana* (Milan: Electa Editrice, 1958) pl. 53. B. Rackham, *Catalogue of Italian Majolica: The Victoria and Albert Museum*, I, 286-287, nos. 862, 863; II, pl. 138, no. 862, pl. 139, no. 863.

44 The Entombment 22.174

Earthenware, tin-glazed. H. 68.6 cm., W. 55.9 cm. Italy, Faenza. Late 15th century AD. Gift of Samuel Mather.

Elaborate relief compositions in glazed terracotta were produced in Faenza in the late fifteenth century. The scene of the Entombment, as our example, and the Adoration of the Child (*Presepio*) were most numerous in a repertory which also included a variety of single figures, religious and profane, either in full or bust length.

In America an *Entombment* particularly close to ours is in the collection of the Boston Museum of Fine Arts (60.943). Another, more involved example, now at The Metropolitan Museum of Art in New York, bears a date of 1487 and thus provides a time mark for our piece. While the technique of these reliefs is based on the precedents of the Florentine shop of the della Robbias of the 1470–1480s, such emotional pieces are stylistically related to the expressive art of Cosimo Tura and Ercole Roberti in nearby Ferrara. Sharp greens and blues are used to heighten the sense of drama. PdeW

LITERATURE J. Chompret, *Répertoire de la majolique italienne,* 2 vols. (Paris: Les Editions Nomis, 1949) I, 64; II, pl. 53. Hanns Swarzenski, "Some Recent Accessions," *Bulletin of The Museum of Fine Arts, Boston,* LVIII (1960) 93. Antonio Corbara, "Le Plastiche fiamminggheggianti del tardo Quattrocento e la 'Linea' Faenze-Ferrara," *Faenza,* LIX (1973) 64-72, pls. XXX-XXXV.

45 Altarpiece: Madonna and Child Enthroned with Saints Francis and Anthony Abbot 21.1180

Earthenware, tin-glazed. H. 200 cm., W. 165 cm. Italy, Florence, Benedetto Buglioni (1461–1521). AD 1510–1520. Gift of J. H. Wade.

Stanniferous, or tin-glazed terracotta, altarpieces came into fashion essentially as a substitute for those, more costly, of carved marble. It was Lucca della Robbia who introduced this medium in monumental sculpture. The art of Benedetto Buglioni — an artist of stature in sixteenth-century Florence, chosen, for example, to be among those who selected a site for Michelangelo's *David* in 1504 — parallels that of the della Robbias. Buglioni seems to have been particularly influenced by the work of Andrea, the younger della Robbia. In his gossipy account of Verrochio's life, Giorgio Vasari suggests that Buglioni secured the secret of glazing from a woman in Andrea's house. Buglioni's style also shows a definite relationship with the oeuvre of Antonio Rossellino.

In the present work, the gracefully sentimental figures are polychromed in sober colors against a light blue enamel ground with cherubs. The egg and dart cornice (partly restored) bears two shields with the arms, according to Marquand, of the Borgherini family. The sculpture probably graced a chapel in Florence owned or endowed by this family. PdeW

PUBLICATIONS William M. Millikin, "An Enthroned Madonna and Child with Saints by Benedetto Buglioni," CMA *Bulletin,* IX (February 1922) 23-26.

LITERATURE Allan Marquand, *Benedetto and Santi Buglioni* (Princeton: Princeton University Press, 1921) esp. p. 120, no. 133.

46 Figure of Dovizia (Plenty) 40.343

Earthenware, tin-glazed. H. 110.2 cm., W. 38.2 cm. Italy, Florence, Giovanni della Robbia (1469–1529?). Ca. AD 1520–1530. Gift of S. Livingston Mather, Constance Mather Bishop, Philip R. Mather, Katherine Hoyt Cross, and Katherine Mather McLean in accordance with the wishes of Samuel Mather.

The inspiration for this figure of Plenty appears to be a famous over life-sized stone statue of Dovizia by Donatello which stood in the old Mercato Vecchio of Florence until the eighteenth century. Dovizia carries a basket of fruits and vegetables on her head while holding other produce in her right hand. The fruits are brightly polychromed in contrast to the figure, entirely glazed in white. Dovizia appears as an idealized young woman bringing the bountiful gifts of nature to the market. The children clinging to either side of the woman bestow on her an added sense of domesticity.

Closely related terracotta figures in the same scale are in the Bardini Museum, Florence. These, as well as our statue, were produced in the della Robbia workshop when it was under the leadership of Giovanni. Instead of the careful lyrical style of his father Andrea or the subtle chromatism of his uncle Luca, Giovanni was more intent on producing pictorial effects. Here, for example, we see a gaping frog among the produce the young woman carries on her head. Yet the striding idealized figure clad in classical drapery evokes most gracefully the Neoplatonist spirit of Renaissance Florence.

PdeW

EXHIBITION Cleveland, 1971: The Cleveland Museum of Art, Florence and the Arts, cat. by E. Pillsbury, no. 33.

LITERATURE Allan Marquand, "A Statuette of Dovizia by Giovanni della Robbia in the Minneapolis Museum," *Art in America*, V (1917) 195-199. Idem, *Giovanni della Robbia* (Princeton: Princeton University Press, 1920) p. 212, no. 213.

47 Maiolica Plate with Maiden 23.1096

Earthenware, tin-glazed with yellow and blue lustre. H. 8 cm., Diam. 41.3 cm. Italy, Deruta. Ca. AD 1515–1520. Gift from J. H. Wade.

This large plate is an outstanding example of maiolica produced in the small town of Deruta, near Perugia, in the early sixteenth century. In this example, a fashionable young woman, seen in three-quarter length, wears her hair in a snood and is dressed in a robe with square-cut neckline. In front of her is a scroll inscribed IV BILLIA BELLA ("Beautiful Jubilia"). The rim is decorated with strong palmette and geometric motifs contrasting with the flowing lines of the feminine figure.

This plate was most probably not intended for use but rather had a decorative purpose. The subject and the inscription suggest that this particular type of dish may have been destined as a gift on the occasion of an engagement, bearing the name of the would-be-bride. Of the several examples known of this type of Deruta plate, a close parallel is to be found in a private collection (see Chompret); others are in the Victoria and Albert Museum. PdeW

LITERATURE J. Chompret. *Répertoire de la majolique italienne*, I, 41-44; II, figs. 200, 204, 205-207. B. Rackham, *Catalogue of Italian Majolica: Victoria and Albert Museum*, I, 158-159, no. 478; II, pl. 74, fig. 478.

48 Plate with the Prodigal Son 50.82

Earthenware, tin-glazed with gold and red lustre. Diam. 21 cm. Italy, Gubbio and Faenza, Maestro Giorgio Andreoli. AD 1528. Purchase from the J. H. Wade Fund.

Chief among the lustre painters in Gubbio was Maestro Giorgio Andreoli. The master's skill in controlling a wide range of tone values raised Renaissance ceramics to fine arts status. The present plate is an example of his work bearing his marks and the date 1528 in lustre on the back. The scene, that of the repentant prodigal son who, having become destitute, is reduced to becoming a swine herder, is a free rendering of an engraving by Albrecht Dürer (Bartsch 28) dated ca. 1496. Dürer's supplicating man has here been turned into a fair-headed youth, but the Italian artist has faithfully copied the German master's rendering of the Bavarian farmhouse.

Though lustred by Maestro Giorgio, the plate and the drawing of its composition may well have been produced in Faenza. The draftsmen of this city seem to have been particularly attracted by, or seem to have gotten hold of, German models, not only those of Dürer but also those of Martin Schongauer. Our plate was produced the very year Dürer died. There is another plate with a rendering of Dürer's *Prodigal Son* bearing the mark of Master Giorgio and the date of 1525, in the Metropolitan Museum of Art (Robert Lehman Collection).

PdeW

EX COLLECTIONS Baron von Goldschmidt-Rothschild, Frankfurt-am-Main; Richard von Passavant-Gontard, Frankfurt-am-Main; Febore.

EXHIBITION Frankfurt-am-Main, 1929: Städelschen Kunstinstitut, Die Sammlung R. v. Passavant-Gontard, no. 211, pl. 70.

PUBLICATIONS R. Schilling, "Ausstellung der Sammlung R. v. Passavant-Gontard im Städelschen Kunstinstitut," *Pantheon*, III (1929) 186. William M. Millikin, "Three Majolica Plates by Maestro Giorgio," CMA *Bulletin*, XXXVII (1950) 211-212, repr. 207. George Szabó, "Dürer and Italian Majolica I, Four Plates with 'The Prodigal Son Amid the Swine,'" *American Ceramic Circle Bulletin*, 1970–1971, pp. 5-28.

LITERATURE Otto von Falke, "Der Majolikamaler Giorgio Andreoli von Gubbio," *Pantheon*, XIV (1934) 328-333. Alan Caiger-Smith, *Tin-Glaze Pottery in Europe and the Islamic World* (London: Faber and Faber, 1973) p. 96, color pl. I. B. Rackham, *Catalogue of Italian Majolica: Victoria and Albert Museum*, I, no. 793; II, pl. 125, no. 793.

49 Dish with Bust of Saint Paul 42.628

Earthenware, tin-glazed with gold and red lustre, and molded decoration. Diam. 25.4 cm. Italy, Gubbio. Ca. AD 1535. Bequest of John L. Severance.

The pottery made in Gubbio in the sixteenth century is famous for its decoration in gold and ruby lustre. Such was the high degree of craftsmanship there attained in this technique that rival kilns from Castel Durante, Urbino, and elsewhere sent wares to Gubbio to receive lustre enrichment over decoration otherwise complete.

The present dish, produced entirely in Gubbio, is an excellent example of Gubbio ware in which high lustre is combined with decoration molded in relief. The central medallion is surrounded by a series of copper-gold lustred pine cones with painted foliage and ruby lustred bosses. PdeW

PUBLICATION *Catalogue of the John L. Severance Collection* (Cleveland: The Cleveland Museum of Art, 1955) p. 23, no. 92.

LITERATURE B. Rackham, *Catalogue of Italian Majolica: Victoria and Albert Museum*, I, nos. 708, 709; II, pl. 101, nos. 708, 709.

50 Pair of Maiolica Salt Cellars 45.126-.127

Earthenware, tin-glazed. H. 20.3 cm., L. 21 cm. Italy, Urbino. Ca. AD 1580–1600. Gift of Mr. and Mrs. Philip R. Mather.

With the establishment of potters such as Orazio Fontana in the second half of the sixteenth century, Urbino assumed the supremacy Faenza had held in the manufacture of maiolica, now often heavily decorated, with an exceptional intensity of pigment, and highly glazed. One important workshop, active towards the end of the sixteenth century and into the early seventeenth, was that of the Patanazzi family and their associates, who by and large followed the style of Fontana but lacked his refinements. The present salt cellars are closely related to the production of the Patanazzi and that of one of their associates, a painter who signed a dish now at the Victoria and Albert Museum with initials F. G. C. Each of our pieces is composed of a boat bearing two seated putti, each adorned with a brown necklace and holding a shell. The surface of the bark which rests on a curvilinear cross-shaped base, is decorated with Neptune's mask in relief and paintings of a flying cupid in four compartments and also in the well. Blue, orange, copper-green, and opaque white are the dominant tonalities. PdeW

EX COLLECTIONS Spitzer, Paris, 1893; Samuel Mather, Cleveland.

PUBLICATION Helen S. Foote, "Gifts to the Majolica Collection," CMA *Bulletin*, XXXIII (April 1946) 36-38, repr. p. 34.

LITERATURE J. Chompret, *Répertoire de la majolique italienne*, I, 192-199. Rackham, *Catalogue of Italian Majolica: Victoria and Albert Museum*, I, 296, nos. 885, 887, p. 304, no. 913.

51 Medici Plate 49.489

Soft-paste porcelain with underglaze blue decoration. Diam. 28 cm. Italy, Florence. AD 1574–1578. Purchase, John L. Severance Fund.

According to a recent count, this is one of only about fifty known examples of soft-paste porcelain produced in Florence at the instigation of Francesco Maria de' Medici, second Grand Duke of Tuscany. Inspired by Chinese Blue-and-White porcelain (see [118, 128]), it was produced in limited numbers and for less than two decades at the factory of the Boboli Gardens. Unlike actual porcelain of petuntse and kaolin, soft-paste was produced with a mixture of white clay and vitreous substances. The latter made for difficulties not only in shaping but also in attaining even surface in the course of firing. The manufacture, which therefore retained an experimental character, closed down shortly after the death of Francesco.

PdeW

EX COLLECTIONS Sir T. Graham Briggs, London; Mrs. Ernest C. Innes, London; E. L. Paget, London.

EXHIBITIONS Florence, 1939: Palazzo Medici, Mostra Medicea, p. 140, cat. 9D. Detroit, 1958–1959: The Detroit Institute of Arts, Decorative Arts of the Italian Renaissance, 1400–1600, p. 50, no. 130. Cleveland, 1971: The Cleveland Museum of Art, Florence and the Arts, cat. by E. Pillsbury, no. 99; Florence, 1980: Palazzo Vecchio, Firenze e la Toscana dei Medici, p. 186, no. 350.

PUBLICATIONS Helen S. Foote, "A Rare Medici Plate," CMA *Bulletin*, XXXVII (November 1950) 193-195, repr. 190. Eros Biavati, "Studio tecnico chimico ceramico della porcellana dei Medici," *Faenza-Bolletino del Museo internazionale delle ceramiche in Faenza*, LIX (1973) 73-79, pl. XXXVI. Victoria Kloss Ball, *Architecture and Interior Design, A Basic History Through the Seventeenth Century* (New York: John Wiley and Sons, 1980) p. 270, fig. 655.

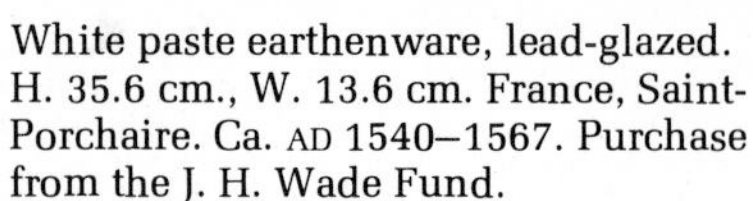

52 Saint-Porchaire Ewer 53.363

White paste earthenware, lead-glazed. H. 35.6 cm., W. 13.6 cm. France, Saint-Porchaire. Ca. AD 1540–1567. Purchase from the J. H. Wade Fund.

This ewer is one of five pieces in the Museum's collection produced in the village of Saint-Porchaire in Poitou by a highly individualistic potter. It is among the best of about sixty known such elaborately shaped specimens — ewers, candlesticks, salts, dishes, and flower holders — of this artist who was active in western France in the mid-sixteenth century. The production of his kiln had no relation to local tradition and was very probably subsidized by the Montmorency-Laval family including the well-known art patron the Connétable Anne de Montmorency, also known to have fostered the ventures of Bernard Palissy (see [54]). Each Saint-Porchaire piece was probably commissioned for a specific occasion, presumably as a gift. The highly decorative finely textured, off-white ware is unlike that of any other ceramics both in its varied shapes and in the dazzling technique of its inlaid ornamentation comprised of intricate arabesques akin to motifs found in Venetian embroidery pattern books. This was produced not only by painting but also by impressing the soft white clay body with metal stamps and filling the indentations with various colored clays, mainly brown, reddish-yellow, black, and blue. This ware, which has also been called Henri II style, is a strikingly sophisticated example of Renaissance Mannerism in France, with an involved and playful vocabulary of forms beginning with the half-figure of the *condottiere* crowning the handle and clasps, the elaborately curved rim, to the many tiered base with masks, garlands, strapwork, frogs, and jewel-shaped ornaments. PdeW

EX COLLECTIONS Monville; Lionel de Rothschild; Edmund de Rothschild, London.

PUBLICATIONS Helen S. Foote, "Saint-Porchaire Pedestal Dish and Ewer," CMA *Bulletin*, XLII (1955) 23-27. Bertrand Jestaz, "Poteries de Saint-Porchaire," *La Revue du Louvre*, XXV (1975) 392, fig. 11.

53 Saint-Porchaire Bouquetier (Flower Vase) 50.125

White paste earthenware, lead-glazed, with molded decoration. H. 45.7 cm., Diam. 17.5 cm. France, Saint-Porchaire. Ca. AD 1520–1540. Purchase from the J. H. Wade Fund.

Another example of the extremely fragile, original, and rare Saint-Porchaire ware, this vase was made as two separate elements, the upper shaft fitting by means of dowel into the globular perforated cup, the whole structure being comparable to the shape of an elaborate candle holder or a diminutive fountain. If Italian Renaissance models such as the Paduan bronzes of Riccio indirectly inspired such configurations, the whim is typical of the French style of Henri II. Included here as part of the intricate ornamentation and antithetical to true Renaissance forms are double-lobed arcades at the base, each with a diminutive Gothic figure.

The impracticality of filling the very fragile oviform cup with water suggests that the piece may have been conceived to hold dry flowers only. Most probably it was in effect primarily considered, as it is today, as a *tour de force* of decorative art. PdeW

EX COLLECTION Colville; Anthony de Rothschild.

PUBLICATION Helen S. Foote, "Three Pieces of Henri II or Saint-Porchaire Ware," CMA *Bulletin*, XXXVIII (June 1951) 132-133, 140-142.

54 Rustic Platter 69.106

Earthenware, lead-glazed with relief decoration. L. 52.4 cm., W. 40.7 cm. France (Paris?), Bernard Palissy (manner of). Ca. AD 1570 (?). Gift of the John B. Putnam Foundation.

An important characteristic of the Mannerist movement is the juxtaposition of real elements and unnatural contexts. Flora, and even more so fauna, became the object of a new fascination, casts often being made of actual insects and plants. In Nuremberg, the workshop of Wenzel Jamnitzer produced a bronze mortar (now CMA 51.444) with such casts of insects. In Paris Bernard Palissy, who worked for the court of Catherine de' Medici, was famed for the spectacular rustic grottoes he had designed for the Tuilleries Garden (fragments now in the Musée Carnavalet) and for the Château of Ecouen, with a large assortment of life-like fauna. The present platter, of which several different versions exist, was produced in that same spirit of awe for the unexpected, the predatory, the living, and the dead.

At center, on a grassy-bed, a realistically rendered snake (head damaged) uncoils, ready to pounce on an oblivious large toad on the brim. A rushing stream carries three fish while a fourth one, dead, has been washed on shore. On the wide brim, in temporary stillness, coiled snakes, lizards and other reptiles, and insects appear as if basking in the sun among seashells and a luxuriant vegetation. The making of such a plate obviously required not only ingenuity but also the greatest skill in modeling and glazing. PdeW

LITERATURE M. J. Ballot, *Musée du Louvre, la Céramique française – Bernard Palissy et les fabriques du XVI*[e] *siècle* (Paris: Editions Albert Morancé: 1924). Carl Christian Dauterman, "Snakes, Snails and Creatures with Tails," *The Metropolitan Museum of Art Bulletin*, XX (1962) 272-285.

55 Tiger-Ware Jug with Gilt Silver Mounts 64.374

Stoneware, salt-glazed. H. 23.8 cm., W. 13.3 cm. Rhineland; England, London. AD 1594–1595. Gift of Robert Hays Gries.

This is a globular tall-necked jug of finely mottled Rhenish stoneware, many examples of which were imported into England in the sixteenth century where they were then set into mounts, usually of silver. The present piece, with loop handle, has a wide gilded silver collar around the neck ornamented with repoussé strapwork and fruit clusters. The hinged dome cover is surmounted by a baluster finial. From a flecked ring around the shoulder, three hinged strapwork members of bearded caryatids and masks connect with the base mount whose decoration matches that of the upper band. The thumbpiece is formed as an angel flanked by cornucopias. The four marks on London plate — the maker's mark (here CB in monogram, also found, according to Jackson, on a communion cup at Saints Peter and Paul, Chingford, Essex, in 1595–1596), the leopard's head, the lion *passant*, and the annual letter (R for 1494–1495) — are found on the lid and on the neck and base mounts. On the interior rim of the silver mount base are etched signs which include VIII and a caduceus (a reference to the weight of the silver?). PdeW

LITERATURE Charles James Jackson, *English Goldsmiths and Their Marks* (London: Macmillan and Co., 1921) pp. 81, 107.

56 Bellarmine or Bartmann Jug

74.43

Stoneware, salt-glazed with applied and impressed decoration. H. 33.3 cm., Diam. 28.3 cm. Germany, Frechen, AD 1608. Purchase, Andrew R. and Martha Holden Jennings Fund.

Late in the sixteenth century the kilns of Cologne were moved to nearby Frechen which became an important center of salt-glazed gray stoneware. Bellarmine jugs are identified with the production of that city, with a bulbous body and a short neck on which there is a molded mask of a bearded man. Below, in a medallion in molded relief, is a coat-of-arms either of a Rhenish city or that of a local nobleman.

The present jug, an impressive one, bears the arms of the Pallant van Culemborg family of Gelders relating either to Floris I or Floris II. Two additional decorative roundels each with a facing man and woman in bust are set at either side of the heraldic shield. The Bellarmine jug (also known as *Bartmann* — "bearded man") was named after Cardinal Bellarmine (1542–1621) — hated in Germany for his Counter-Reformational zeal — because of his supposed resemblance to the awesome bearded masks on the neck of the jars.

Such vessels were glazed by throwing common salt into the kiln when it reached 1200–1400°C. Melting, the salt coated the ware with a thin glossy film, leaving the surface slightly pitted with a characteristic orange-peel texture. PdeW

EX COLLECTION Duc d'Arenberg.

LITERATURE Karl Koetschau, *Rheinisches Steinzeug* (Munich: Kurt Wolff Verlag, 1924) pls. 6-7. Ekkart Klinge, *Deutsches Steinzeug der Renaissance und Barockzeit*, exhib. cat. (Düsseldorf: Hetjens Museum, 1979) p. 22, nos. 24, 25.

61 Cachepot. France, Paris, Mennency-Villeroy Factory. Ca. 1735–1740.

65 Faience Tureen with Platter. France, Strasbourg, Hannong Factory. Mid-18th century.

66 Tureen with Platter. France, Sèvres. 1757.

57 Pilgrim Bottle 51.451

Stoneware, polished red with silver gilt mounts and applied decoration. H. 16 cm., W. 9.5 cm. Germany, Meissen. Ca. AD 1715. Purchase from the J. H. Wade Fund.

True porcelain was first produced in Europe by the royal Saxon factory at Meissen. Although several persons participated in its discovery, Johann Friedrich Böttger is given primary credit. About 1708, as a by-product of his efforts to produce porcelain, Böttger developed a fine red stoneware inspired by the example of Chinese ceramics. So hard was this stoneware that it could be polished on a lapidary's wheel, as was the body of this small bottle. The form and decoration of Meissen red stoneware are generally based upon contemporary metalwork. Stoneware played an important role in the earliest productions of the Meissen factory, until about 1720, and it continued to be made there into the 1730s.

The form of the pilgrim bottle is a traditional one based upon the shape of dried gourds in which drinking water was carried (see [43]). Their function was, by the eighteenth century, largely decorative, and they were made in a variety of materials. The form of the present example was, like most Meissen stonewares, almost certainly derived from a piece of contemporary silver. The vessel and its applied ornament would have been separately cast in molds, assembled, and then polished.

Painted in black on the base of this bottle is a mark which appears to be a monogram dominated by the letter "T." This mark bears a resemblance to certain pseudo-Chinese marks used on Meissen ceramics, but it does not seem to have been recorded as a factory mark and is perhaps that of a collector. On the cover of this bottle there was originally a small round knop from which the silver gilt chain was suspended. It is now missing.

HH

78 Seated Figure. Mexico, Zapotec Culture, style of Monte Alban II. Late first millennium BC.

58 Maiolica Plate 20.422

Earthenware, tin-glazed with polychrome decoration. Diam. 48 cm. Italy, Castelli, decorated by Liborio Grue. Signed: "L.G.P." *(Liborio Grue Pinxit).* Second quarter 18th century AD. Gift of J. H. Wade.

In a cartouche at the bottom of the plate is inscribed not only the initials of the decorator but also the subject of its chief decoration, "Polifemo." The scene, which is copied from one of Annibale Carracci's famous ceiling decorations of the Farnese Palace in Rome, shows the jealous Cyclops Polyphemus preparing to kill with a rock the fleeing Acis, accompanied by Galatea, whose rejection of Polyphemus in favor of Acis caused the altercation. Although lacking in originality, the decoration of this plate is carefully executed in the palette of high temperature colors which had traditionally been used by Italian Maiolica decorators [42-43, 47-50]. It represents one of the last significant examples of that tradition. Only the charming putti and the flowers which decorate the border of the plate indicate that it was made toward the middle of the eighteenth century. HH

59 Faience Plate 66.221

Earthenware, tin-glazed and decorated in underglaze blue. Diam. 44.2 cm. France, Nevers. Late 17th century AD. The Norweb Collection.

Tin was added to the glaze of earthenware in order to produce an opaque white surface resembling that of porcelain. The technique was invented in the Middle East in the ninth century. It was introduced into Europe through Spain and from there spread first to Italy, where such wares were known as maiolica, and then to northern Europe. In France and Germany, tin-glazed earthenwares are called "faience," in Holland and England "delftware."

In the center of this large plate is a quite abstract representation of the heavens, presumably in the form of an armillary sphere. Several circular bands are shown, one of which is decorated with symbols of the signs of the zodiac. On the framing band is inscribed *Moderata . durant*, meaning "Constant Regulation" and undoubtedly referring to the astrological belief that the position of the stars plays a determining role in human affairs. The border of the plate is decorated with flowers and two small vignettes of landscapes, in one of which appear human figures. This plate is distinguished both by its large size and by the unusual subject of its decoration. HH

EX COLLECTION Mme. Antonin Durand.

EXHIBITION Paris, 1932: Musée des Arts Decoratifs, La Faience Française de 1525 à 1820, no. 1074.

PUBLICATIONS Dr. Joseph Chompret, Jean Bloch, Jacques Guérin, and Paul Alfassa, *Rèpertoire de la faience française*, II (Paris: Serge Lapina, 1933) Nevers, pl. 33E.

LITERATURE Marjatta Taburet, *La Faience de Nevers et le miracle lyonnais au XVIe siècle* (Paris: Sous le Vent, 1981).

60 Poterat Vase 47.63

Soft-paste porcelain decorated in underglaze blue. H. 20.5 cm., Diam. 11.7 cm. France, Rouen, Poterat Factory. Ca. AD 1690. Purchase from the J. H. Wade Fund.

Soft-paste porcelain was first made in France at Rouen in a factory owned by the Poterat family. Faience (tin-glazed earthenware) was the chief product of this factory. Contemporary records are sparse, and there is disagreement among experts on the identification of Rouen porcelain, but this vase belongs to a small group of porcelains commonly ascribed to the Poterat family's factory. Its decor in underglaze blue with designs inspired by the work of the Berains — ornamentalists active around 1700 — is typical of this class of soft-paste porcelain.

This variety of decoration — often termed "grotesque" — can be traced back through Raphael and other artists of the Renaissance to ancient Roman painted interiors. They were found in subterranean ruins, popularly known in Italy as "grotte," hence the name "grotesque," which was later applied to all sorts of strange, unexpected forms. HH

EX COLLECTIONS Karrick Riggs; his daughter Pauline Oothout Riggs Noyes.

PUBLICATIONS Helen S. Foote, "French Soft-Paste Porcelain," CMA *Bulletin*, XXXIV (December 1947) 249-250. Idem, "Soft-Paste Porcelain of France," *Art Quarterly*, XI (Autumn 1948) 335-347. Hermann Jedding, *Europäisches Porzellan* (Munich: Keysersche Verlagsbuchhandlung, 1971) p. 264, no. 818.

61 Cachepot 47.60

Soft-paste porcelain decorated with polychrome enamels. H. 15.6 cm., Diam. 21.9 cm. France, Paris, Mennecy-Villeroy Factory. Mark "D.V" painted in purple beneath base. Ca. AD 1735–1740. Purchase, John L. Severance Fund.

Cachepot is a French term taken over into English to designate a vessel designed to hold, and thus hide, an ordinary terracotta flower pot. Pieces of this size and shape were also used to cool wine. Although its form is European, the painted decoration of this cachepot is based upon Oriental models. The specific model was probably Chinese lacquer.

This cachepot and its pendant in the Cleveland Museum (47.61) are relatively large and early examples of the soft-paste porcelain produced in the factory patronized by the Duc de Villeroy. It was set up in Paris in 1734, transferred to the town of Mennecy in 1748 and then to Bourg-la-Reine in 1773. HH

EX COLLECTIONS Karrick Riggs; his daughter Pauline Oothout Riggs Noyes.

EXHIBITIONS San Francisco, 1966: California Palace of the Legion of Honor, Cathay Invoked: Chinoiserie, A Celestial Empire In the West, no. 64. Cincinnati, 1979: The Taft Museum, Chinoiserie: The Chinese Influence, pp. 3, 7.

PUBLICATIONS H. S. Foote, CMA *Bulletin*, XXXIV (December 1947) 249-250. Idem, *Art Quarterly*, XI (Autumn 1948) 335-374. H. Jedding, *Europäisches Porzellan*, p. 256, no. 786.

See also color plate following page 54.

62 Seated Chinese with a Pot 47.62

Soft-paste porcelain decorated with polychrome enamels. H. 16.7 cm., W. 18.8 cm. France, Chantilly. Mark: hunting horn in red on bottom. Ca. AD 1740. Purchase, Grace Rainey Rogers Fund.

The decoration of this piece is characteristic of the Chantilly factory and is based upon eighteenth-century Japanese porcelain of the Kakiemon variety (see [161-162]). The figure itself is probably derived from a Chinese example in ceramic or some other material. Other examples of this model are known, but it is seldom encountered in such excellent condition as the present example. HH

EX COLLECTIONS Karrick Riggs; his daughter Pauline Oothout Riggs Noyes.

EXHIBITION Cincinnati, 1979: The Taft Museum, Chinoiserie: The Chinese Influence, pp. 3, 8.

PUBLICATIONS H. S. Foote, CMA *Bulletin*, XXIV (December 1947) 249-250. Idem, *Art Quarterly*, XI (Autumn 1948) 335-347. H. Jedding, *Europäisches Porzellan*, p. 253, no. 768.

63 Covered Bowl 44.225-a

Soft-paste porcelain decorated with polychrome enamels. H. 15.2 cm., Diam. 15.7 cm. France, Vincennes. Ca. AD 1745. Purchase from the J. H. Wade Fund.

This covered bowl is one of the earliest surviving examples of Vincennes porcelain, the forerunner of the royal French porcelain factory at Sèvres. Its decorations, particularly the lacey borders, show the influence of Meissen porcelain, but already an individual note is struck in the extreme delicacy and coloristic restraint of the painting of the landscape scenes. The metal band around the foot is probably a later addition to hide a break. HH

EX COLLECTION J. Pierpont Morgan.

EXHIBITION New York, 1914-1915: The Metropolitan Museum of Art.

PUBLICATIONS Comte X. de Chavagnac, *Catalogue des Porcelains Françaises de M. J. Pierpont Morgan* [Paris, 1910] 49-50, no. 54. Helen S. Foote, "Early French and German Porcelain Formerly in the J. Pierpont Morgan Collection," CMA *Bulletin*, XXXI (November 1944) 160-162. H. S. Foote, *Art Quarterly*, XI (Autumn 1948) 335-347. Henry Hawley, "Vincennes-Sèvres Porcelain at The Cleveland Museum of Art," *Antiques*, LXXXV (March 1964) 322-325. H. Jedding, *Europäisches Porzellan*, p. 278, no. 868.

64 Tureen 52.3

Soft-paste porcelain decorated with polychrome enamels. H. 25.7 cm., W. 38.4 cm. France, Vincennes. Model by Claude-Thomas Duplessis. Mark: Ornamented double "L." Ca. AD 1752. Purchase, John L. Severance Fund.

This tureen was one of the earliest large-scale works made at the French royal porcelain factory, which was located at Vincennes until 1756 and then moved to Sèvres. Its model is described in the factory records as the "terrine Saxe," clear evidence of the influence of Meissen porcelain on the early productions of the Vincennes-Sèvres factory. Duplessis has been credited with its authorship on the basis of an extant drawing of his which can be related to the platter which often accompanies tureens of this model. A very similar tureen with a damaged platter at the Museé National de Ceramique de Sèvres is thought to have been made as a pair to the one in Cleveland. According to the dealer from whom ours was purchased, the two tureens were given by Louis XV to his Connétable de France, but in publications of the Sèvres Museum theirs is not so described, and this tradition may be apocryphal.

This tureen is sumptuously decorated both inside and out with birds and plants naturalistically colored. Its decoration clearly demonstrates the varied palette of enamel colors available at the Vincennes factory at a comparatively early date. The melting surface of the warm white soft-paste porcelain displays these rich colors to maximum advantage. The pride of the craftsmen in their technological and aesthetic achievement finds reflection in the careful detail with which the various motifs of decoration have been rendered.

HH

PUBLICATION Helen S. Foote, "Vincennes and Meissen Porcelain," CMA *Bulletin*, XXXIX (June 1952) 124-127. H. Hawley, *Antiques*, LXXXV (March 1964) 322-325. H. Jedding, *Europäische Porzellan*, p. 278, no. 867.

65 Faience Tureen with Platter 76.52 a, b

Earthenware, tin-glazed and decorated with polychrome enamels. Platter: W. 38.6 cm., D. 33.3 cm.; Tureen: H. 21.2 cm., W. 37.8 cm. France, Strasbourg, Hannong Factory. Mid-18th century AD. Purchase, Andrew R. and Martha Holden Jennings Fund.

The tureen with handles in the form of eagle heads is a well-known model of the Hannong factory in Strasbourg, but seldom found in as good condition as the present example. This factory is famous for its imaginative forms in the rococo style and for its use of strong colors in their decoration. Their wares were strongly influenced by German porcelain; for example, the naturalistic flower used to decorate the center of this platter was directly inspired by the so-called "deutsche Blumen" of Meissen porcelain, which were imitated at Strasbourg beginning about 1750. HH

See also color plate following page 54.

66 Tureen with Platter 53.25a, b

Soft-paste porcelain with pink ground and flowers in polychrome enamels in reserved panels edged in gold. Tureen with cover: H. 24.1 cm., W. 28.2 cm.; platter: W. 34.3 cm., D. 40.6 cm. France, Sèvres. Mark: Trace only beneath tureen. AD 1757. Purchase, John L. Severance Fund.

This tureen and its companion in The Cleveland Museum of Art (53.26) are almost certainly parts of a large dinner service with a pink ground color, popularly known as "rose Pompadour," which was made at the Sèvres factory in 1757. Thus, though this particular tureen and platter bear only a trace of a mark, their date and place of manufacture can be precisely identified on the basis of the marks on other related pieces. A very similar tureen, without platter, was formerly in the Lurcy Collection, and a somewhat larger example is in the Tuck Collection, Musée du Petit Palais, Paris.

The pink ground color was introduced at the Sèvres factory in 1757, the year these pieces were made. They exhibit the characteristics of the early Sèvres production. Clearly the factory had not yet achieved technological mastery, as can be witnessed by the firing cracks and inconsistency of the ground color of this example. But the sophisticated style of the French royal factory and the high quality of its decorations in gold and colored enamels are already fully apparent. HH

EX COLLECTION Countess Redorte, Paris.

PUBLICATIONS Helen S. Foote, "A Pair of Soft-Paste Tureens and Platters," CMA *Bulletin*, XL (November 1953) 200-202. H. Hawley, *Antiques*, LXXXV (March 1964) 322-325. H. Jedding, *Europäisches Porzellan*, p. 268, no. 832.

See also color plate following page 54.

67 Potpourri Vase 44.230

Porcelain decorated with polychrome enamels, with gilt bronze mounts. H. 38.1 cm., W. 33.6 cm. Germany, Meissen. Mark: crossed swords in underglaze blue on bottom. Mounted France, Paris. Porcelain dated AD 1749 in decoration. Purchase from the J. H. Wade Fund.

Meissen porcelain of this kind with small blue or white forget-me-nots in relief and cartouche-shaped reserves painted with figures in landscape settings in the manner of Watteau were popular toward the middle of the eighteenth century. The inscription of a date on an obelisk included in one of the painted scenes is unusual, but 1749 is precisely the date one would expect for its manufacture. A number of pieces with decor of this style exist with contemporary French mounts in gilt bronze. On 3 June 1752, the Parisian dealer Lazare Duvaux sold to Mme. du Pompadour, for use in her library at Crecy, four matching vases of Meissen porcelain "à fleurs de relief, avec des cartouches de miniatures, montés en bronze doré d'or moulu." It is conceivable that this vase and its mate, also in Cleveland (44.229), may be identical with two of those owned by Pompadour. Another similar pair, but slightly earlier in date and smaller in size, is in the Wrightsman Collection, New York. HH

EX COLLECTION J. Pierpont Morgan.

PUBLICATIONS H. S. Foote, CMA *Bulletin*, XXXI (November 1944) 160-162. George W. Ware, *German and Austrian Porcelain* (Frankfurt am Main: Lothar Woeller Press, 1953) pp. 47-48, fig. 35. F. J. B. Watson, *The Wrightsman Collection*, II (New York: The Metropolitan Museum of Art, 1966) 474-475, no. 267A, B.

68 Pipe Head 80.7

Porcelain decorated with polychrome enamels and gilding. H. 6.3 cm., W. 6 cm. Germany, Nymphenburg Factory. Modeled by Franz Anton Bustelli. Ca. AD 1760. Purchase, Norman O. Stone and Ella A. Stone Memorial Fund.

Although unmarked, this pipe bowl has been identified on the basis of its style as the product of the Nymphenburg Factory and its most famous modeler, Franz Anton Bustelli. Of the style of the latter, W. B. Honey has written: "Its outstanding characteristics are extreme simplifications of form, supple movement, a sensitive rhythmical play of line, giving expression to a temperament at once humorous and fanciful in an essentially rococo idiom." Despite its small size, this pipe bowl offers an accurate illustration of the style of Bustelli, who can reasonably be described as the outstanding European modeler of rococo porcelain.

In its design, the bowl incorporates a typically Germanic visual conceit of dividing a single head into two expressively distinct halves, one cheerful, the other quizzical. Although the porcelain itself is in good condition, the piece has suffered from the loss of intended adjuncts — a gilt metal cover and an attachment, probably of the same material, for the bowl to be joined to a stem. HH

LITERATURE W. B. Honey, *European Ceramic Art* (London: Faber and Faber, Ltd., 1952) p. 460.

69 Print Seller 50.570

Soft-paste porcelain, glazed. H. 20.3 cm., W. 9.5 cm. Italy, Naples, Capo-di-Monte. Model attributed to Giuseppe Gricci. Mark: Impressed *fleur-de-lis* beneath base. Ca. AD 1744–1745. Gift of Judge Irwin Untermyer.

Inspired by the example of Meissen, a porcelain factory was founded by the King of Naples at his palace of Capo-di-Monte in 1743. However, unlike its German predecessor, the Italian factory produced artificial soft-paste porcelain, not the true porcelain which the Meissen factory had discovered, inspired by the ambition to imitate the Chinese. Soft-paste porcelain, made of finely ground glass held together with clay, looks like true porcelain but lacks its strength and durability.

Despite her tattered clothing and bare feet, the dignity of the posture of the *Print Seller* imparts to this figure an inherent nobility far removed from the humor or sentimentality with which poverty is frequently associated in works of this sort. Its thick, unctuous glaze seems particularly appropriate to its jagged forms. Very likely this figure is from a series "representing poor people" which the modeler Gricci is documented as having executed between 1744 and 1745. HH

PUBLICATIONS Helen S. Foote, "Important Additions to the Porcelain Collection," CMA *Bulletin*, XXXVIII (October 1951) 199-200. H. Jedding, *Europäisches Porzellan*, p. 284, no. 886.

70 The Itinerant Musician 55.176

Soft-paste porcelain decorated with polychrome enamels and gilding. H. 19.8 cm., D. 14 cm. England, Chelsea. AD 1758–1759. Gift of Mr. and Mrs. Lesley Sheafer.

The porcelain factory at Chelsea, a London suburb, was one of the first to be established in England and its products can be counted among the most significant produced there during the eighteenth century. *The Itinerant Musician*, a very rare model, represents a transitional piece between the period of the factory's early maturity between 1749 and 1756 (when Meissen porcelain was closely imitated) and the full rococo style of the 1760s (inspired by French models, particularly Sèvres porcelain). The simplicity of dress and activities of its figures is characteristic of the earlier mode, while the scrolled and gilded base points toward the more elaborate taste evidenced in the following decade. HH

PUBLICATIONS Helen S. Foote, "A Chelsea Figurine," CMA *Bulletin*, XLIV (November 1957) 204-205. Frank Stoner, *Chelsea, Bow and Derby Porcelain Figures* (Newport, England: The Ceramic Book Company, 1955) pl. 18.

71 Punch Bowl 38.331

Artificial porcelain with underglaze scale blue ground and birds and plants in polychrome enamels in reserved panels. H. 11.5 cm., Diam. 27.6 cm. England, Worcester, Dr. John Wall factory. Mark: Fretted square in underglaze blue beneath base. Ca. AD 1770. Given in memory of John MacGregor, Jr. and Mary Folger MacGregor, by Mrs. John F. McGuire.

Like early French and Italian porcelain, that made in England in the eighteenth century was of an artificial soft-paste, not the true, hard-paste porcelain which had first been made in Europe at the Meissen factory, following the inspiration of Chinese ceramics. Unlike their Continental contemporaries, the English learned early on that the additon of bone ash to their ceramic medium produced wares which had much of the strength and durability of true porcelain. The factory which was established at Worcester in 1751 by Dr. John Wall and others was among the most successful English porcelain manufactories of its day. The shape of this bowl was based upon Chinese prototypes. Its decoration consists of a dark blue underglaze ground color with a scale pattern in lighter blue against which are reserved broad irregularly shaped panels of white porcelain. The panels are enframed with gilt rococo scrolls and within them are to be found exotic birds and plants painted in polychrome enamels. This species of decoration is that most characteristic of the Worcester factory, here applied to an unusually large but simple form which permits its most significant expression. HH

PUBLICATIONS Helen S. Foote, "A Worcester Punch Bowl," CMA *Bulletin,* XXV (November 1938) 164-165. H. Jedding, *Europäisches Porzellan,* p. 251, no. 762.

72 Cupid Carried by the Graces 66.235

Unglazed porcelain (biscuit). H. 25.4 cm., W. 14 cm. France, Sèvres factory. Modeled by Josse-François-Joseph le Riche after a design by François Boucher. Model executed AD 1768. The Norweb Collection.

Beginning in the early 1750s the French royal porcelain factory, first at Vincennes and later at Sèvres, made figures of unglazed, biscuit porcelain. This material closely resembles white marble, and with the growing taste for things classical, porcelain figures made of it soon became widely popular and were imitated by almost every major European factory. The intrinsic beauty of Sèvres porcelain combined with the skills of French designers and sculptors made such figures the most important of their kind during the last half of the century. The present example combines a classical subject and drapery style with a playful mood and movemented forms which remain thoroughly rococo in spirit. HH

73 Ewer and Basin 53.277

Soft-paste porcelain decorated with polychrome enamels. Ewer: H. 23.9 cm., W. 18 cm.; basin: H. 7.5 cm., W. 33.3 cm. France, Chantilly. Mark: hunting horn and "P" in red-brown beneath base on both pieces. Ca. AD 1770. Purchase, John L. Severance Fund.

The porcelain factory at Chantilly was established in 1725 at the chief seat of the Orleans branch of the Bourbon family, the ruling house of France. It is most famous for the wares made during its first quarter century, particularly those reflecting the style of Japanese Kakiemon porcelains [62]. The factory continued in operation until after the Revolution, and this ewer and basin represent rare later evidence of efforts at aesthetic excellence on the part of its administrators. The simplified forms of these vessels and the use of classically inspired motifs, such as ribbons, indicate a date of manufacture well into the second half of the century. The combination of painted and relief decoration which these pieces exhibit is unusual, and no other examples of this pattern have come to light. The ewer may have originally been equipped with a cover of ceramic or metal. HH

74 Cup and Saucer 50.387-a

Porcelain decorated with polychrome enamels and gilding. Cup: H. 5.8 cm., W. 6 cm.; saucer: Diam. 14.3 cm. Austria, Vienna. Mark: Beehive in underglaze blue and the numerals "806" incised on both pieces. Ca. AD 1806. Gift of R. Thornton Wilson in memory of his wife, Florence Ellsworth Wilson.

Following Meissen's lead, the second European factory to make true porcelain was established in Vienna in 1719. After producing some distinctive wares during the first half of the century, the factory slipped into a period of relative decline after mid-century until a wool manufacturer, Konrad von Sorgenthal, assumed direction of it in 1784. He revived it as a commercial enterprise, and in the first decade of the nineteenth century, the porcelain produced at Vienna in the neoclassic style was perhaps the most distinguished being made anywhere in Europe. This cup and saucer, with its geometrically inspired forms and its principal decoration based quite literally on ancient Roman mosaics, constitutes an excellent example of Viennese porcelain in the neoclassic style. HH

EXHIBITION Cleveland, 1964: The Cleveland Museum of Art, Neo-Classicism: Style and Motif, cat. by Henry Hawley, no. 176.

PUBLICATION H. S. Foote, CMA *Bulletin*, XXXVIII (October 1951) 199-200.

75 The MacMahon Vase 79.40

Porcelain decorated in white *pâte-sur-pâte*, blue and gray ground colors and gilding, with gilt bronze mounts. H. 89.2 cm., W. 43.8 cm. France, Sèvres, Alfred-Thompson Gobert, decorator; Jules Archelais, decorator; Emile-Bernard Rejoux, gilder; Jean-Denis Larue(?), sculptor; Constantin (called Constant) Renard, potter. Design perhaps suggested by Albert Carrier-Belleuse. Marks: "S74" printed in green; "Decore a Sèvres 74" with "RF" printed in red; "CR 72 6" and "CR 72 9" incised; "NL" incised; "ABF" scratched; "Gob r/Sèvres" and "JA" conjoined, both in white *pâte-sur-pâte*. AD 1872–1874. The Thomas L. Fawick Memorial Collection.

This vase is an excellent example of the elaborate porcelains produced by the French national factory at Sèvres during the nineteenth century. It was made in honor of and first owned by Marie Edmé Patrice Maurice de MacMahon (1808-1893), Duke of Magenta, Marshall of France, and second President of the Third Republic. His medallion portrait in low relief *pâte-sur-pâte* decoration dominates its primary side. The style of the piece, particularly its sculptural elements — such as its handles in the form of heads of Minerva — suggests that the sculptor Albert Carrier-Belleuse may have participated in its design, though he is not documented as having done so. The vase may originally have had a cover. HH

EX COLLECTIONS President MacMahon, purchased by him from the Sèvres factory for 3000 francs in 1874; his descendents (in the United States?).

EXHIBITION Paris, 1874: Palais des Champs Elysées, Produits de Manufactures Nationales . . ., p. 5, no. 23.

PUBLICATION Henry Hawley, "The MacMahon Vase," CMA *Bulletin*, LXVII (September 1980) 220-227.

AMOR PATRIA
SAPIENTIA
FORTITUDO
Gob.R.

76 Vase with Lustre Glazes 79.8

Earthenware, decorated with lustre glazes. H. 28.6 cm., W. 26.5 cm. France, Golfe Juan, Clement Massier Factory. Designed by and decoration executed by Lucien Levy-Dhurmer. Marks: "Clement Massier/Golfe Juan/L. Levy" painted on bottom; "Clement Massier/Golfe Juan/ AM/L. Levy" impressed on bottom. AD 1887–1895. The Mary Spedding Milliken Memorial Collection, Gift of William Mathewson Milliken.

In 1887 Clement Massier hired the young painter, Lucien Levy, to work at the ceramics factory which he had established at Golfe Juan in the South of France in 1872. Massier had the ambition to create ceramics of aesthetic distinction and, with Levy's help, succeeded in becoming one of the front runners in French efforts at renewing their traditions in this medium. After a disagreement with Massier, Levy resigned in 1895, added Dhurmer to his surname to avoid confusion with other artists named Levy, and went on to become a leading member of the symbolist movement in painting.

The form of the Cleveland vase, with its four evenly spaced appendages, was designed by Lucien Levy and produced by casting in a mold. He then decorated it by painting feathers in purple lustre and allowing green and amber lustre glazes to drip over the surface. This style of ceramic production was continued by the Massier firm long after Levy-Dhurmer's departure. HH

LITERATURE *Autour de Lévy-Dhurmer Visionnaires et Intimistes en 1900*, exhib cat. (Paris: Grand Palais, 3 March-30 April 1973).

Pre-Columbian

77 Stirrup Spouted Vessel 68.192

Earthenware with polished brown surface. H. 22.7 cm., W. 15.4 cm. Peru, North Coast, Cupisnique Valley, Chavin style. 1st millennium BC. Purchase, Bequest of Helen Humphries.

Human habitation of the Western Hemisphere is quite ancient. The peoples who first settled these continents are presumed to have come from Asia across the Bering Strait and gradually to have infiltrated farther and farther south. Strangely enough, the earliest settlements presently known are in South America. There the archaeological sequence begins with pre-ceramic cultures of the third millennium BC. Ceramics are first encountered late in the second millennium, but techniques for forming vessels of fired clay soon became widespread. Ceramics of great stylistic and technical diversity were produced in the Americas during the two and half millennia before the arrival of Europeans, but one Old World ceramic technique of great importance was never employed — the raising of vessels by throwing the clay on a fast spinning wheel. In fact, with the exception of children's toys, wheels were completely unknown before Columbus.

The Chavin style is typical of the earliest sophisticated ceramics from Peru. The stirrup spout, presumably initiated to facilitate handling, became ubiquitous in Peruvian ceramics. This vessel is decorated with two small and four large reliefs which are abstract representations of heads, probably of a jaguar. The decoration of a monochromatic ceramic vessel entirely in relief is unusual, but this piece indicates that it can be aesthetically quite successful. HH

EXHIBITION Norfolk, Virginia, 1970: Norfolk Museum of Arts and Sciences, The Arts of Pre-Hispanic America.

78 Seated Figure 54.857

Earthenware with polished red-brown surface, slight remains of red pigment, and white in the incised glyphs. H. 32.3 cm., W. 17.6 cm. Mexico, State of Oaxaca, Zapotec Culture, style of Monte Alban II. Late 1st millennium BC. Gift of Hanna Fund.

Less well known than their neighbors, the Mayas, the people who occupied the region which includes the modern Mexican state of Oaxaca nevertheless produced a rich culture which, in the visual arts, is notable particularly for its architecture and its sculpture in clay. Archaeologists have applied the names Monte Alban (from an important ceremonial center near the modern city of Oaxaca) and Zapotec (the name of a still extant, linguistically identifiable group of this region) to the ancient culture of the Oaxaca region.

This *Seated Figure* belongs to a small number of sculptures thought to be among the earliest surviving pieces from Oaxaca. It has been assigned to the cultural phase designated as Monte Alban II, and probably dates from the end of the pre-Christian era, roughly from the third to the first centuries before Christ. The cross-legged position of this figure, with its hands and arms symmetrically arranged, corresponds to the posture of ceramic figures made in the Oaxaca region over a very long span of time. The later examples are, however, more complex, with the symbolic ornaments, here included as incised glyphs on the figure's chest and headdress, transformed into three-dimensional decorations of clay. These designs undoubtedly served as the identifying attributes of particular deities. It is the simplicity of modeling of the *Seated Figure,* combined with the hieratic pose and the representational distortions of the eyes and mouth, which endow this image with a forcefulness of expression commonly found in the early manifestations of significant artistic traditions.

This and a very similar figure in the Oaxaca Museum are two of the most famous Monte Alban style ceramic sculptures. Both are distinguished by realism combined with expressive intensity. HH

See also color plate following page 54.

EXHIBITION New York, 1970-1971: The Metropolitan Museum of Art, Before Cortes, Sculpture of Middle America, cat. by Elizabeth Kenney Easby and John F. Scott, p. 194, no. 155, repr.

PUBLICATIONS William M. Milliken, "Two Pre-Columbian Sculptures," CMA *Bulletin*, XLII (April 1955) 57-61. Esther Pasztory, "Artistic Traditions of the Middle Classic Period," in *Middle Classic Mesoamerica: A.D. 400–700*, ed. Esther Pasztory (New York, Columbia University Press, 1978) pp. 113-114, fig. 6.

79 Head 40.11

Gray-brown terracotta, pupils of the eyes indicated with black pigment. H. 28.1 cm., W. 26.4 cm. Mexico, southern State of Veracruz, Papaloapan River Basin. Mid-first millennium AD.. Purchase from the J. H. Wade Fund.

In the first millennium AD., there flourished in what is today the eastern Mexican state of Veracruz, a culture related to the classic civilizations of central and southern Mexico, but distinct from them. One of the frequently encountered manifestations of the classic Veracruz culture was the production of quite large, almost life-size figures made of terracotta, sparsely decorated with black pigment. This head is presumably a fragment of such a figure. It represents a man wearing a headdress which makes of him the personification of an animal, probably feline, deity. Although realism of detail frequently characterizes classic Veracruz art, this head is unique in its accurate representation of human physiognomy combined with an impression of arrested action which imparts a convincing sense of aliveness to the image. HH

PUBLICATIONS William M. Milliken, "A Pre-Columbian Mexican Head," CMA *Bulletin*, XXVII (July 1940) 107-108. Pal Keleman, *Medieval American Art* (New York: MacMillan Company, 1943) I, 168; II, pl. 117b. William Spratling, *More Human than Divine* (Mexico City: Universidad Nacional Autonoma de Mexico, 1960) pls. 22, 23. Henry Hawley, "Pre-Columbian Art at Cleveland," *Apollo*, LXXVIII, no. 22 (December 1963) 489-493. Idem, "Classic Veracruz Sculptures," CMA *Bulletin*, LXI (December 1974) 321-330.

80 Jar 55.173

Earthenware with polished orange ground decorated in red, dark brown, yellow, gray, and white. H. 36.7 cm., Diam. 23.5 cm. Peru, South Coast, Tiahuanaco style. After AD 600. Gift of William R. Carlisle.

This jar is an unusually large and richly decorated example of Tiahuanaco style ceramics. That style is presumed to have originated in the southern highlands of Peru and around the shores of Lake Titicaca, and to have spread from there to the coastal regions of southern Peru during the second half of the first millennium AD. The style is characterized by complex, "baroque" forms painted in polychrome. This vessel has an anthropomorphic character which makes of it an arresting object. Visually, it can in its entirety be read as a human figure, but the "arms" of that figure are themselves made up of other recognizable elements — a human head and arms holding a serpent-like creature. HH

PUBLICATION Wendell C. Bennett and Junius B. Bird, *Andean Culture History* (New York: American Museum of Natural History, 1949) p. 192.

82 Footed Bowl 51.317

Earthenware with red-orange surface; exterior decorated in brown, orange, yellow, and black. H. 14.6 cm., Diam. 18.1 cm. Mexico, State of Pueblo, Vicinity of Cholula, Mixtec Style. Ca. AD 1300–1500. Purchase, John L. Severance Fund.

This footed bowl is a well-preserved example of perhaps the finest ceramic type made in Mexico at the end of the pre-Columbian sequence. Although related stylistically and iconographically to the Mixtec culture, it was made during the period of Aztec dominance of central Mexico. This ceramic type is typified by precisely rendered geometric decorations, frequently, as in this example, executed in several colors. HH

PUBLICATION George Kubler, *The Art and Architecture of Ancient America,* The Pelican History of Art (Harmondsworth, Middlesex, England: Penguin Books, 1962, 1975) p. 103, pl. 56A.

81 Vase 67.203

Earthenware, decorated in black, white, red, gray, and mauve on an ochre ground. H. 19 cm., Diam. 10.8 cm. Mexico or Central America, Maya. Ca. AD 800. Gift of Edgar A. Hahn.

The class of Maya ceramics to which this vase belongs is characterized by rather tall, beaker-shaped vessels with polychrome decoration showing scenes of tribute being paid to a figure of authority. As in this example, the latter is usually shown facing a procession of standing figures. This vase has unfortunately been damaged. Approximately 5 centimeters are missing from its upper edge. It is, nevertheless, an important piece because the quality of its painting is unexcelled in Maya art. HH

American Indian

83 Mimbres Bowl with Antelope 30.50

Earthenware with slip decoration. H. 11.8 cm., Diam. 31.2 cm. America, New Mexico, Mimbres Valley. Ca. AD 1000–1200. Purchase, The Charles W. Harkness Endowment Fund.

Since the potters wheel was unknown in Pre-Columbian America, American Indian ceramics were made by a hand coiled method. The shaping and polishing were all done by hand with special stones which were highly prized and handed down from generation to generation. This coiling method was used by the prehistoric Indians such as those of the Mimbres valley and continued into modern times.

Mimbres pottery is noted for its imaginative use of design motifs and its strong sense of realism and narrative presentation. It is decorated with either life forms or geometric designs. Often the two are combined as in this bowl. Here a wide band of zigzag design frames the antelope in the center of the bowl. These figures are usually seen in profile and the eye is depicted by a dot within a white circle. The use of abstract design on the body of the animal is typical of the style.

Bowls such as this example were found in burial sites and are commonly broken or "killed" in the center. VC

EX COLLECTION Museum of New Mexico, Santa Fe.

EXHIBITION New Haven, 1956: The Yale University Art Gallery, Mimbres Pottery.

PUBLICATION Wesley Bradfield, *Cameron Creek Village* (Santa Fe: El Palacio Press, 1931) p. 87, pl. LXVIII, no. 248.

84 Mimbres Bowl with Fish 73.165

Earthenware with slip decoration. H. 8.8 cm., Diam. 20.3 cm. America, New Mexico, Mimbres Valley. Ca. AD 1000–1200. Purchase, James Albert and Mary Gardiner Ford Memorial Fund.

Though black-on-white decoration was the most common for Mimbres pottery, some red-on-white was produced. This bowl is a fine example of the naturalistic design using life forms. The fish appears to be leaping across the white ground of the bowl. It is placed slightly above center, perhaps to avoid being marred by the "kill-spot." The narrow banding around the rim is typical of the composition of these bowls and leaves ample space for the figural decoration. VC.

EX COLLECTION Larry Frank, Santa Fe, New Mexico.

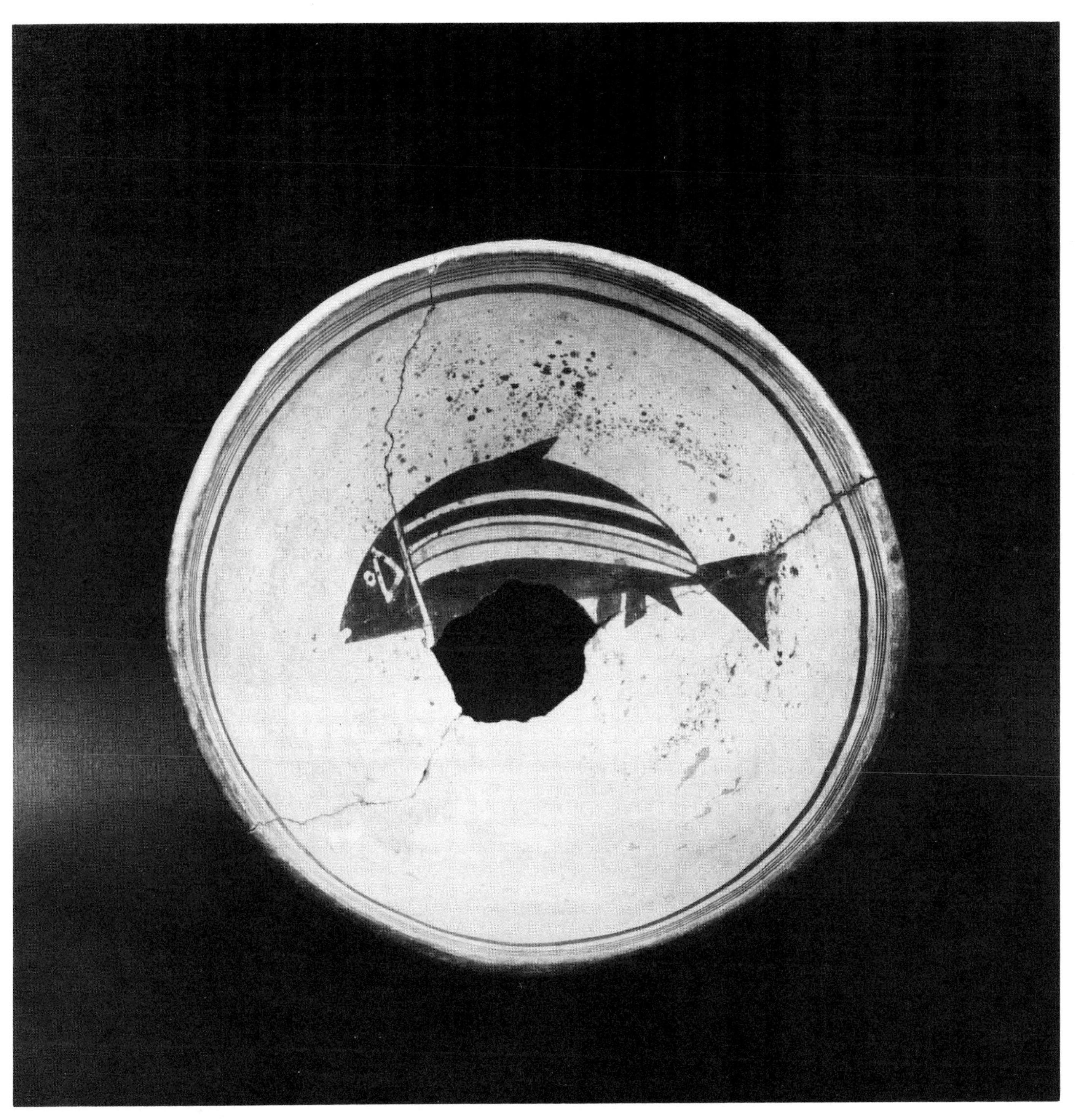

85 Zuni Jar 23.1082

Earthenware with slip decoration. H. 25.9 cm., W. 37.2 cm. America, New Mexico, Zuni Pueblo. Late 19th century AD. Gift of the Smithsonian Institution.

This jar illustrates the classic Zuni design. The shape of the jar with the high shoulder and sharply indented neck became common about 1880. The red underbody paint, however, has been used since prehistoric times. Zuni decoration is always divided into three parts, neck designs being different than those of the body, and is typically linear in style. The designs are drawn freehand against the white ground, with some attempt at a balanced, but not static, arrangement. The motif on the body of this jar has been called the "rain-bird" by H. P. Mera, who traces it through centuries of ceramic development. He also points out that the interrupted line-break, seen here on the shoulder band, is traditional, but its significance is no longer known. Some claim that it is used to release the spirit of the jar. The motifs on the neck are stylized feathers. Zuni pottery has rather thick walls and coarse surfaces. But the designs are quite sophisticated showing sensitivity in the shaping of the lines and the fine hatching used to fill in the triangles making this pottery among the finest produced in the Southwest. VC

LITERATURE H. P. Mera, *The "Rain Bird," A Study in Pueblo Design* (Santa Fe: Laboratory of Anthropology, 1938).

86 Acoma Jar 37.897

Earthenware with slip decoration. H. 28.4 cm., W. 35.6 cm. America, New Mexico, Acoma Pueblo. Ca. AD 1900. Gift of Amelia Elizabeth White.

Technically, Acoma pottery is among the finest produced in the Southwest; it has the thinnest walls of all American Indian pottery. Around the turn of the century, Acoma jars developed a high shoulder with a gently curving neck resulting in a continuous design over the vessel. Acoma geometric style is quite intricate, filling most of the surface of the jar. There is more use of hatching as filler, and designs are less linear than in Zuni pottery [85]. The design motifs on this jar are arranged vertically and repeated alternately around the body of the jar, unlike Zuni decoration which tends to be arranged and divided into horizontal bands. VC

87 San Ildefonso Plate 51.363

Earthenware, matte-black-on-polished-black. Diam. 38.5 cm. America, New Mexico, San Ildefonso Pueblo, Maria Martinez (1887–1980) and Santana Martinez. Signed: Marie & Santana. Ca. AD 1950. Purchase, The Harold T. Clark Education Extension Fund.

The process for making black-on-black ware was developed by Maria Martinez and her husband Julian in 1919. Maria formed and polished the clay body, while Julian painted the design with a red clay slip. The piece was then fired producing the black color. The feather motif on this plate was adapted from Mimbres pottery decoration. It and the Avanyu ("serpent") motif were the two most popular designs used by Julian. After his death in 1943, Maria continued to make pottery with her daughter-in-law, Santana, a partnership that lasted until 1956. Basically it was an extension of the earlier Maria-Julian period producing the same type and style of pottery.

Black-on-black ware is extremely successful commercially and has been made by other San Ildefonso potters, but Maria was the most well known, traveling extensively and becoming a famous spokesperson for her people. VC

LITERATURE Richard L. Spivey, *Maria* (Flagstaff, Arizona: Northland Press, 1979).

Chinese

88 Double-Handled Beaker 71.228
(Shuang-ta-erh kuan)

Buff earthenware, burnished. H. 12 cm., Diam. of mouth 8.2 cm. China, type-site at Ch'i-chia-p'ing, Kansu Province. Neolithic Period, Ch'i-chia Culture, ca. 2000–1500 BC. Purchase, Edward L. Whittemore Fund.

The cultural diversity of neolithic China is most vividly attested by regional styles in ceramics. This tautly contoured beaker is distinctive to a northwestern farming culture centered in the loess highlands of Kansu Province and extending to Ch'inghai, Ninghsia, and Inner Mongolia. Its delicately hand-modeled form conjoins a bi-conical body with a funnel-shaped neck. The concentric striations visible around the outer rim suggest that the piece was finished on a revolving turntable. Flat strap handles, pressed against a plaitwork, are luted onto the rim and shoulder. The fine-grained buff clay is partly coated with a thin layer of slip and lightly pared to smooth and accentuate the profile. Whereas overall lustre was probably achieved by burnishing the damp clay with a pebble, the random patches of reddish brown resulted inadvertently from irregular oxidation during firing.

Beakers of similar scale but different proportions have been excavated from both cemeteries and dwelling sites. Generally more carefully shaped and of finer clay than accompanying pots for cooking and storage, they probably served as drinking cups before being interred as mortuary gifts. In 1924 the Swedish geologist Johan Gunner Andersson first recognized a "Ch'i-chia culture" near the village of Ch'i-chia-p'ing in Kansu Province but dated it too early in the neolithic sequence. Extensive, stratigraphic excavations, supplemented by radiocarbon tests, have determined that in approximately 2000 BC, the Ch'i-chia succeeded other communities distinguished by boldly painted urns. Small objects of copper and bronze, recently unearthed from Ch'i-chia sites, confirm this late neolithic dating but raise new questions about the potters' possible inspiration from neighboring metalsmiths. Despite their hardedged clarity in thin handles and sharp curves, these clay vessels have yet to find a metal prototype. EP

EX COLLECTION Walter Hochstadter.

LITERATURE Margrit Bylin-Althin, "The Sites of Ch'i Chia P'ing and Lo Han T'ang in Kansu," *Bulletin of the Museum of Far Eastern Antiquities* [Stockholm], XIX (1946) esp. 383-418 (publication of Andersson's early discoveries). Kansu Archaeological Team, "Excavation of the Remains of Ch'i-chia Culture at Ta-ho-chuang in Yung-ch'uang in Yung-ch'ing County, Kansu," in Chinese with English summary, *K'ao-ku hsüeh-pao,* 1974 / 2, pl. 6:1, 2 (beaker of similar proportions). Chang Kuang-chih, *The Archaeology of Ancient China,* 3rd edition rev. (New Haven and London: Yale University Press, 1977) pp. 195-199. Clarence F. Shangraw, *Origins of Chinese Ceramics,* exhib. cat. (New York: China House Gallery, 1978) pp. 29-30 (comparative survey of Ch'i-chia and other neolithic wares).

89 Cylindrical Jar 48.214
(Lien or Tsun)

Buff earthenware, lead-glazed with molded relief decoration. H. 26.7 cm. Diam. 27.3 cm. China. Han Dynasty, 206 BC–AD 220. Purchase from the J. H. Wade Fund.

The well-furnished Han Dynasty tomb included earthenware substitutes for vessels of more valuable materials, buried in sets for the use and comfort of the deceased. This cylindrical shape was common to both cosmetic boxes *(lien)* of lacquer and wine warmers *(tsun)* of bronze. Bronze versions clearly inspired these squatting bear feet and ogre-mask ring-

handles, the latter free-swinging and functional in metal, but here immobile and decorative. They are centered on two molded relief panels joined along vertical seams. The originally crisp relief is softened by a lead glaze; its thickness is visible in drops which accumulated along the rim when the vessel was fired upside-down. Unlike most Han Dynasty glazes colored green by copper oxide, this yellowish-brown glaze probably contains iron absorbed from the clay body. Centuries of burial have decomposed the glaze into thin layers, which reflect light with a slight iridescence.

Similar cylinders are often called "hill jars" since many survive with conicial covers molded in rising peaks. Their relief bands most frequently depict an animal chase along rolling hills or waves. By contrast this extraordinary terrain — wavelike hills and precipitous peaks sprouting foliage — is populated with a menagerie of real and imaginary creatures. Rambling amid the animals are wispy semihuman elves, who achieved eternal life in cults of Taoist mysticism prevalent during the Han Dynasty. Their legendary homelands in distant eastern and western realms are suggested by the dragon and tiger — directional symbols of Han cosmology — stalking opposite sides of the jar. Unrolled, this panorama may describe a paradise of immortality idealized in popular cults and sought for the deceased in burial offering. But regardless of symbolism or function, this sculptural landscape provides rare evidence for contemporary paintings in more fragile media, now lost. EP

EX COLLECTION Dikran G. Kelekian.

EXHIBITIONS Chicago, 1917: The Art Institute of Chicago, The Kelekian Collection of Ancient Chinese Potteries, cat. by John Getz, no. 121. Cleveland, 1954: The Cleveland

Drawing traced from an ink rubbing of the molded relief decoration.

Museum of Art, Chinese Landscape Painting, cat. by Sherman E. Lee (2nd edition, rev., 1962), no. 4.

PUBLICATIONS Michael Sullivan, *The Birth of Landscape Painting in China* (London, Berkeley, and Los Angeles: University of California Press, 1962) p. 55, pl. 40. *Kodai Chugoku* [Ancient China], comp. Aida Yuji et al., vol. III of *Sekai rekishi shirizu* [The world history series] (Tokyo: Sekai Bunka sha, 1967) 202.

LITERATURE Berthold Laufer, *Chinese Pottery of the Han Dynasty* (Leiden: E. J. Brill, 1909; 2nd edition, Rutland, Vt.: C. E. Tuttle, 1962) pp. 198-212 (examples of typical hill jars in the Field Museum of Natural History, Chicago). René-Yvon Lefebvre d'Argencé, *Bronze Vessels of Ancient China in the Avery Brundage Collection* (San Francisco: The de Young Museum Society, 1977) pl. LX, lower right (gilt bronze wine warmer with relief landscape).

90 Jar *(Hu)* 54.370

Reddish gray stoneware, iron-glazed with incised and applied decoration. China, probably Chechiang Province (Shao-hsing type). H. 45.7 cm., Diam. 39.4 cm. Early Eastern Han Dynasty, 1st century AD. Edward L. Whittemore Fund.

Since the turn of this century, archaeological excavations have unearthed a closely related group of jars from Han burials to the north and south of the Yangtze River. They are usually found in pairs and, in fact, a partially damaged jar almost identical to the Cleveland vessel is in the Shanghai Museum. Characteristic of this ceramic family are their trumpet-shaped necks and globular bodies. Many also exhibit raised relief decoration in the form of horizontal rope bands and non-functional loop handles suspended from animal masks (cf. [89]) — features borrowed from the decorative vocabulary of Chinese bronzes. The two bands of spirals terminating in bird forms incised on the shoulder of the Cleveland and Shanghai jars occur also in recently excavated examples as well as those preserved in various museum collections outside China. However the lowest incised register of rhomboid lozenges (a motif common to Han textiles and lacquer) alternating with a domino-like configuration (so far found only in Kuangtung ceramics) is unique within this family of jars. Equally unprecedented is the sheer finish of the Cleveland and Shanghai jars. Unlike many of their counterparts, they exhibit a smooth outer surface, terminating in a tall, elegantly modulated ring foot which has virtually no peer in other surviving members of this group.

The kiln site actually responsible for such refinement has so far not been located. Shao-hsing, Chechiang Province, is commonly considered their point of origin since so many jars have been unearthed from tombs in that district. This jar and its counterparts do exhibit the iron-rich gray fabric burnt red in firing which characterizes later Shao-hsing, products. The inconsistency in glaze color within the group — from yellow through gray-green to reddish brown — is also the result of iron subjected to unpredictable kiln atmospheres. It would take until the late third century for the potters of Chechiang to reduce the amount of oxygen in their kilns to the extent necessary for the formation of the glaze color which we call celadon green. HJK

EX COLLECTION Mrs. Louis Wannieck.

PUBLICATIONS Sherman E. Lee, "The Celadon Tradition," CMA *Bulletin*, XLIII (March 1956) fig. 1. J. Mayuyama and H. Igaki, "Chinese Ceramics in the Collection of The Cleveland Museum of Art," in Japanese, *Tosetsu*, no. 41 (August 1956) p. 42, pl. 1. *Kodai Chugoku*, vol. III of *Sekai rekishi shirizu* (1967) 203. Margaret Medley, *The Chinese Potter: A Practical History of Chinese Ceramics* (Oxford: Phaidon Press, 1976) p. 49, fig. 29. Katherine R. Tsiang, "Glazed Stonewares of the Han Dynasty: Part One — The Eastern Group," *Artibus Asiae*, XL, 2/3 (1978) 150, fig. 21.

LITERATURE Chiang Hsüan-i and Ch'in T'ing-yü, *Chung-kuo tz'u-ch'i fa-ming* [The invention of Chinese porcelain; study of early ceramics excavated in Shao-hsing, Chechiang Province], in Chinese (Shanghai: I-yüan chen-sheng she, 1956) p. 10, lower plate (Shanghai Museum). Chu Po-ch'ien, "Shao-hsing Li-chu ti Han mu" [The Han tombs at Li-chu, Shao-hsing], in Chinese, *K'ao-ku hsüeh-pao*, 1957 / 1, pl. IV, 1-3. Mary Tregear, *Catalogue of Chinese Greenware: Ashmolean Museum, Oxford* (Oxford: Clarendon Press, 1976) p. 17, pl. 11.

91 Jar with Tiger Head Spout: Yüeh Ware 70.152

Gray stoneware, iron-glazed, with applied, carved, and incised decoration. H. 20.5 cm., Diam. 17.2 cm. China (southern). Western-Eastern Chin transition, late 3rd–5th centuries AD. Purchase from the J. H. Wade Fund.

The gray bodied and celadon glazed porcelains of Chechiang and Chiangsu provinces are called Yüeh ware, after the small kingdom which rose in the sixth century BC to control that region. The abundance of kiln sites and burial remains excavated there indicates that the Yüeh ceramic industry experienced a sudden expansion of activity from the third century onward. This phenomenon can be attributed in part to a change in Chinese drinking habits. By the third century, tea replaced grain wine as the staple liquid refreshment in the Yangtze River region. Significantly the provinces within the boundaries of the old Yüeh kingdom were also blessed with prosperous tea plantations. By the fourth century the quality of this local tea as well as the pottery made to serve it was so great that contemporary poets came to praise Yüeh products in their tea poetry.

The Yüeh potter did not limit himself to teacups alone. A variety of utilitarian objects survive, many of which were decorated with and even formed into the shape of animals. In this pouring vessel, a playfully ferocious tiger's head serves both as a functional spout and as the chief focus of ornament, complemented only by lightly incised string bands and rope-patterned handles. The jar deserves our attention because its tiger-headed spout is a rare survivor from the Six Dynasties period. Beyond that remain purely ceramic considerations. Note how, from its thinly potted neck, the vessel swells, then constricts to a narrow concave base. These springing rhythms in its profile create a linear grace attained by the most talented Chinese potters in the fourth and succeeding centuries. Likewise, the fairly uniform yellow-green glaze coating this jar and other contemporary Yüeh vessels represents a technological improvement over the unpredictable glaze colorations of the preceding Han Dynasty (cf. [90]). This pale green glaze, which won the admiration of fourth-century poets, also functioned as the backbone of Chinese ceramic manufacture for the next thousand years. HJK

EXHIBITION Los Angeles, 1952: Los Angeles County Museum of Art, Chinese Ceramics from the Prehistoric Period through Ch'ien Lung, cat. by Henry Trubner, no. 51.

LITERATURE René-Yvon Lefebvre d'Argencé, *Chinese Ceramics in the Avery Brundage Collection* (San Francisco: The de Young Museum Society, 1967) pl. XV. The Nanking Museum, "Cultural Objects Unearthed from Six Dynasties Burials in the Nanking Vicinity," in Chinese, *K'ao-ku* 1955/8, pl. VIII (tomb dated AD 293). Idem, ed., *Chiang-su Liu-ch'ao ch'ing-tz'u* [Celadon wares of the Six Dynasties excavated in Chiangsu Province] (Peking: Wen-wu ch'u-pan she, 1980) pl. 43.

99 Harpist.
China (northern).
T'ang Dynasty,
second quarter 8th century.

110 *Kuan* Ware Basin. China, Chechiang Province. Southern Sung — Yüan dynasties, 12th–14th centuries.

126 Stem Cup with Design of Sea Monsters. China, Ching-te-chen, Chianghsi Province. Ming Dynasty, mark and reign of Hsüan-te (1426–1435).

127 Wine Cup with Decoration of Children Playing. China, Ching-te-chen, Chianghsi Province. Ming Dynasty, mark and reign of Ch'eng-hua (1465–1487).

136 Vase with Decoration of Golden Pheasants. China, Ch'ing Dynasty, mark and reign of Ch'ien-lung (1736–1795).

92 Chicken-Headed Ewer: Yüeh Ware 73.84

Gray stoneware, iron-glazed, with applied, carved, and incised decoration. H. 23.5 cm., Diam. 15.5 cm. China, Chechiang Province (Hsiao-shan type). Six Dynasties period, mid-5th century AD. Gift of Mr. and Mrs. John D. MacDonald.

Although the tiger-head jar (see [91]) appears rarely, the chicken-headed ewer must have been the bread and butter of the Yüeh potter. This shape, sometimes sporting a clay coil handle in the form of a dragon, surfaces frequently at the Yüeh kiln sites and burials in southern China excavated in recent years. In fact the motif became so popular during the Six Dynasties period that it was imitated by potters working far to the north and to the south of the Yüeh kilns. However, this ewer is one of the few in Western collections. Rarer still is the lotus petal band carved and incised around its body. The motif so far has been found only at the Shan-tung kiln, recently excavated in Hsiao-shan district, Chechiang Province.

In addition to its archaeological interest, this pairing of animal with flower has iconographical importance. The chicken, the tiger, and the dragon are three of the twelve animals which represent the zodiac within the Chinese cosmological system. By the end of the Six Dynasties, the twelve animal heads would be joined to earthenware statuary of human form and placed in northern Chinese burials. The lotus, on the other hand, is a purely Buddhist symbol: just as the flower unfolds spotlessly from the muddy waters surrounding it, so does the enlightened disciple of the Buddhist way rise above the entrapping world of the senses. Buddhism traveled the sea and silk routes from India and began to infiltrate the Chinese empire about two hundred years before this vessel was made. In order that the Indian scriptures be translated and the message of the Buddha's path of salvation be accepted, Buddhist adepts in the Yangtze region often borrowed the vocabulary of Confucianism and Taoism to translate the Indian scriptures. The potter of this vessel probably did not mean to provide a deep philosophical insight when combining symbols from indigenous and foreign cosmologies to decorate its surface. The presence of the Buddhist lotus on this and other Shan-tung kiln products simply indicates a measure of acceptance which the foreign religion enjoyed among the Chinese south of the Yangtze River. HJK

EXHIBITION Los Angeles, 1952: Los Angeles Country Museum of Art, Chinese Ceramics from the Prehistoric Period through Ch'ien Lung, cat. by Henry Trubner, no. 52.

LITERATURE Feng Hsien-ming, "Basic Information on Ceramics," in Chinese, *Wen wu*, 1960/4, pp. 81-83 (Development of the chicken-headed ewer). *Chugoku bijutsu gosen-nen ten* [Exhibition of 5000 years of Chinese art], exhib. cat (Osaka: Osaka Municipal Museum, 1966) no. 4-15. Albert le Bonheur et al., *Musée Guimet*, vol. VIII of *Oriental Ceramics: The World's Great Collections*, ed. Fujio Koyama and John A. Pope (Tokyo: Kodansha, 1977) monochrome pl. 12. Huang T'i, ed., *Shang-hai po-wu-kuan ts'ang tz'u hsüan-chi* [Selected porcelains from the collection of the Shanghai Museum] (Peking: Wen-wu ch'u-pan she, 1979) pl. 16. G. St. G. M. Gompertz, *Chinese Celadon Wares*, 2nd edition rev. (London: Faber and Faber, 1980) p. 45, pl. 7B (Japanese collection).

93 Candlestand 30.322

Cream-white stoneware, feldspathic glaze, with applied and carved decoration. H. 29.8 cm., Diam. of base 15.5 cm. China. Sui or early T'ang Dynasty, ca. 7th century AD. Charles W. Harkness Fund.

Throughout early Chinese history, candle or oil lamps were manufactured in styles ranging from the simple and functional to the complex and ornamental. This lamp is typical of the pedestaled version prevalent during the brief Sui Dynasty (589–618 and at the beginning of T'ang (618–906). The underlying form is wheel-thrown in sections: the base an inverted bowl, the shaft a narrow cylinder emphasizing the ridges and grooves of the throwing process, the candle container combining a tubular socket and a shallow dish for the dripping wax. Applied elements enliven it as an imaginative sculpture: open lotus petals, a pair of identical writhing dragons, and acanthus-like leaves. Most striking are the dragons, their elongated bodies formed of alternately coiled ropes of clay. Each grasps the trunk of its partner with one forepaw and upholds a leaf with the second. Powerfully carved leg muscles and clawed feet contrast with the more delicate heads with tapered snouts and curved eyebrows, echoing the elegantly upturned leaves. While dragon-head handles are standard features of sixth- and seventh-century amphorae (cf. CMA 54.371), these are among the earliest clay creatures rendered fully from head to looped tail.

The lotus base was more pervasive in decorative art at this time — common to secular vessels and tomb figures as well as the Buddhist statuary from which it originally derived. Its combination with a coiled dragon shaft is known from Buddhist stone lanterns, most notably a late T'ang Dynasty example in the Ansho-ji temple near Kyoto, Japan. Whether our lotus-and-dragon candlestand originally served a Buddhist function is open to question. Related examples include a dish-shaped base below the dragon shaft and lotus blossom container above (Musée Guimet, Paris; Museum of Fine Arts, Boston) and censers with conical perforated covers for releasing fragrant smoke (e.g., Tohata collection, Kobe, Japan). Alongside plain examples, candlestands with lotus bases have been found in tombs and probably were made for special domestic use before burial. Both aromatic and graduated ("time telling") candles figure prominently in T'ang poetry.

High relief appliqués partly inspired by Buddhist art ornament numerous stoneware vessels of the sixth and seventh centuries — both whitewares and gray-green celadons. This minutely crazed glaze, transparent but tinged yellow-green where thick, may agree with the Chinese description of "crab shell" celadon. But it also corresponds with one of various white-glazed stonewares found in northern Chinese tombs of the early seventh century. Within the next hundred years, technical refinements of this body and glaze culminated in the development of the first true white porcelain. EP

EXHIBITIONS Los Angeles, 1952: Los Angeles Country Museum of Art, Chinese Ceramics from the Prehistoric Period through Ch'ien Lung, cat. by Henry Trubner, no. 92. New York, 1953: China House Gallery, T'ang Art.

PUBLICATIONS *Zui-To hen* [Sui-T'ang], vol. IX of *Sekai toji zenshu* [Ceramic art of the world], ed. Koyama Fujio et al. (Tokyo: Kawade Shobo, 1956) fig. 46. Kobayashi Taichiro, *To-So no Hakuji* [White Porcelain of the T'ang and Sung dynasties], vol. XII of *Toki zenshu* [Complete catalog of ceramics] (Tokyo: Heibonsha, 1959) pl. 3 (as "Hsing ware"). Fujioka Ryoichi, "Green Glazed Hill Censer with Two Coiling Dragons" [Tohata collection, Kobe], in Japanese, *Yamato bunka,* no. XXXIV (March 1961) fig. 4; cf. figs. 3 (candlestand or censer, Museum of Fine Arts, Boston) and 5 (stone lantern, Ansho-ji). Hasebe Gakuji, ed., *Toji* [Ceramics], vol. V of *Chugoku bijutsu* [Chinese art in Western collections], ed. Akiyama Terukazu et al. (Tokyo: Kodansha, 1973) color pl. 14. Madeleine Paul-David, "Un chandelier chinois du début du VIIe siècle au Musée Guimet," *La Revue du Louvre et des Musées de France,* XXVI (1976) fig. 3; cf. figs. 1, 2.

LITERATURE Yutaka Mino, *Pre-Sung Dynasty Chinese Stonewares in the Royal Ontario Museum* (Toronto, 1974) no. 50.

94 Ewer *(Hsiao-k'ou hu)* 66.145

Buff stoneware, iron-brown patches under alkaline glaze, with applied relief decoration. H. 22.5 cm., Diam. 16.3 cm. China, T'ung-kuan kiln complex, Hunan Province (Wa-cha-p'ing type). T'ang Dynasty, 8th–9th centuries AD. 50th Anniversary Gift.

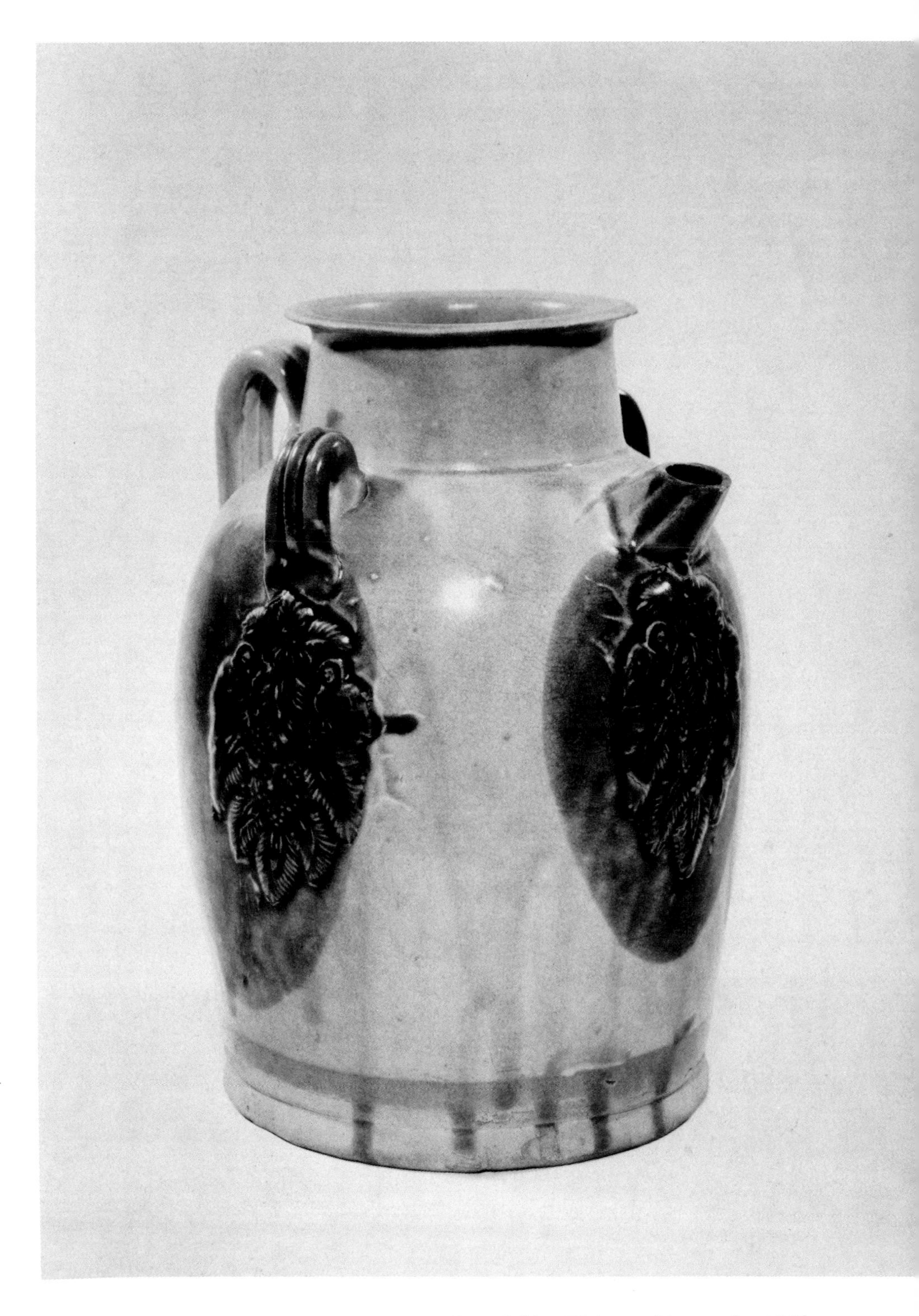

This stout jug belongs to a coherent group provisionally dated to the T'ang Dynasty since the 1940s, when examples were reportedly collected from tombs in the Ch'angsha municipality of southern Hunan Province. In 1956 the search for local production ended at Wa-cha-p'ing north of Ch'angsha, where the discovery of kiln ruins brought to light one center of a progressive ceramic industry. Here potters forfeited refinements of material for inventive experiments with surface design. The regional clay was slightly gritty, and their low-fired alkaline glaze characteristically thin and pale. But applied over molded reliefs and metallic oxide pigments, it effectively sheathed contrasting textures and colors. Such forthright if inelegant decoration enhances vigorous shapes like this bulging cylinder with its articulated neck, rimmed mouth, polygonal spout, and triple-strand handles. Few examples share this vessel's secure volume and just proportions, its solid contours accented by symmetrically repeated relief appliqués and firm but uneven patches of iron brown — a glazelike slip probably applied with a pad. The relief motifs vary widely. These confronted birds and leaves, common also to textiles and metalwork, illustrate T'ang Dynasty taste for heraldic motifs of ultimately Persian derivation. Among similar ewers in North American collections, the appliqués incorporate fruit, fish, flowers, and human figures.

Competent and surprisingly lightweight potting made these utilitarian ewers a staple kiln product with widespread demand in China, Korea, Indonesia, and the Near East. Among the Korean imports, a few are inscribed with the surnames of family studios, the vessel name, *hsiao-k'ou* ("small mouth"), and a commercial promotion such as "famous under heaven" or "first under heaven." Islamic merchants who established trading posts along China's southern coast shipped them to Nishapur in Iran, where excavations initially suggested a ninth-century date. Recent Chinese surveys of the broader environs of Wa-cha-p'ing indicate that production may have begun at least one century earlier. EP

PUBLICATIONS Thomas Shafer, *Pottery Decoration* (New York: Watson-Guptill, 1976) repr. p. 69. M. Medley, *The Chinese Potter*, fig. 68 (erroneously captioned "Chinese Government"). Idem, *T'ang Pottery and Porcelain* (London: Faber and Faber, 1981) pl. 88.

LITERATURE Hsien-ch'i Tseng and Robert Paul Dart, *The Charles B. Hoyt Collection in the Museum of Fine Arts, Boston* (New York: October House, 1964) I, no. 110. R.-Y. L. d'Argencé, *Chinese Ceramics in the Avery Brundage Collection*, pl. XIX:A. Mino, *Pre-Sung Dynasty Chinese Stonewares in the Royal Ontario Museum*, no. 59. *Hsin Chung-kuo ch'u-t'u wen wu: Historical Relics Unearthed in New China* (Peking: Wai-wen ch'u-pan she, 1972) no. 158 (Similar jug excavated in 1958 from kiln ruins at Wa-ni-tuan near Wa-cha-p'ing). Ch'eng Te-k'un, "T'ang Ceramic Wares of Ch'angsha," *Journal of the Institute of Chinese Studies* [The Chinese University of Hong Kong], III, no. 1 (September 1970) 1-53, esp. pls. 66, 75 (for related ewers). Ch'angsha Municipal Cultural Bureau, "An investigation of T'ung-kuan Kiln-Sites of the T'ang Dynasty at Ch'angsha," in Chinese with English summary, *K'ao-ku hsüeh-pao*, 1980/1, pp. 67-96 — the Chinese classify this and similar Ch'angsha wares with underglaze painting as celadons.

95 Jar *(Kuan)*: Huang-tao Ware 15.381

Grayish-white stoneware with blended iron and ash-phosphoric glazes. H. 29.3 cm., Diam. 26 cm. China, probably Chia district, Honan Province. T'ang Dynasty, 8th–9th century AD. Gift of Ralph King.

The balanced wheel-thrown form of this ovoid jar is a standard for the middle and late T'angDynasty. Numerous sturdily potted jars in earthenware and stoneware vary only in more elongated or globular profile. Here, the expansive contours swell upward from the beveled foot to an extra full hemispherical shoulder, then contract into a short concave neck and everted rim. Two layers of glaze enhance its bursting rotundity: a lustrous brown-black that thins to finely crazed olive-brown and a cream shading to violet-blue mottled with tan. The first, applied by dipping the vessel upside down, coats the interior and stops unevenly above the foot to prevent sticking to the kiln floor. The second, splashed or poured over four overlapping areas of the shoulder, cascades in diagonal streaks as if pulled by the momentum of a rotating wheel.

While this shape and the dense brown-black glaze are characteristic of widespread T'ang production, the unusual bluish suffusions most closely resemble opaque blue and purple-stained glazes of Chün ware developed in the subsequent Sung and Chin dynasties (cf. [105]). Consequently, this and similarly glazed vessels were often misidentified as imitations of Chün before kiln ruins established their origin in the T'ang Dynasty at Huang-tao and other sites in central and western Honan Province. Since Chün kilns are located in this vicinity, Huang-tao ware is now generally recognized as an innovative precursor to Chün ware. But the chemistry of its abstract color patterns has yet to be consistently analyzed. The suffusions are alternately described as feldspathic or ash (containing phosphorous, like Chün), and the metallic colorant as cobalt, iron, or copper. Moreover, diverse examples suggest variations in glaze formulas as well as application and firing conditions: The brown-black may have a mat finish, and the bluish suffusions may be thicker and more viscous, patterned in even patches or allowed to stream down and gather in frothy-looking drops. More rarely, dark suffusions overlay a pale blue-gray glaze. EP

PUBLICATIONS Sherman E. Lee, "Two Basement Excavations, A Twelfth-Century Bargain, and a Gift," *Far Eastern Ceramic Bulletin,* IX, nos. 1-2 (March–June 1957) pl. 1. Henry J. Kleinhenz, "Porcelains for Imperial Use: The Sung Dynasty," CMA *Bulletin,* LXV (April 1978) fig. 9.

LITERATURE John Ayers, *The Seligman Collection of Oriental Art,* vol. II: *Chinese and Corean Pottery and Porcelain* (London: Lund Humphries, 1964) no. D57, pl. XXIII. Mino, *Pre-Sung Dynasty Chinese Stonewares in the Royal Ontario Museum,* no. 63. Celia Carrington Riely, *Chinese Art from the Cloud Wampler and Other Collections in the Everson Museum* (New York: Frederick A. Praeger, 1968) no. 25 (discussion of the Huang-tao glaze). In addition to Huang-tao in Chia district, kiln sites for T'ang black ware with blue "mottles" have since been reported in the neighboring districts of Yu and Lu-shan. However, many examples in Chinese museums (Palace Museum, Peking, and Shanghai Museum) were excavated from tombs rather than kiln sites in Honan.

96 Polo Player 64.181

Buff earthenware with remains of polychrome slip decoration. H. 30.4 cm., L. 38.4 cm. China, probably Shenhsi or Honan Province. T'ang Dynasty, late 7th–early 8th century AD. Severance A. and Greta Millikin Collection.

Like a star the ball hits the field
Like a new moon the stick turns it up.
Ts'ai Fu, T'ang Dynasty

Once introduced from Tibet or Persia early in the T'ang Dynasty (618–906), polo instantly became a favorite recreation of Chinese nobility. It was patronized by successive emperors who accepted foreign tribute gifts of polo ponies, sponsored matches in the imperial theater, and opened polo grounds in the palace complex of Ch'angan (831). The sport was decreed an exercise for military troops but popularized by men and women of all ages — described by contemporary poets as "moon batters" after the crescent-shaped tip of the T'ang polo stick. Its form is most graphically illustrated in wall murals depicting a polo match in the tomb of Chang-huai, a crown prince reputed as a skillful player and buried in the outskirts of Ch'angan (present-day Hsian, Shenhsi) in 706.

That polo was deemed an appropriate subject of tomb painting is symptomatic of the T'ang Dynasty — an exuberant age when even funerary artists replicated daily life and its current fashions with keen observation and style. Decades before the 1971 excavation of Chang-huai's tomb, randomly collected burial figures had been identified as polo players by animated pose and gesture, despite loss or disintegration of their sliver-thin sticks. The Millikin figure, turned sharply in the saddle with arm poised for a downstroke, probably represents a young Chinese woman of ca. 800 dressed in a man's riding habit of "barbarian" origin — then considered exotic, daring, and hence very chic. Clothing features are clearly carved in low relief and detail, but their original color must be envisioned from traces of slip-pigment. Her large peaked hat with upturned brim, appropriated from felt styles of Central Asia or the Near East, was painted red to match the tunic fitted over tight orange sleeves; pale green breeches overlay pink trousers and black boots. The once florid saddle blanket now shows only a few red blossoms faintly outlined on one side. Traces of white slip remain on the horse's mane, head, and tail, and on the rider's face.

Her spirited mount runs in a "flying gallop," all four legs outstretched as if in mid-leap. This unrealistic but convincing portrayal of intense speed was a convention used by Chinese painters for centuries but newly adopted by ceramic sculptors. It required a complex assembly of molded and hand-modeled parts, disguised when finished by smoothing and detail: full-round contours lightly pared, arched neck and tense leg muscles deeply grooved. The hollow trunk, probably molded in left and right halves, has been perforated with a small hole under the hind legs to prevent explosion in the kiln. This structurally differs from a set of four polo players in the Nelson Gallery-Atkins Museum in Kansas City, where each has a large hole in its belly for insertion of a pedestal support. Here, the original pedestal may have cradled the belly like its modern wood replacement. EP

EX COLLECTION John L. Severance.

LITERATURE Carl Diem, *Asiatische Reiterspiele* (Berlin: Deutscher Archiv-Verlag, 1941) p. 145 (poem) and figs. 67-72. Ch'en Wan-li, *T'ao Yung* [Pottery figures] (Peking: Chung-kuo ku-t'ien i-shu ch'u-pan she, 1957) pl. 54. Jane Gaston Mahler, *The Westerners among the Figurines of the T'ang Dynasty of China* (Rome: Instituto Italiano per Il Medio Ed Estremo Oriente, 1959) pl. XXX (polo players, Nelson Gallery-Atkins Museum, Kansas City). *Han T'ang pi-hua: Murals from the Han to the T'ang Dynasty* (Peking: Foreign Languages Press, 1974) pls. 78-80 ("polo playing" mural, tomb of Crown Prince Chang-huai).

Ezekiel Schloss, *Ancient Chinese Ceramic Sculpture from Han through T'ang* (Stamford, CT: Castle Publishing Co., 1977) esp. p. 59, drawing no. 11 (reconstruction of the multipiece mold used to form an equestrian group). *Chuka Jimmin Kyowakoku shiruku rodo bunbutsu ten: Sansei, Kanshuku, Shinkyo shutsudo* [Exhibition of ancient art treasures of The People's Republic of China: Archaeological finds of the Han to T'ang Dynasty unearthed at sites along the Silk Road], exhib. cat. (Tokyo: Tokyo National Museum, 1979) no. 104 (male polo player unearthed in Turfan).

97 Bactrian Camel 67.147

Light buff earthenware, lead-glazed. H. 79.4 cm., L. 61 cm. Base probably modern. China, probably Shenhsi or Honan Province. T'ang Dynasty, late 7th–first half 8th century AD. Purchase, John L. Severance Fund.

Ceramic figures made exclusively for burial reached their most opulent proportions between the late seventh and mid-eighth centuries. At the height of T'ang Dynasty prosperity, noble society constructed elaborate underground tombs and populated them with colorful replicas of cosmopolitan life. Bactrian camels were vital to such conspicuous wealth. Indispensable for caravan traffic, they carried luxurious burdens across the desert silk routes between northwest China and the Near East. Models of this size and sturdy bearing have been excavated primarily from cemeteries sur-

rounding the T'ang capital sites of Ch'angan in Shenhsi and Loyang in Honan. Usually paired with figures of Central Asian grooms, they may be aligned in a main chamber or crowded into niches specially dug to contain them.

Such large, hollow figures were composed of interchangeable piece-molds probably assembled on an armature. A herd of camels in this typical posture of braying may have been roughly shaped by molds taken from a common model, but hand smoothing and carving distinguished individual beasts. On the exterior of this camel, joins are visible only in the humps, either cast separately or cut off, hollowed, and re-applied with seams and knife marks for alignment left exposed. Ridges inside the neck and along the thighs indicate other points of assembly. The ungainly animal is otherwise abstracted to a sleek play of contours, its neck slightly twisted out of absolute profile. Facial features, angular and furrowed, are observed from anatomy yet stylized by deep grooves that also appear on the neck and forelegs.

The glossy amber coat sheathing this compact silhouette represents seventh-century improvement in lead glaze chemistry (cf. [89]). Red lead and silica were melted and reground to form a fluid, transparent, and non-toxic base, colored by the measured addition of powdered metal oxides. Different proportions of an iron oxide similar to rust yielded a range of hues from yellow to deep brown. While exact recipes for this medium amber tone probably varied among potters, almost all coated the body with an underlying white slip to assure true and vivid color. Modern repairs on the lower neck and four legs approximate this color, but not the fine network of surface crazing formed over centuries of burial in damp earth. EP

LITERATURE *Tokyo Kokuritsu Hakubutsukan zuhan mokuroku: Chugoku kotoji-hen* [Illustrated catalog of the Tokyo National Museum: Chinese ceramics] (Kyoto: Benrido, 1965) no. 137 (camel of similar scale and modeling with polychrome glaze). Margaret Medley, *T'ang Pottery and Porcelain*, pp. 45-63.

Technical note: Laboratory examination with the base removed indicates that the camel was fired directly on its feet. The pad of each foot has been dug with a small hole, apparently for insertion of a stilt, and washed with a talclike substance. These two procedures would have elevated the figure and prevented its sticking to the kiln floor.

98 Caparisoned Horse 55.295

White earthenware, with three-color (*san-ts'ai*) lead glaze. H. 76.8 cm., L. 80.3 cm. China, probably Shenhsi or Honan Province. T'ang Dynasty, first half 8th century AD. Anonymous Gift.

Purebred horses were never so admired as during the T'ang Dynasty, when Arabian steeds were imported for imperial stables and ceramic models commissioned for aristocratic tombs. Among innumerable horses mass-produced for burial retinues, this vigilant animal belongs to an unusually large and elaborately caparisoned stock, sculpted with convincing volume and spirit. The few excavated examples of comparable scale and known age come from tombs of civil and military elite dated by epitaph to the early and mid-eighth century. In remarkably consistent fashion, all stand firmly foursquare with neck and head turned leftward. Their mechanical piece-mold assembly is disguised by details hand-modeled in leather-hard clay: fully rounded muscular flanks, hogged mane, parted forelock, and tied tail. Relief trappings are the main distinction between one well-groomed figure and another. Here pendant medallions, resembling actual brass examples of the period, are stamped and applied under thin harness straps firmly luted to hind- and forequarters. Bridle straps are so carefully fitted as to be pulled with some tension under the cheeks.

Neatly apportioned colors illustrate one conservative option of the versatile polychrome glaze — this a typical "three color" palette of amber, brown, and green. The subtle contrast in tone between saddle and horse is a measure of control achieved most precisely between relief boundaries. Only over the lower legs are contrasting colors allowed to streak and overlap — a natural quality of fluid lead glazes exploited on similar horses for quite different, splashy effects.

By the eighth century, the demand for funerary figures was so great that imperial edicts were issued to limit the size and number allowed for privileged officials. Tomb finds prove that production far exceeded these quotas. But for many years, kiln site evidence for T'ang polychrome glazing was limited to a few fragmentary vessels found in Kung-hsien east of Loyang, Honan. This evidence has recently been supplemented by more complete vessels as well as small figures and molds, which offer promise for locating the sculpture studios in this area. EP

PUBLICATIONS Glenn C. Nelson, *Ceramics: A Potter's Handbook*, 3rd edition (New York: Holt Rinehart and Winston, 1971) color pl. 1. Robert Tichane, *Those Celadon Blues* (Painted Post, NY: New York State Institute for Glaze Research, 1978) p. 20, fig. 3.8. Janet Gaylord Moore, *The Eastern Gate* (Cleveland and New York: William Collins, 1979) repr. pp. 73, 86 (color). Sherman E. Lee, *A History of Far Eastern Art*, 4th edition (Englewood Cliffs, NJ, and New York: Prentice-Hall and Harry N. Abrams, 1982) p. 285, repr. p. 279, color pl. 23.

LITERATURE John G. Ayers, *Victoria and Albert Museum*, vol. VI of *Oriental Ceramics: The World's Great Collections* (Tokyo: Kodansha, 1976) color pl. 13 (horse of almost identical proportions with similar trappings but different saddle and free-flowing three-color glaze). *T'ang Ch'ang-an ch'eng chiao Sui T'ang mu: Excavation of the Sui and T'ang Tombs at Xi'an* [Hsian], in Chinese with English abstract (Peking: Wen-wu ch'u-pan she, 1980) color pl. 1 (similarly modeled, slightly smaller horse from tomb of Hsien-yu Ting-hui, dated AD 723).

99 Harpist 31.450

Reddish-gray earthenware, slip-coated under three-color (*san-ts'ai*) lead glaze and polychrome slip decoration. H. 32.1 cm., W. 14.4 cm. China (northern). T'ang Dynasty, second quarter 8th century AD. Purchase, Edward L. Whittemore Fund.

After four centuries of political turmoil and social disorder, a reunited China during the first half of the T'ang Dynasty (618–906) was an age of unprecedented prosperity, vitality, and creativity. The self-confident spirit of the time was reflected vigorously by the T'ang potters in their innovation with lead-silicate glazes. The lead glazes were nothing new in monochromed wares since the Han Dynasty, but mixing them with multiple colorants for ceramic decoration was a T'ang development. Fired in an oxidizing atmosphere at relatively low temperature, these glazes produced a rich pallete of the "three colors" (*san-ts'ai*) whose aesthetic appeal is frankly down-to-earth, exuberantly bourgeois and sensuous, and unparalleled in any other period. The usual flamboyant impression, however, is quietly subdued in the case of this seated musician, partly as a result of glaze deterioration which has left only a small part of the original bright yellow on the long, high-waisted skirt. The white slip underneath thus exposed is also flaking in some areas, revealing the chalky reddish-gray body. The upper garment is colored in amber-brown, with traces of cobalt blue remaining on the collars and scarves. The face and hair were not glazed but delicately painted. Despite the loss of color the figure retains its original

Caparisoned Horse [98]

air of natural elegance so typical of "high T'ang" ceramic sculpture. This is achieved by the ease of its sitting posture and the simplicity of the free flowing folds gathered gracefully at the feet of the young lady. She is sitting on a plinth shaped like a narrow-waisted drum (*yao-ku*), with one foot raised and resting on a garden rock to balance the musical instrument she is playing in a seemingly meditative mood. Her hair is well groomed in a stylish coiffure surmounted by a high chignon dangling precariously over her forehead. Her delicate eyebrows, thin nose, small lips, and round face, together with the narrow, tight "barbarian" sleeve of her robe are all indicative of the vogue during the reign of Emperor Hsüan-tsung (r. 712–756), who was well known for his taste in Rubenesque beauties and the Central Asian style in woman's fashion. These characteristics relate the Cleveland harpist closely to the numerous earthenware figurines excavated in recent years from a group of T'ang tombs outside Hsian which are all precisely dated to the second quarter of the eighth century.

The musical instrument involved is a *shu K'ung-hou* (an upright *K'ung-hou* as opposed to the reclining type), or an angular harp. It is a plucked string instrument with twenty-three strings, which by the mid-eighth century, probably owing to the personal interest of the emperor, occupied a prominent position in court orchestras.

The Cleveland harpist is unique among known ceramic tomb figurines from the eighth century. Not only is she the only seated harpist so far discovered from T'ang tombs, but she also represents a class of more accomplished musicians from the *Chiao-fang* rarely represented in Western collections. She was most likely selected not merely for her talents but also for her youth and beauty. In his famous series of one hundred poems describing life in the palace, the mid-T'ang poet Wang Chien wrote about one of these young girls:

> At thirteen, she began to learn playing the angular harp.
> Among the many students she was chosen to be retained.
> Yesterday she moved into her Palace quarters for the new musicians,
> And there she sat quietly, allowing her roommate to re-do her hair.

WKH

See also color plate following page 86.

PUBLICATIONS O. Sirén, "Stilentwicklung der Chinesischen Grabfiguren," *Winner Beitrage in Kunst und Kultur Asiens*, VI (1931). Howard C. Hollis, "A T'ang Dynasty Tomb Figure," CMA *Bulletin*, XIX (January 1932) 7-8, repr. p. 2. Warren E. Cox, *The Book of Pottery and Porcelain* (New York: Crown Publishers, 1944) I, pl. 30. *Daito no han-ei* [The prosperity of the great T'ang], vol. VII of *Sekai rekishi shirizu*, color repr. p. 30. Thomas Munro, *Oriental Aesthetics* (Cleveland: The Press of Western Reserve University, 1965) pl. V, facing p. 54. Giuseppe Eskenazi, *Ancient Chinese Sculpture*, sale cat. (London, 1978) fig. 13. William Watson, *L'art de l'ancienne Chine*, Editions D'art Lucien Mazenod (Paris: Lucien Mazenod, 1979) color pl. 52, pl. 409, p. 418 (detail). S. E. Lee, *A History of Far Eastern Art*, 4th edition, p. 385, fig. 374.

100 Covered Box *(Ho)*: Yüeh Ware 72.95

Gray stoneware, iron glazed, with molded, carved, and incised decoration. H. 4.5 cm., Diam. 13 cm. China, reportedly from kiln site at Shang-lin-hu, Yü-yao district, Chechiang Province. Five Dynasties period, Wu-Yüeh kingdom, or early Northern Sung Dynasty, second half 10th century AD. Gift of Mary B. Lee, C. Bingham Blossom, Dudley S. Blossom III, Laurel B. Kovacik, and Elizabeth B. Blossom in memory of Elizabeth B. Blossom.

In 1936 the Chinese ceramic historian Ch'en Wan-li illustrated the lid of this box in an album of decorated celadon wares collected in the Hangchou Bay area of Chechiang Province in southeastern China. The reported find site, a complex of kiln ruins along the shores of Shang-lin-hu (Shang-lin Lake), had recently been investigated by Chinese, Japanese, and American scholars. All sought to identify the finest kiln wasters with Yüeh ware, described by ninth-century poets as strong, resonant, and a jadelike shade of blue-green. Tenth-century texts celebrated the superiority of the *pi-se* ("secret color") variety, reserved for exclusive use and distribution by emperors of the independent Wu-Yüeh kingdom and their Sung Dynasty overlords, who took over the kilns following the Wu-Yüeh abdication in 978.

Such vivid accounts provide few clues to appearance beyond the allusion to a transparent celadon glaze improved over the centuries at many southern kilns (cf. [91, 92]). Yet initial discoveries at Shang-lin-hu (1935–1937), which included this piece, revealed an unprecedented range of molded, carved, and incised surface patterns, and some modification of long-established vessel shapes. This shallow covered basin *(ho)*, first perfected in lacquer cosmetic boxes of the Warring States period (third–second centuries BC), was common to polychrome-splashed earthenware and monochrome stoneware by the mid-T'ang Dynasty (eighth century AD). But most elegant styling was achieved by contemporary gold- and silversmiths, who embellished the surface with repoussé (beaten relief) and chased (delicately chiseled) decoration. That this ceramic lid was partly inspired by metalworking is suggested not only in its profile, molded like a rim beaten flat and soldered around the circumference, but also in the designs carved and incised in the clay, resembling the shadows of respoussé and chasing as the glaze collects and darkens in the sloping cuts and fine grooves.

This combination of raised pattern and patterned background characterizes only a few of the most intricately decorated Yüeh wares, which probably represent the climax of production at Shang-lin-hu and affiliate kilns. The carved parrot is a larger and bolder version of common incised or carved birds, all with profile heads, gently outspread wings, and upswept tailfeathers. Its closest relative, rising above a similar ground of fluently incised feather scrolls, is a phoenix filling the top roundel of a *ho* lid in the Hakone Art Museum, Kanagawa, Japan.

The splayed foot rim of both the Cleveland and Hakone basins is typical of but not exclusive to the finest vessels found at Shang-lin-hu. However, since kilnsite wasters show that *ho* basins generally were fired in saggers with their lids in place, the contrasts in glaze color and texture indicate that this Cleveland example may consist of two originally separate sections that happen to fit perfectly together. EP

EX COLLECTION Mr. and Mrs. Alfred Clark, Ivan Heath, England.

EXHIBITIONS Paris, 1937: Musée de l'Orangerie, Arts de la Chine Ancienne, cat. introd. by Georges Salles, no. 404 (ground pattern described as "dragon"). London, 1955: Oriental Ceramic Society, Loan Exhibition of The Arts of the T'ang Dynasty, cat. essays by

Basil Gray, Harry M. Garner, and S. Howard Hansford, no. 252, pl. 14a. Los Angeles, 1957: Los Angeles County Museum, The Arts of the T'ang Dynasty, cat. introd. by Henry Trubner, no. 262.

PUBLICATIONS Ch'en Wan-li, *Yüeh-ch'i t'u-lu* [Pictorial record of Yüeh ware] (Hangchou, preface dated 1936) pl. 3: retouched photo or line drawing. Basil Gray, *Early Chinese Pottery and Porcelain* (London: Faber and Faber, 1953) pl. 14. H. J. Kleinhenz, CMA *Bulletin*, LXV (April 1978) 137, fig. 2, a. M. Medley, *T'ang Pottery and Porcelain*, pl. 108.

LITERATURE Chin Tzu-ming, "Excavation Report on Celadon Kiln Sites in Yü-yao District, Chechiang," in Chinese, *K'ao-ku hsüeh-pao*, 1959/3, esp. fig. 1 (covered box with incised lid from Huang-shan-shan site at Shang-lin-hu); English abstract by Hin-cheung Lovell and Judith Moorhouse, *Yüeh Ware Kiln-sites in Chekiang*, Victoria and Albert Museum and Oriental Ceramic Society, Chinese Translations no. 6 (London, 1976). *Zui-To hen*, vol. IX of *Sekai toji zenshu* (1956) color pl. 4 (covered box, Hakone Art Museum). M. Tregear, *Catalogue of Chinese Greenware: Ashmolean Museum, Oxford*, pp. 45-46, pls. 148-160 (covered boxes esp. pl. 157 with carved parrots). G. St. G. M. Gompertz, *Chinese Celadon Wares*, 2nd edition rev., pp. 50-66 (survey of Shang-lin-hu).

101 Jar: Hsing Type 57.29

Porcelain with underglaze incised decoration. H. 12.5 cm., Diam. 12.5 cm. China (northern). Late T'ang or Liao Dynasty, 10th century AD. Purchase, John L. Severance Fund.

The taut profile and compactness of this jar combine with the comblike incised underglaze decoration to make a most satisfying pot. The body is an off-white porcelain; the overall color, with the transparent covering glaze, is a very slightly warm white not unlike Ting ware of the Northern Sung Dynasty (see [103]).

Date and provenance remain somewhat puzzling. In all respects except the decoration the piece corresponds well with many porcelains, including an excavated "spittoon" from Hsian, and can be included under the heading Hsing ware, the late T'ang white porcelain that laid the foundation for all Sung white production in the North. The decoration corresponds with that found on several excavated Liao pieces with colored lead glazes over a stoneware body. The question then becomes one of the extent of Liao borrowings from immediately preceeding Chinese accomplishments in the very areas closest to Liao hegemony. Since trade and diplomatic communications were common to Liao-Chinese relations, the possibility of Chinese imports into the Chinese culturally oriented Liao areas is very strong. There are only two possible answers and they are so close together as to make the distinction an academic one at best. SEL

EX COLLECTIONS Edward Chow, Hongkong; Men-chu Wang, San Francisco.

EXHIBITON New York, 1973: China House Gallery, Ceramics in the Liao Dynasty, cat. by Yutaka Mino, p. 66, no. 40.

PUBLICATION Michel Beurdeley, *The Chinese Collector Through the Centuries, From Han to the Twentieth Century* (Vermont and Tokyo: Charles E. Tuttle Co., 1966) no. 28, repr. p. 223.

LITERATURE *The Genius of China*, exhib. cat. (London: The Royal Academy, 1973–1974) p. 142, no. 288 (spittoon from Hsian). Li I-yu, "Introduction to the Excavation of an Old Tomb in T'u-ch'eng-tzu, Ho-lin-ko-erh [Inner Mongolia]," in Chinese, *Wen wu*, 1961/9, p. 32, pl. 2:1, as cited by Mino, *Ceramics in the Liao Dynasty*. Hunan Provincial Museum, "T'ang and Sung Tombs Excavated in Northeastern Ch'angsha [Hunan Province]," in Chinese, *K'ao-ku*, 1959/12, pl. 2:1 (box cover with similar decorative motif), also as cited by Mino.

102 Ewer in the Form of a *Sheng* Player 53.248

Buff stoneware, slip-coated with underglaze incised and oxide decoration. H. 21.2 cm., Diam. 10 cm. China (northern). Liao Dynasty, late 10th–early 11th century AD. Purchase, John L. Severance Fund.

While ewers in animal form or with tiger-head or chicken-head spouts (see [91, 92]) are known, ewers in human form are extremely rare. Besides our example, only two have previously been published: a mermaid and a man astride a monster, both with a white Ting type glaze. A fourth example, recently excavated, permits a firm localization and date in the Liao Dynasty (907–1125) of northern China and Manchuria.

Pouring a liquid from an ewer in human form presents a psychological barrier that may account for the rarity of the type in China and for the repulsiveness of the well-known "Toby jug" type in the West. Nevertheless, the *Sheng*-player ewer has its attractive features. Conceived as a wheel-thrown ewer shape, the metamorphosis into female form is accomplished with some humor. Rotund and smiling while she plays, she only alludes to the fashionably plump court musicians of the T'ang Dynasty (such as [99]). The basic ceramic form is not violated and the spout is restricted to the dimensions of the vertical reed mouth-organ known as the *sheng*. Her phoenix-head cap becomes the mouth of the vessel, while her trefoil-toe slippers are mere appliqués at the base of the ewer. The incised drapery and cloth patterns are reinforced by an iron-oxide brown color in the straw-colored glaze. It is both a useful and amusing utensil.

The conservative Liao court continued T'ang style arts and techniques, whether in roof tiles, ceramic shapes and glazes, or Buddhist forms and subjects. This accounts for the appearance of the *sheng* player and also for the more up-to-date influences from the Yüeh wares of southern China to be seen in the incising and glaze color of the piece. Long a puzzling and heterodox problem piece, her place as a major example of Liao ceramic seems assured. SEL

PUBLICATIONS Sherman E. Lee, "The 'Sheng' Player: A T'ang Wine Pitcher," *Far Eastern Ceramic Bulletin*, VI, no. 3 (September 1954) 6-11. Hasebe Gakuji, "Chinese Ceramics of the Tenth Century," in Japanese, *Tokyo Kokuritsu Hakubutsukan kiyo: Proceedings of the Tokyo National Museum*, III (1967) 216, fig. 27.

LITERATURE Robert L. Hobson, *The George Eumorfopolous Collection* (London: E. Benn, 1925–1928) III, c219, pl. x61 (mermaid ewer). Robert L. Hobson, B. Rackham, and W. King, *Chinese Ceramics in Private Collections* (London: Hatton and Smith, 1931) p. 42, fig. 88 (ewer in the form of a man astride monster). Su T'ien-chün, "Excavation of the Remains of the Liao Dynasty Ching-kuang Stupa Foundation at Shun-i District, Peking," in Chinese, *Wen wu*, 1964/8, p. 50, fig. 2 (ewer datable to 1007–1014 representing an official).

103 Conical Bowl: Ting Ware 29.995

Porcelain with underglaze carved and incised decoration. H. 6.4 cm., Diam. 20.3 cm. China, probably Ch'ü-yang district, Hopei Province. Northern Sung Dynasty, early 12th century AD. Dudley P. Allen Collection.

A transparent ivory-toned glaze barely distinct from its elegantly potted body identifies this bowl as Ting ware, the preeminent white porcelain of the Sung Dynasty (960–1279). Throughout this period, the enormous kiln industry of ancient Ting prefecture (modern Ch'ü-yang district, southwest of Peking) produced a wide range of whitewares alongside smaller quantities of colored glazes. But in the late eleventh and early twelfth centuries, the finest white porcelain was reserved for dishes and bowls — graceful and useful table wares esteemed by the imperial court and elite society for whom sensitivity to materials and to nature was a scholarly pursuit. If fragile form and smooth glaze immediately appealed to the touch, designs delicately incised and carved in the paste invited the same close scrutiny as bird-and-flower studies then meticulously painted at the Imperial Academy.

In Ting ware comparably idyllic scenes began as concise and large-scale outlines decoratively adjusted to the concave interior of open vessels. Ducks and reeds were a standard motif of master draftsmen, judging by several superior examples that vary slightly in composition but share remarkable linear fluency and rhythm. All define setting by a few undulating waves executed with a fine-tooth comb and by twisting reeds cut with an upright point and gently slanted blade. Each shows the spontaneity of firsthand drawing — a quality that disappeared later in the twelfth century when Ting decorators adopted carved molds to mass-produce more elaborate patterns in relief. The visual distinction between incised-carved and mold-impressed surface decoration is aptly likened to that between a free sketch and a calculated textile design.

Typically, the glazed Ting bowl was dried upright on its foot but stacked and fired upside-down within a tiered sagger. Chinese connoisseurs of later centuries noted two technical shortcomings of this process as virtues of authenticity: "tear stains" of excess glaze congealed down the exterior walls; and a lip wiped clean of glaze to prevent sticking to the firing support. Both features are visible in this example. The bare rim reputedly discredited Ting in the discriminating eyes of Emperor Hui-tsung (r. 1101–1125), but numerous vessels bound with metal bands illustrate an attractive solution that assured continued and widespread appreciation of this luxury ware. EP

EXHIBITIONS Cleveland, 1929: The Cleveland Museum of Art, Exhibition of Far Eastern Art. New York, 1974, Asia House Gallery: The Colors of Ink, cat. by Sherman E. Lee, no. 57.

PUBLICATIONS H. J. Kleinhenz, CMA *Bulletin*, LXV (April 1978) fig. 4. J. G. Moore, *The Eastern Gate*, p. 75.

LITERATURE Hin-cheung Lovell, *Illustrated Catalogue of Ting Yao and Related White Wares in the Percival David Foundation of Chinese Art*, School of Oriental and African Studies, University of London (London, 1964) nos. 100, 160. Jan Wirgin, "Sung Ceramic Designs," *Bulletin of the Museum of Far Eastern Antiquities* [Stockholm], XLII (1970) pl. 65 (bowl, Museum of Fine Arts, Boston).

104 Ewer with Lion Spout: Northern Celadon Ware, Yao-chou Type 48.220

Gray porcelain with celadon glaze and carved and incised decoration. H. 18.3 cm., Diam. 19.1 cm. China, probably Huang-pao-chen (Yao-chou), Shenhsi Province. Northern Sung Dynasty, late 10th–early 11th century AD. Purchase from the J. H. Wade Fund.

Decades of speculation, flimsily based on literary sources and descriptions applied to a particularly refined Northern Celadon ware, have been verified by recent excavations in China at Yao-chou in Shenhsi Province. Carved and incised peony decoration on sherds and a jar from Yao-chou are so similar to those found on the Cleveland ewer as to preclude any reasonable doubt as to its origin. Previously called by many *tung* ware (a still legendary ware supposedly made in the vicinity of the capital, K'aifeng), this ewer has been published and exhibited many times because of its completeness, careful and skillful manufacture, and elaborate decoration.

The body is a hard, porcelaneous gray covered by an even pale gray-green iron glaze with some veiled blue overtones. This places the ewer in the overall category of Northern Celadon produced in rivalry to the Yüen ware of the T'ang and early Sung dynasties (see [100]). The decoration consists of two registers of relief carved and incised large peony scrolls, one on the shoulder, the other on the lower body. A small lion seated on a small lotus flower makes the spout, while the handle has an incised lozenge pattern with an overlay of flying birds and dragons in molded relief. The shape emphasizes the discrete parts of the ewer — neck, spout, handle, upper and lower halves of the body, and a high spreading foot with a deep rim and convex bulging base. The ewer type and the peony scrolls are related to those of Northern Sung carved Tz'u-chou ware (see [116]), while the incising technique and particularly the bird and dragon motif have affinities with tenth-century Yüeh ware (see [100]). The thin, even walls of the ewer are remarkable as is the scalloped projecting waistband. These elements, with the straplike handle, recall the metal — especially silver — dishes and jars of late T'ang and early Sung dynasties. All of the elements discussed above confirm a late tenth- to early eleventh-century date for this important ceramic. SEL

EX COLLECTION Dikran G. Kelekian.

EXHIBITIONS Los Angeles, 1952: Los Angeles County Museum of Art, Chinese Ceramics from the Prehistoric Period through Ch'ien Lung, cat. by Henry Trubner, p. 80, no. 172. Tokyo, 1955: Takashimaya Department Store, So-ji meihen ten [Exhibition of Sung ceramics], organized by The Japan Ceramic Society, no. 4. Paris, 1956: Musée Cernushi, La Chine des Sung, 960–1279.

PUBLICATIONS Madeleine David, "Céramiques Song," *Cahiers de la Ceramique et des Arts du Feu*, V (Winter 1956–1957) 15, color cover (as "Tung ware" from Honan). Jean Roger Rivière, "El Arte del La China," *Summa Artis Historia General del Arte*, XX (1966) 325, repr. 326, fig. 267. Hasebe Gakuji et al., *So* [Sung], vol. XII of *Sekai toji zenshu* (1977) color pl. 183. Fujio Koyama, *Seiji* [Celadon ware] (Tokyo: Heibonsha, 1978) pl. 64. G. St. G. M. Gompertz, *Chinese Celadon Wares*, 2nd edition rev., p. 102, repr. color pl. C, p. 104, fig. 40 (detail). S. E. Lee, *A History of Far Eastern Art*, 4th edition rev., p. 370 fig. 496.

LITERATURE Shenhsi Institute of Archaeology, *Shen-hsi T'ung-ch'uan Yao-chou yao* [Yao-chou ware from T'ung-ch'uan, Shenhsi] (Peking: Science Press, 1965) pl. XII:1. H.-c. Tseng and R. P. Dart, *The Charles B. Hoyt Collection in the Museum of Fine Arts, Boston*, II, no. 56. Cheng Shao-tsung, "Excavation Report on Liao Tombs at Ta-ying-tzu, Ch'ih-feng [Inner Mongolia]," in Chinese, *K'ao-ku hsüeh-pao*, 1956 / 3, pl. 7:1, left (comparable ewer shape from Liao Dynasty tomb dated AD 959).

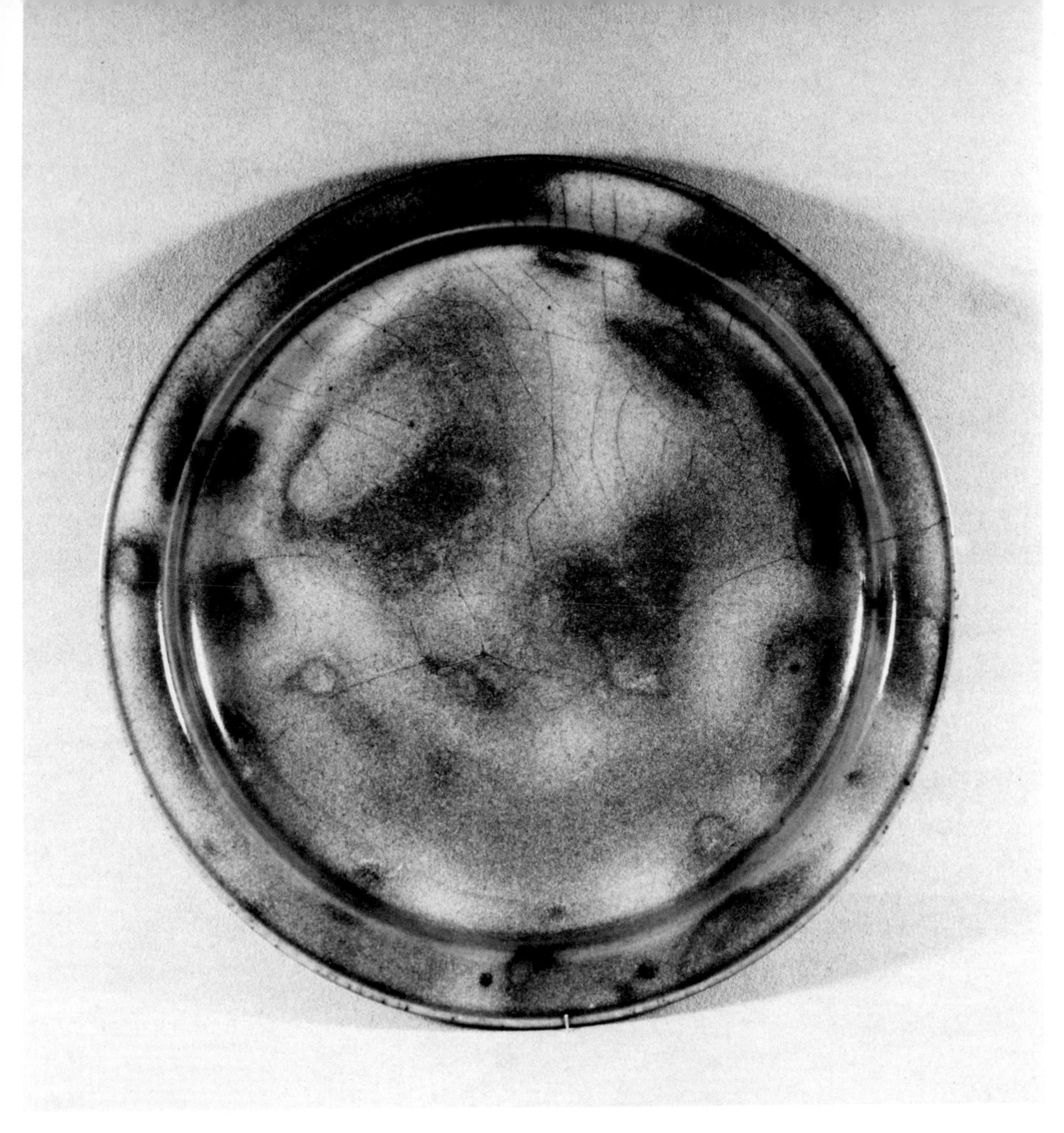

105 Plate *(Che-yüan tieh):* Chün Ware *42.665*

Light gray stoneware with mottled glazes. H. 2.5 cm., Diam. 18.1 cm. China (northern). Northern Sung or Chin Dynasty, 12th–13th centuries AD. Bequest of John L. Severance.

This uniquely glazed plate is a fine example of the probably earlier type of Chün ware found at many different kiln sites in northern China with Yü-hsien in Honan Province as center for the best, perhaps court-commissioned products. The small shallow plate is visually dignified by a wide, flat projecting rim abruptly curved-in which echoes and stabilizes the broad flat base, a shape originating in the bronze *p'an* of the Ch'in and early Han periods (third–second centuries BC). This simple and unpretentious classical shape is boldly contrasted by its exuberant decoration, its ash glaze of deep sky blue being accentuated and enlivened by the splashes of purplish copper-red, creating a seemingly free design which is particularly pleasing to modern eyes. The somewhat opalized thick glaze, thinned and burnt at the outer lip, covers all surfaces of the plate including the exterior base which is usually unglazed, or only partially glazed, in the later type of the fourteenth century. The successful application of the elusive copper over or under the glaze layer in a high temperature, reducing fire was an important technological breakthrough of the Sung and Chin potters. Its special effect in coloration, known as *yao-pien* (a controlled "kiln accident") or *yohen* in Japan, has been fondly compared with the early evening sky adorned with floating clouds edged by the glows of purplish or rosy red. The technique of *yao-pien*, despite its discontinuation in most northern kilns after the Yüan Dynasty, had a profound and lasting influence on Chinese ceramic art in the south, especially in the Ching-te-chen (Chianghsi) and Shih-wan (Kuangtung) kilns.

Chün is one of the five most famous wares of the Sung Dynasty. But more controversial than the other four, its main problem is one of dating. A Yüan date had previously been assigned to the Cleveland dish by some specialists, partly on the strength of the three unglazed spur marks on its base, but we are still in an early stage of establishing a chronology for the Chün ware which depends on further and more conclusive archaeological finds. WKH

PUBLICATION *Catalogue of the John L. Severance Collection, Bequest of John L. Severance, 1936* (Cleveland: The Cleveland Museum of Art, 1942) no. 136, pl. XXX.

106 Brush Washer: Ju Ware 57.40

Buff stoneware with phosphoric glaze. H. 3.5 cm., Diam. 12.9 cm. China, probably Honan Province. Northern Sung Dynasty, late 11th–early 12th century AD. Purchase, John L. Severance Fund.

Often mentioned within Chinese ceramic literature is a ware supposedly fired in present-day Lin-ju district, Honan Province, for the exclusive use of the Northern Sung imperial court. Although the kiln that produced it has never been located, ceramic specialists have isolated a unified ceramic group conforming to the literary descriptions of Ju ware. This unpretentious brush washer — one of but thirty-odd examples outside the former imperial collections — illustrates the characteristics most frequently cited for this very special ware: firing scars (called *spur marks*) shaped like sesame seeds on its base and a fine web of crackle within its soft sea-green glaze.

Spur marks result from a firing method seldom employed in the Sung ceramic industry. Normally, potters would protect a fine glazed porcelain from the open flame and sooty kiln atmosphere by standing it on its foot or lip in a heat-resistant clay container called a sagger. After the fired porcelain was removed from its sagger, all surfaces would be covered with glaze except the foot — in the case of Yao-chou ware (see [104]) — or the lip — as found in Ting ware (see [103]). The disadvantage of this method was the chance that sandy particles in the sagger would adhere and cause a roughened lip or foot after firing. To avoid this, Ju potters placed the base of this glazed dish on five tiny ovoid clay stilts or spurs inside the sagger. The removal of these supports after firing left sesame seed-shaped scars which reveal a buff-colored body clay underneath an otherwise uninterrupted expanse of glaze.

This celadon glaze is as unusual as spur marks within the northern ceramic technology of Sung China. Excavations in Shenhsi (see [104]) and Honan have unearthed a closely related group of olive-green glazed ceramics which imitated the shapes and thin, transparent glazes of Five Dynasties and Sung Yüeh ware imported from the south (see [100]). The thick, opalescent, and blue-green tonality which separates the Ju glaze from this tradition first appeared in the north during the late T'ang Dynasty with the blue-splashed decor of Huang-tao wares, made about seven miles from Lin-ju (see [95]). The glaze was popularized with Chün ware — a ceramic type which may have developed at the same time as Ju (see [105]) and was manufactured at the same Lin-ju district kilns which produced Yüeh-type celadons. The manufacture of Huang-tao and Chün types in the vicinity of Lin-ju district therefore seems to justify the tradition that the rare imperial ware was also made there, even though not a sherd of Ju has yet been found.

The final feature of Ju ware, mentioned as early as the fourteenth century, is the presence of crackle in its glaze. Crackle can be a flaw that develops as the result of different rates of stress the porcelain body and its glaze covering undergo from firing and cooling, or it can be controlled for decorative effect. The phenomenon can occur in a newly fired piece or develop after centuries of exposure to the atmosphere. It was admired because the tiny network adds to its jadelike glaze color an almost palpable resemblance to the stone so greatly revered in Chinese culture. HJK

EX COLLECTION Men-chu Wang.

PUBLICATIONS Suzanne G. Valenstein, *A Handbook of Chinese Ceramics* (New York: The Metropolitan Musem of Art, 1975) p. 75, fig. 30. H. J. Kleinhenz, CMA *Bulletin*, LXV (April 1978) 140, fig. 6, a. R. Tichane, *Those Celadon Blues*, p. 27, fig. 3.14. S. E. Lee, *A History of Far Eastern Art*, 4th edition, p. 369, repr. p. 340, color pl. 36, bottom.

LITERATURE Sir Percival David, "A Commentary on Ju Ware," *Transactions of the Oriental Ceramic Society*, XIV (1936–1937) 18-69. Osvald Sirén, *Kinas Konst Under Tre Artusenden* (Stockholm: Natur och Kultur, 1942–1943) II 366, fig. 324 (A. Øigaard collection, Copenhagen). *Ju Ware of the Sung Dynasty*, vol. I of *Porcelain of the National Palace Museum* (Hongkong: Cafa Company, 1961) pp. 43-47, pls. 13-17. G. St. G. M. Gompertz, *Chinese Celadon Wares*, 2nd edition rev., pp. 84-98, p. 89, pl. 32B (Percival David Foundation, University of London).

107 Conical Bowl: *Ch'ing-pai Ware* 64.210

Porcelain with underglaze incised and carved decoration. H. 5.7 cm., Diam. 14.6 cm. China. Sung Dynasty, late 11th–early 12th centuries AD. Severance A. and Greta Millikin Collection.

The fine-grained "sugary" body of this earliest refined porcelain is composed of white clay (kaolin) and crushed feldspathic rock (petuntse mined from granite). The feldspar integral to the glaze fused with that of the body to form a translucent glassy surface. Its strength and hardness supported remarkably crisp, thin-walled vessels like this straight-sided conical bowl which exemplifies the most fragile Sung Dynasty potting. In reduction firing, traces of iron oxide and titania in the glaze imparted a faint blue-green tinge, described as *ch'ing-pai* ("bluish-white") by thirteenth- and fourteenth-century historians and *ying-ch'ing* ("shadow blue") by twentieth-century dealers.

However imprecise, *ch'ing-pai* is visually descriptive of this glassy blue-green glaze, applied to wares of diverse form and quality produced at widespread kilns between the ninth and fourteenth centuries. While published kiln wasters are too sparse to distinguish specialized wares of individual sites, the finest Sung *ch'ing-pai* is usually attributed to Ch'ing-te-chen in southeastern Chianghsi Province, where huge local deposits of kaolin and petuntse supplied a thriving private industry as they later supplied vast imperial factories of the Ming and Ch'ing dynasties. Since 1950 *ch'ing-pai* wares datable to the Sung Dynasty have been reported from numerous kiln sites in Chianghsi as well as in other southern provinces (Chechiang, southern Anhui, Fuchien, Kuangtung, and Yunnan). Consequently, *ch'ing-pai* is usually regarded as a southern counterpart to Ting, the ivory-toned whiteware made in far-northern Hopei (see [103]). However, this evidence recently has been supplemented, and such assumptions may be modified, by the discovery of *ch'ing-pai* at a Sung kiln site in north-central Honan which also produced Chün (see [105]), Northern Celadon (see [104]), and Tz'u-chou type wares (see [115–117]).

This bowl is entirely glazed except over the slightly recessed base, stained reddish-brown from a disc-shaped kiln support which probably contained iron and oxidized with the influx of air after firing. The blue-green color deepens where it pools in the center and in the lines of floral sprays lightly incised and carved, barely skimming the clay body. Stylized peony blossoms of thin overlapping petals, curved stalks, and bud-tendrils emerge and dissolve amid a background filled with dotted lines — a stippled variation of the combing technique common to Ting (see [103]) and other contemporary wares. This restrained decor, more abstract and elusive than on Ting vessels, characterizes the most delicate *ch'ing-pai* bowls initially made as a domestic luxury ware, but not patronized by the imperial court.

This example probably predates bowls with molded designs, introduced in increasing volume over the twelfth century. A similar floral scroll and dotted background appear in mold-impressed *ch'ing-pai*, whose thicker body — required by that new technique — could be shaved thin after the impression was taken. Toward the end of the Sung Dynasty, however, heavier and more durable vessels were favored for export to Southeast Asia, Indonesia, and the Near East; and surface designs, whether cut or molded under the glaze, became bolder and more elaborate. EP

LITERATURE B. Gray, *Early Chinese Pottery and Porcelain*, pl. 76B (British Museum). Bo Gyllensvard, *Chinese Ceramics in the Carl Kempe Collection* (Stockholm: Almqvist & Wicksell, 1964) no. 540 (conical), no. 543 (rounded bowl with foliate rim). J. Wirgin, *Bulletin of the Museum of Far Eastern Antiquities*, XLII (1970) 48-74. Honan Provincial Museum, "Discovery of a Kilnsite at Chün-tai, Yu-hsien, Honan," in Chinese, *Wen wu*, 1975 / 6, fig. 10:3 (conical bowl with similar molded decoration). M. Medley, *The Chinese Potter*, fig. 124 (Victoria and Albert Museum).

108 Cup and Stand (*chan, chan-t'o*): *Ch'ing-pai* Ware — 80.185, a

Porcelain with underglaze incised and perforated decoration. Cup: H. 4.8 cm., Diam. 10.3 cm.; stand: H. 4 cm., Diam. 14 cm. China, probably Ching-te-chen, Chianghsi Province. Sung Dynasty, ca. 12th century AD. Gifts of Laurence H. Norton, Robert G. Norton, and Mrs. Miriam Norton White in memory of Mr. and Mrs. D. Z. Norton; Mrs. A. S. Chisholm; Horace E. Potter; and the John Huntington Art and Polytechnic Trust by Exchange.

The origin of the cupstand in China is credited by one Sung Dynasty scholar to the daughter of an eighth-century official; she devised a dish of melted wax with a ring in the center to support the foot of her hot teacup. Her father thereafter commissioned a lacquer reproduction of the custom-fit saucer, *t'o* (Ch'eng Ta-ch'ang, *Yen-fan-lu,* AD 1181). While tomb finds of bronze and stoneware cupstands appear as early as the Southern Dynasties (fifth–sixth centuries), this story accurately reflects the new T'ang Dynasty vogue for tea drinking that inspired luxurious utensils in lacquer, silver, and porcelain. Two types of cupstands in different media current by the late T'ang took standard form in the subsequent Sung Dynasty: one fitted with a globular bowl that partially contained the cup as an eggcup contains an egg; the second fitted with a ridge or pedestal to elevate the cup on its foot.

By Ch'eng Ta-ch'ang's time, both types were common to porcelain with *ch'ing-pai* glaze (cf. [107]). They probably were used indiscriminately for tea, still a prestigious beverage, and for wine, customarily drunk after each course of a Sung feast. Alongside ewers-in-basins used to heat wine, cup-and-stand sets are clearly depicted in Sung paintings of elegant banquets, catered in the capital by "tea and wine kitchens."

The pedestal type seen in this cupstand has close antecedents in Yüeh ware of the ninth and tenth centuries, whose style ultimately derives from T'ang examples in beaten silver. The central of three stacked and luted section is a dish with a shallow well and flat, six-lobed rim — a distinctly metallic form probably imitated in ceramic by pressing the clay between a revolving mold and template. The center of the dish is perforated as a vent for gases that otherwise would be trapped inside the pedestal attached above. Below, a flat slab of clay is wound in a high footring and notched in six panels, each pierced with a decorative trefoil. This complex of sturdy volumes offsets simple delicacy in the cup, its fragile walls flaring like an open flower to a sharply everted lip, pinched in discreet petals and lightly incised with exterior lobes.

The high plasticity of the *ch'ing-pai* body allowed such cups to be potted to translucent thinness, distinguishing them from tea or wine sets of all other contemporary wares. These include the more eminent "imperial" wares of Ting (see [103]), Ju (see [106]), and *kuan* (see [110, 111]) as well as Korean celadons and white porcelains based on Chinese imports. Within the course of the Sung, Koryo Dynasty potters avidly adopted the Chinese cup and stand, and modified it to Korean taste. EP

EX COLLECTION Mr. and Mrs. Eugene Bernat.

EXHIBITION Manchester, New Hampshire, 1959: Currier Gallery of Art, Chinese Ceramics of the Sung Dynasty, cat. no. 66.

PUBLICATION Harry M. Garner and Margaret Medley, *Chinese Art in Three-Dimensional Color* (New York: The Asia Society for The Gruber Foundation, 1969) III, 210, reel 29, no. 5.

LITERATURE Feng Hsien-ming, "Literary Examination of T'ang, Sung, and Later Fashions in Tea Drinking and the Changes in Ceramic Vessels Used for Tea," in Chinese, *Wen wu,* 1963/1, p. 10 (*Yen-fan-lu*), fig. 6. J. Ayers, *The Seligman Collection of Oriental Art,* vol II: *Chinese and Corean Pottery and Porcelain,* no. D223, D233A (similar cup with different foliate stand). B. Gyllensvard, *Chinese Ceramics in the Carl Kempe Collection,* no. 536 (similar stand with straight-rimmed cup). Wang Shan-ts'ai and Ch'en Hung-shu, "Excavation of a Northern Sung Tomb [AD 1113] at Ma-ch'eng, Hupei," in Chinese, *K'ao-ku,* 1965/1, pl. V:3. John Ayers, *The Baur Collection, Geneva,* vol. I: *Chinese Ceramics* (Geneva: Collections Baur, 1968) no. A120. Hasebe et al., *So,* vol. XII of *Sekai toji zenshu* (1977) color pl. 156 (pair of cup and stand sets, Tokyo National Museum).

109 Brush Washer: Lung-ch'üan Ware 64.363

Porcelain with celadon glaze. H. 5.7 cm., Diam. 16.5 cm. China, Chechiang Province. Southern Sung Dynasty, 13th century AD. Sundry Purchase Funds.

During the ninth and tenth centuries, the Yüeh kilns in northeastern Chechiang Province set a standard of technical excellence imitated by the whole celadon industry south of the Yangtze River. Their pride of place was due to patronage by the local princely house which had broken with the disintegrating T'ang government in northern China to establish an independent government centered in the city of Hangchou. However, after the last ruler of the region surrendered to the northern house of Sung in 978, the level of quality at various Yüeh kilns to the east of Hangchou dissipated quickly. By the end of the eleventh century, innovation within the Chechiang celadon industry shifted to Lung-ch'üan district in the southwestern section of the province.

Archaeological investigation during the past few years confirms the grand scale of Lung-ch'üan production during the Sung Dynasty. Some of the excavated kilns could hold as many as twenty-five thousand vessels in a single firing. Given the difficulty of controlling the level of oxygen in so large a kiln complex, it is remarkable that Lung-ch'üan potters could produce a uniformly colored glaze. The brush washer in this collection, however, exhibits a gray-green glaze identical in hue to many other extant Lung-ch'üan wares of the thirteenth century. This marks a technological advance over tenth-century Yüeh production, where uniformity of glaze color — even within a single piece — was a rarity (see [100]). Equally innovative was the method of glazing employed by Lung-ch'üan potters. Because the Yüeh potter applied only one layer of glaze to a vessel before firing, a thin and transparent glassy surface resulted. The Lung-ch'üan potter applied many coats of glaze and allowed each to dry before adding another. With firing, the glaze matured to a thick and cloudy gray-green layer remarkably like the texture and hue of the finest jade.

In addition to color, the beauty of Lung-ch'üan wares resides in their refined forms, as illustrated in this vessel by the subtle counterplay of angled planes in its lip, body, and foot rim. It is also one of the rarest forms within the Lung-ch'üan repertoire — few such vessels have so far been published from Western collections and none have yet appeared at any kiln site so far excavated. The potter who designed the vessel may have been inspired by a metal prototype, but a prototype distinctly foreign to the Chinese tradition. The possibility remains that this essential tool of the Chinese scholar's table owes its appearance to Near Eastern metalwork, imported into China by the large Arab population that had settled in Hangchou and the ports along the Chechiang coast during the Sung Dynasty. In fact it was their ships which transported Lung-ch'üan and other southern wares to Indonesia, Southeast Asia, and the wealthy Islamic caliphates in Africa, where many Chinese ceramics have been preserved intact to the present century. HJK

LITERATURE R. L. Hobson, *Chinese Pottery and Porcelain in the Collection of Sir Percival David* (London: Stourton Press, 1934) pl. XXXV. *Lung-ch'üan Ware of the Sung Dynasty,* vol. XVIII of *Porcelain of the National Palace Museum* (Hongkong: Cafa Company, 1962) p. 61, pl. 18. Chu Po-ch'ien and Wang Shih-lun, "Report on the Excavation of Lung-ch'üan Celadon Kiln Sites in Chechiang," in Chinese, *Wen wu,* 1963/1, 27-35; English translation by Hin-cheung Lovell, Victoria and Albert Museum and Oriental Ceramic Society, Chinese Translations no. 2 (London, 1968). Chou Jen, Chang Fu-k'ang and Cheng Yung-fu, "Technical Studies on Lung-ch'üan Celadons of Successive Dynasties," in Chinese, *K'ao-ku hsüeh-pao,* 1973/1, 131-156; English translation by Patty Proctor, Victoria and Albert Museum and Oriental Ceramic Society, Chinese Translations no. 7 (London, 1977). G. St. G. M. Gompertz, *Chinese Celadon Wares,* 2nd edition rev., pp. 147-172.

110 Basin: *Kuan* Ware 57.48

Dark gray porcelain with celadon glaze and copper rim. H. 6 cm., Diam. 24.2 cm., China, Chechiang Province. Southern Sung-Yüan dynasties, 12th–14th centuries AD. Purchase, John L. Severance Fund.

With the loss of northern China to the Chin invasion of 1127, remnants of the Sung house reestablished a court to the south in the Chechiang provincial capital of Hangchou. Later writers on ceramics mention that a *kuan* or "official" ware was eventually designed for imperial use. Early in this century, one of the kilns recorded in the traditional literature as the source for the ware was excavated in the suburbs of the city, near the imperial sacrificial altars. The sherds unearthed there were potted from a porcelaneous clay so rich in iron that its dark coloration can be seen in unglazed or thinly glazed areas. In addition, the glaze itself was webbed with a mesh of crackle described in the literature on *kuan* ware. This simply designed basin, the largest of fifteen such wares represented in Cleveland, conforms to these "Suburban Altar" sherds. However, it and its neighbors in this collection (cf. [111]) also seem identical to a crackle ware only recently discovered at five kilns in Lung-ch'üan district, far to the south of the former imperial capital.

Technical studies on these Lung-ch'üan crackle wares have broadened our understanding of the Southern Sung imperial wares. Microscopic analysis of broken *kuan* wares preserved in the former imperial collections and excavated specimens from Hangchou and Lung-ch'üan indicate that the glaze — sometimes reaching a thickness greater than the porcelain body which supports it — was built up through successive applications before firing. This layering technique may explain the richness of the crackle levels within this large basin: the gold to brown webbing is the result of iron seepage from the charcoal gray body clay into the fissures within the various glaze levels. In addition, the limpid gray-green background in which the crackle is suspended comes quite close in hue to the uncrackled and glaze layered wares which formed the bulk of Lung-ch'üan production (see [109]).

We have noted earlier that it is difficult to determine if the crackle in the glaze of Northern Sung Ju ware developed during firing or over centuries (see [106]). The Lung-ch'üan excavations indicate that southern potters produced crackle at will. They used different types of clay — from coarse yellow-gray to a dense purple brown — to control the expansion and contraction of body and glaze during firing, thereby increasing or decreasing the size and density of crackle. This spectrum of colored clays and varied crackle also occurs in the Cleveland *kuan* collection.

Archaeological investigation has still not advanced enough for us to ascertain whether this distinctive crackle ware developed first in Hangchou or in Lung-ch'üan. However, since the same shapes recur in both ceramic groups, we have become more familiar with their period of manufacture. This basin, for example, is joined by two others of the same shape in the former imperial collections, now in the National Palace Museum, Taipei. Both were fired on a circular clay ring, whereas the Cleveland basin was fired on spurs. Second, a dragon in raised relief appears beneath the glaze on the interior base of the Chinese basins whereas the Cleveland example is undecorated. Raised relief and clay ring firing characterize Lung-ch'üan wares from the Yüan Dynasty (see [121]). It is therefore possible that this very special Chechiang crackle ware continued to be made under the Mongol occupation. HJK

EX COLLECTION The Manchu Imperial Household.

PUBLICATIONS Junkichi Mayuyama, *Chinese Ceramics in the West* (Tokyo: Mayuyama & Company, 1960) pl. 51. Hasebe, ed., *Toji, vol.* V *of Chugoku bijutsu* (1973) color pl. 43. Hasebe et al., *So*, vol. XII of *Sekai toji zenshu* (1977) 224, fig. 78. H. J. Kleinhenz, CMA *Bulletin*, LXV (April 1978) 144-145, 150, fig. 17, a.

LITERATURE *Kuan Ware of the Southern Sung Dynasty*, vol. XIII of *Porcelain of the National Palace Museum* (Hongkong: Cafa Company, 1962) Book I, Part II, pp. 122-125, pls. 36-37. G. St. G. M. Gompertz, *Chinese Celadon Wares*, 2nd edition rev., pp. 126-146.

See also color plate following page 86.

111 Incense Burner *(Lu)*: *Kuan* Ware 57.63

Dark reddish-brown porcelain with celadon glaze. H. 7.3 cm., W. 15.6 cm. China, Chechiang Province. Sung-Yüan Dynasty, 12th–14th centuries AD. Severance A. and Greta Millikin Collection.

The Sung Dynasty is best remembered for its artistic and literary pursuits. Less known to the public are its scientific studies. Reflecting the generalized Sung spirit of humanism is the stride made in the archaeological study of ancient bronzes — an approach which is truly modern in conception. Sung scholars were the first to separate these archaic forms from the superstitious associations with mythical kings and supernatural events characteristic of bronze studies from earlier Chinese epochs. Instead, they collected different types and recorded and deciphered inscriptions so as to understand the continuity of Chinese culture from the Shang through the Sung period. The vocabulary they developed to describe the shapes within the Sung imperial and private bronze collections as well as their methods for deciphering the inscriptions on these vessels still provide a useful fund of knowledge for today's bronze specialist.

This fondness for ancient forms also influenced the Sung world of ceramics. Many of the shapes common to uncrackled Lung-ch'üan and the *kua* wares from Chechiang are based on ancient bronzes. This incense burner of squat proportions and flattened handles illustrates a bronze shape and is known in only a few crackled celadon examples. Characteristic of the diversity within the *kuan* group, its thinly potted clay is a deep brown whereas the *kuan* basin in this collection [110] exhibits a charcoal gray fabric. The incense burner also bears a more opaque and pronounced bluish glaze with a single layer of red-stained crackle, whereas the glaze of the basin is translucent green with a many layered gold-stained crackle. However, both were fired on clay spurs, further testimony to the very special care with which the ware was fired.

To date, this bronze shape has yet to appear within any of the published fragments of crackle wares excavated from either the Hangchou or Lung-ch'üan kilns, but an incense burner of identical shape was excavated from the Jen family tombs in Chiangsu Province. The tomb inscriptions are dated between 1338 and 1351, suggesting that the *kuan* type wares could have continued into the Yüan Dynasty. This discovery is important to Clevelanders for another reason. Among the various Jen family tomb epitaphs, one belongs to Jen Jen-fa, the celebrated Yüan painter of horses, whose handscroll *Three Horses and Four Grooms* (CMA 60.181) can be seen in our collection. HJK

EX COLLECTION The Manchu Imperial Household.

PUBLICATIONS Sherman E. Lee, "Contrasts in Chinese and Japanese Art," *Journal of Aesthetics and Art Criticism*, XXI (Fall 1962) 9, fig. 14. Idem, "Janus in Limbo," CMA *Bulletin*, L (January 1963) 3, fig. 1. H. J. Kleinhenz, CMA *Bulletin*, LXV (April 1978) 144-145, 146, fig. 12, a. Glenn C. Nelson, *Ceramics: A Potter's Handbook*, 4th edition (New York: Holt, Rinehart and Winston, 1978) p. 182, pl. 358 (right). J. G. Moore, *The Eastern Gate*, repr. p. 76 and p. 86 (color). S. E. Lee, *A History of Far Eastern Art*, 4th edition, p. 374, repr. p. 390, color pl. 38 (right).

LITERATURE Nanking Museum and Chiangsu Provincial Museum, *Chiang-su sheng ch'u-t'u wen-wu hsüan-chi* [Collection of cultural objects unearthed in Chiangsu Province] (Peking: Wen wu ch'u-pan she, 1963) pl. 193 (incense burner from Jen family burial). Margaret Medley, *Percival David Foundation of Chinese Art*, vol. VII of *Oriental Ceramics: The World's Great Collections* (Tokyo: Kodansha, 1976) color pl. 25, monochrome pl. 33.

112 Tea Bowl: Chien Ware 48.206

Purplish-brown stoneware with iron slip glaze. H. 8.7 cm., Diam. 17.8 cm. China, Fuchien Province. Southern Sung Dynasty, 12th–13th centuries AD. Purchase from the J. H. Wade Fund.

The tea bowls from Chien-yang district, Fuchien, have been mentioned in Chinese literature since the end of the T'ang Dynasty. This bowl, along with several examples from collections throughout the world, is a shape that seems to have been popular during the Southern Sung Dynasty, though its large size is quite rare. Actually it is the ware, not the shape, that is unique within the ceramic history of China for the same impure and iron-rich local clay used to form its body was also applied as an aqueous slip coating to form its glaze. When fired, the body took on a characteristic deep purple-brown hue which hardly varies from one example to another. The enjoyment of Chien rests with the iron imperfections in its glaze which matured with firing into subdued reddish brown spots and streaks upon a rich blue-black ground.

Sung poets and even the Sung Emperor Hui-tsung (r. 1101–1126) called these iron formations "hare's fur marks" when describing Chien bowls in their tea poetry. Recent excavations at selected sites in Chien-yang and neighboring districts in Fuchien affirm the ware's popularity with Sung tea tasters since many kilns limited their output exclusively to tea bowls. Equally informative is the confirmation of imperial patronage for these simple shapes — some of the sherds unearthed at the Shui-chi kiln in Chien-yang district actually bear the stamp *kung-yu* ("purveyed to the emperor"). The popularity which the ware enjoyed during the Sung period can be traced to the fact that Fuchien also produced a much admired local tea. The leaves were dried and fermented in a brick shape. When infused with hot water and whisked, a foamy white layer would form. At their literary gatherings, Sung scholars would make a game of trying to drain their cups so as to leave that trace of white foam on the side of the bowl. What fairer way could there be to decide the winner than to use a darkly glazed bowl such as this. HJK

EX COLLECTION Dikran G. Kelekian.

EXHIBITIONS Cleveland, 1953: The Cleveland Museum of Art, Early Japanese Ink Painting. New York, 1963: Asia House Gallery, Tea Taste in Japanese Art, cat. by Sherman E. Lee, no. 9.

LITERATURE Fujio Koyama, *Temmoku*, vol. XXVI of *Toki zenshu* (1962) pl. 33. Museum of Anthropology, Amoy University. "Brief report on excavations of Sung Dynasty Chien ware kilns at Shui-chi, Chien-yang, Fuchien," in Chinese, *K'ao-ku*, 1964/4, pp. 191, 193, pl. VII: 3. *Tokyo Kokuritsu Hakubutsukan zuhan mokuroku: Chugoku kotoji-hen*, p. 85, pl. 349; p. 86, pl. 353. James Marshall Plumer, *Temmoku: A Study of the Ware of Chien*, ed. Caroline I. Plumer (Tokyo: Idemitsu Art Gallery, 1972).

113 Tea Bowl: Northern Black Ware

Buff stoneware with iron-brown slip and "oil spot" glaze. H. 4.4 cm., Diam. 8.9 cm. China (northern). Northern Sung–Chin Dynasty, 12th–13th centuries AD. Severance A. and Greta Millikin Collection.

This rare variety of lustrous black-glazed stoneware may have originated in northern China in experimental attempts to emulate Chien ware of southern Fuchien (cf. [112]). One clue to northern provenance is the buff unglazed base, camouflaged with iron brown slip to resemble the natural purplish-brown Fuchien clay. But the silvery "oil spot" glaze, known to Chien and other black wares, required specific kiln conditions met either by accident or careful control. Toward the end of the firing cycle, a change in atmosphere from oxidation to reduction caused excessive iron in the slip-glaze to rise to the surface and erupt in tiny iridescent pools, like drops of oil suspended in water.

Together with the more common "hare's fur" variety of Chien and its northern counterparts, this ware is popularly designated *temmoku*, the Japanese name of a mountain in south China and site of a Buddhist monastery where Japanese Zen monks admired such bowls in tea drinking rituals. "Oil spot" or *yuteki temmoku* was particularly esteemed by the Japanese, who imported the Fuchien bowls and passed them from generation to generation for their own, more formalized tea ceremony. The Shogun Ashikaga Yoshimasa (1435–1490), a noted tea master and connoisseur, devoted part of his collection catalog to *temmoku* and its varied glaze patterns. He rated *yuteki* second only to *yohen temmoku*, distinguished by larger spots encircled by iridescent blue and universally recognized today in only three examples preserved in Japan. Unlike oil spot *temmoku* — fired with occasional success by modern American and Japanese potters — the technical mysteries of *yohen* have never been duplicated.

In its small dimensions, rounded profile, and pale clay body, this Millikin bowl is typical of oil spot wares traditionally attributed by Western scholars to Honan Province and labeled Honan *temmoku*. Lacking positive kilnsite evidence from this area, the more recently accepted and intentionally vague label of "Northern black ware" is applied here. EP

LITERATURE A. L. Hetherington, *Chinese Ceramic Glazes* (Cambridge: Cambridge University Press, 1937) pp. 31-32. Charles L. Harder, "A Letter About the Temmoku Glaze," *Far Eastern Ceramic Bulletin*, VII, no. 1 (March 1955) 19-25. J. G. Ayers, *Victoria and Albert Museum*, monochrome pl. 106. Hasebe Gakuji and Seizo Hayashiya, *Tokyo National Museum*, vol. I of *Oriental Ceramics: The World's Great Collections* (Tokyo: Kodansha, 1976) color pl. 27. Kazuo Yamasaki and Fujio Koyama, "The Yohen Temmoku Bowls," *Oriental Art*, XIII, no. 2 (Summer 1967) 1-5.

114 Bottle Vase (*Yü-Hu-Ch'un*) 30.310

Buff stoneware with iron slip-glaze and overglaze iron oxide decoration. H. 27.3 cm., Diam. 17.4 cm. China, Honan Province. Chin or early Yüan Dynasty, 13th–14th centuries AD. Purchase, Charles W. Harkness Endowment Fund.

Numerous black or brown glazed stonewares in vase or bowl types with bodies close to or identical with those found on Tz'u-chou wares of similar date (cf. [116, 117]) have been variously described as Northern black ware, Honan *temmoku*, or, more appropriately, as a variety of the rich and varied Tz'u-chou production. The shape of this piece is a free and plastic one, natural to the wheel throwing process and therefore difficult to date. Comparable shapes are to be found in Ting wares of Sung, *ch'ing-pai* wares of late Sung and Yüan, celadons of Yüan and early Ming, in excavated silver wares of early Yüan, and in middle Yüan Blue-and-White examples. Shapes of the same

general nature exist in earlier and later wares, but this particular profile, evenly narrowing from wide lip to a short neck and swelling to an ample and rotund body with a quick retreat to a spreading foot, is clearly thirteenth or fourteenth century in date. The simple brushed on iron-oxide slip decoration of floral spray has its counterpart in black or brown on white Tz'u-chou decoration of the same time span. The simple flowing shape and restrained decoration combine to silence extended description. SEL

LITERATURE W. B. Honey, *The Ceramic Art of China and Other Countries of the Far East* (London: Faber and Faber, 1945) pl. 54b (Victoria and Albert Museum). Municipal Museum of Wuhsi, "Cultural Relics Unearthed from a Yüan Dynasty Tomb in Wuhsi, Chiangsu Province," in Chinese, *Wen wu*, 1964 / 12, pl. VI:3 (silver bottle vase from tomb of Chien Yu, died AD 1320). Margaret Medley, *Yüan Porcelain and Stoneware* (London: Faber and Faber, 1974) p. 122, pl. 109A (British Museum, formerly Oppenheim collection, London).

115 Baluster Vase: Tz'u-chou Ware 48.226

Buff gray stoneware with incised underglaze slip decoration. H. 41.5 cm., Diam. 12.7 cm. China, probably Honan Province. Northern Sung Dynasty, 10th–11th centuries AD. Purchase from the J. H. Wade Fund.

Tz'u-chou is the name of a ceramic producing district in Hopei Province associated with a fascinating group of wares now known to have been produced in many northern provinces from the ninth through the sixteenth centuries. Their common characteristic is the presence of clay slip decoration. Slip is an aqueous solution of very finely prepared clay which sometimes coats the whole surface of Tz'u-chou vessels to hide an undesirable color or coarseness in the clay used to form the body. This baluster vase represents the more visually rewarding Tz'u-chou type, where the potter took decorative advantage of contrasts between the color of the body clay and its slip covering. The light gray clay body of this vase first seems to have been etched with a stylus to form a feather band at the shoulder, then, a wide floral scroll border above a leaf meander surrounding the lower portion of the vase. Next, the potter applied a light aqueous slip coating, allowed it to dry, then polished off the slip layer until the underlying body clay was exposed where the designs were etched. Finally, a clear colorless glaze was applied. After firing, the slip covered por-

tions assumed a soft ivory color, while the exposed clay body was transformed from light gray to warm cinnamon brown.

The potter's fascination with a clear-cut curving line in the slip decoration on this vase also appears in his conception of its shape. Sharp divisions between lip, neck, shoulder, body, and foot result from playing one curve of mass against another. Such a viewpoint seems more suited to the intractable medium of metalwork than to the malleable nature of clay. For the Chinese archaeologist, this interest in metallic form indicates that the potter lived during the late tenth or early eleventh century. More general considerations of clay type and decoration help to pinpoint his activity in Honan Province, probably to the kiln of Tang-yang-yü in Hsiu-wu district or Ch'ü-ho in Teng-feng district. For the twentieth-century connoisseur, the consummate control of material and unusual sensitivity evident in its form and decoration place this vase at the highest level of the Tz'u-chou potter's art. HJK

EX COLLECTION Dikran G. Kelekian.

EXHIBITIONS Cleveland, 1940: The Cleveland Museum of Art. Los Angeles, 1952: The Los Angeles County Museum of Art, Chinese Ceramics from the Prehistoric Period through Ch'ien Lung, cat. by Henry Trubner, no. 228. Tokyo, 1955: Takashimaya Department Store, So-ji meihen ten [Exhibition of Sung ceramics], organized by The Japan Ceramic Society, no. 102. Tokyo, 1970: Tokyo National Museum, Toyo toji ten: Chugoku, Chosen, Nihon [Exhibition of Far Eastern ceramics: Chinese, Korean, and Japanese], no. 45. New York, 1974: Asia House Gallery, The Colors of Ink, cat. by Sherman E. Lee, no. 51. Indianapolis, 1980–1981: Indianapolis Museum of Art, Freedom of Clay and Brush Through Seven Centuries in Northern China: Tz'u-chou Type Wares, 960–1600 AD, cat. by Yutaka Mino, no. 13.

PUBLICATIONS James Marshall Plumer, "The Potter's Art at Cleveland," *Magazine of Art*, XXX (April 1940) 213. Fujio Koyama, "Hsiu-wu Ware in the Northern Sung Dynasty," in Japanese, *Bijutsu kenkyu*, VI, no. 161 (1951) pl. IV. Hasebe Gakuji, *So no Jishuyo* [Tz'u-chou ware of the Sung Dynasty], vol. XIII of *Toki zenshu* (1958) pl. 31. Mayuyama, *Chinese Ceramics in the West*, pl. 36. Hasebe, *Tokyo Kokuritsu Hakubutsukan kiyo*, III (1967) 213, fig. 22. J. Wirgin, *Bulletin of the Museum of Far Eastern Antiquities*, XLII (1970) pl. 40-1 (cf. pl. 41-1: jar, Buffalo Museum of Science). Hasebe Gakuji and Seizo Hayashiya, eds., *Chugoku kotoji* [Ancient Chinese ceramics] (Tokyo: Mainichi Newspapers, 1971) I, pt. 1, color pl. 152; pt. 2, p. 24. Hasebe, ed., *Toji*, vol. V of *Chugoku bijutsu* (1973) repr. p. 226. Idem, et al., *So*, vol. XII of *Sekai toji zenshu* (1977) pl. 110. S. E. Lee, *A History of Far Eastern Art*, 4th edition, p. 366, fig. 488.

116 Vase *(Mei-p'ing):* Tz'u-chou Ware 40.52

Dark gray stoneware with carved underglaze slip decoration. H. 34.3 cm., Diam. 20.7 cm. China (northern). Northern Sung-Chin Dynasty, 12th century AD. Purchase from the J. H. Wade Fund.

A short neck and a flowing pear-shaped body identify this durably potted vessel as a *mei-p'ing* or prunus vase. Although its slip decoration and shape place this *mei-p'ing* within the Tz'u-chou ranks of the twelfth century, no specific kiln site has yet been isolated for its place of manufacture. Wherever it was made, several procedures must have been necessary for the potter to achieve the decoration on the surface of the vase. The first step may have been to dip the vessel in white slip to mask the coarse gray body clay. After the white layer dried, a dark iron-saturated slip was applied. Then the potter incised a register of overlapping lotus petals around the neck, scrolling peony branches to cover the shoulder and body, and a band of overlapping chrysanthemum petals along the foot. Next, portions of iron slip were carved away to reveal the underlying white slip which forms the background to the peony branches. A few areas of white on black overlapping within that register suggest that the potter reinforced the background with another application of white slip before sealing the surface with a colorless glaze. By firing the vessel in an oxygen-rich kiln atmosphere, the potter produced a rich black silhouette of curving floral forms against a warm white background at the lip and around the body. HJK

EXHIBITIONS Cleveland, 1940: The Cleveland Museum of Art, Chinese Ceramics. Los Angeles, 1952: Los Angeles County Museum of Art, Chinese Ceramics from the Prehistoric Period through Ch'ien Lung, cat. by Henry Trubner, no. 236. New York, 1974: Asia House Gallery, The Colors of Ink, cat. by Sherman E. Lee, no. 54.

PUBLICATIONS J. M. Plumer, *Magazine of Art,* XXX (April 1940) repr. 213. Howard C. Hollis, "A Tz'u-chou Vase," CMA *Bulletin,* XXVII (November 1940) 142-143, repr. 130. J. G. Moore, *The Eastern Gate,* repr. p. 75.

LITERATURE J. Wirgin, *Bulletin of the Museum of Far Eastern Antiquities,* XLII (1970) p. 106, pls. 50:c, 50:d.

117 Petal-Rimmed Baluster Vase 42.656

Gray stoneware, slip-coated with lead glaze. H. 32.6 cm., Diam. 13.5 cm. China (northern). Northern Sung-Chin Dynasty, 12th century AD. Bequest of John L. Severance.

The degraded green glaze covering this petal-rimmed vase at first seems to have nothing in common with the two elegant slip-decorated vases previously discussed [115, 116]. Yet this vase does illustrate a phenomenon in Tz'u-chou decoration rarely encountered in twelfth-century burial or kiln excavations. After forming the body from coarse gray clay, the potter applied a white slip and fired the vase at about 1400° C, the temperature necessary for the formation of porcelain. When the vase cooled, all the outer surfaces except the rounded foot rim were painted with a lead based glaze containing copper. After refiring the vase at a much lower temperature, the glaze matured to what must have been a bright leaf green. Unfortunately eight hundred years of exposure to the atmosphere have dimmed the intensity of hue and caused a finely meshed crackle to form within the glaze layer.

Traditional Chinese collectors of ceramics usually dismiss the whole Tz'u-chou group as an ubiquitous people's pottery of northern China because no imperial or scholarly interest was recorded in the ware during the periods when Tz'u-chou flourished. However, Western interest has been high and has led to a re-evaluation of the ware by modern Chinese collectors. The double firing which this green-glazed vase underwent represents a significant expenditure of human energy and fuel resources. When hours are spent in firing and refiring or adding and removing slip for no purpose beyond the decorative enhancement of surface, such products could hardly have been within the economic reach of the Chinese peasant. If not emperor or scholar, then possibly the wealthy mercantile class provided the necessary market for the Tz'u-chou potters. Perhaps future archaeological investigations will help to clarify our understanding of the patronage at these northern kilns. HJK

PUBLICATION *Catalogue of the John L. Severance Collection: Bequest of John L. Severance, 1936* (Cleveland: The Cleveland Museum of Art, 1942) no. 132, pl. XXIX.

LITERATURE Yutaka Mino, *Freedom of Clay and Brush through Seven Centuries in Northern China: Tz'u-chou Type Wares, 960–1600 AD*, exhib. cat. (Indianapolis: Indianapolis

Museum of Art, 1980–1981) no. 96 (Indianapolis Museum of Art); cf. fig. 279 (vase from tomb near T'ai-yüan, Shanhsi, dated twelfth century by excavators).

118 Blue-and-White Stem Bowl *(Kao-tsu wan)* 64.169

Porcelain decorated in underglaze blue *(ch'ing-hua)*. H. 11.8 cm., Diam. 13.3 cm. China, Ching-te-chen, Chianghsi Province. Yüan Dynasty, 14th century, probably before AD 1350. Severance A. and Greta Millikin Collection.

In 1976 when a Chinese shipwreck was found off the coast of Sinan, South Korea, intensive scholarly interest was aroused by the great quantity of Yüan porcelains recovered from the ship. Among the 6,457 salvaged items the majority by far were celadons and white wares. To everyone's surprise, there was not a single piece of Blue-and-White *(ch'ing-hua)*. The absence of Blue-and-White ware suggests that it was still a newcomer in the early part of the Yüan Dynasty.

The shape of the stem cup (a smaller version of the stem bowl) can be traced through the silver and gold of the T'ang Dynasty and even into neolithic times, in elegant thin-shelled vessels in black pottery. It became increasingly popular under the Mongols and was quickly adopted in Korean *mishima* and white sacrificial wares. Because its top-heavy shape made it particularly suitable for being held in the hand, it was given the appropriate name, *pa-pei* ("cup for holding"). It appears that at some point in the fourteenth century, the potters in Ching-te-chen began to borrow this shape as well as the molded interior designs of dragons and clouds from the *ch'ing-pai* and *shu-fu* wares, and added the painted decorations on both the exterior and interior. Quality of the underglaze design varies from fine brushwork in deep grayish-blue to casual sketches in uneven or blurred color. The Millikin stem bowl, while typical though slightly larger than most examples, is one of the finest pieces distinguished by its draughtmanship and the superb technical control of its underglaze cobalt decoration.

At the time the Millikin stem bowl was acquired in 1958, it was probably one of no more than a half dozen examples known to the West. Today, as one of twenty some pieces known in the world, it is still one of the rarest of early Chinese Blue-and-White ceramics. It represents the budding stage of the *ch'ing-hua* technique which reached its full bloom in the fifteenth century, and was the true glory of Ming porcelain. WKH

EX COLLECTION Geoffrey Stevenson.

EXHIBITIONS Philadelphia, 1949: Philadelphia Museum of Art, Ming Blue and White, cat. *Philadelphia Museum Bulletin*, XLIV, no. 223 (Autumn 1949) no. 8, repr. p. 23. Cleveland, 1968: The Cleveland Museum of Art, Chinese Art Under the Mongols: The Yüan Dynasty (1279–1368), cat. by Sherman E. Lee and Wai-kam Ho, no. 156.

PUBLICATION M. Medley, *The Chinese Potter*, fig. 139.

119 Blue-and-White Jar *(Kuan)* with Lion Head Handles 62.154

Porcelain decorated in underglaze blue. H. 39.7 cm., W. at handles 37.5 cm., China, Ching-te-chen, Chianghsi Province. Late Yüan Dynasty, second half 14th century AD. Purchase, John L. Severance Fund.

The invention of "Blue-and-White" porcelain occurred in China during the Yüan Dynasty (1279–1368). Although there is vague evidence for some relatively crude predecessors in the late Sung Dynasty (960–1279), the first securely dated examples (1327) are in the Percival David Foundation, University of London, and from recent excavations in mid-Yüan contexts at Peking. The invention was of great importance and established a porcelain genre that dominated later Chinese wares and even European production imitating the originals. It is no coincidence that the purity inherent in the combination of Blue-and-White paralleled the rise of the revolutionary literati *(wen-jên)* tradition of ink painting on paper from the mid-fourteenth century onward. The early Blue-and-White wares do not have imperial marks as a basic part of their fabric, as is so characteristic of later productions from the imperial kilns at Ching-te-chen in Chianghsi Province. However, many of the Yüan wares have added, engraved inscriptions indicating their use in imperial contexts. The present exam-

ple has the characters *Nan-kung* ("South Palace") engraved on one side, probably a reference to the storage or display place for this *kuan* in a Chinese or Manchurian imperial palace, or that of a dowager empress.

The Cleveland *kuan*, one of some thirteen known examples, is an outstanding jar with a noble and strong profile, particularly clear color, and firm delineation of the decorative motifs. It embodies many of the most characteristic motifs of the Yüan potters: lion mask handles, squared spirals, waves, lotus arabesque, cloud collars containing phoenix among chrysanthemums and crape-myrtle, large peony arabesques, classical interlocking scrolls, and "rising gadroons." SEL

EXHIBITION Cleveland, 1968: The Cleveland Museum of Art, Chinese Art Under the Mongols: The Yüan Dynasty (1279–1368), cat. by Sherman E. Lee and Wai-kam Ho, no. 156.

PUBLICATIONS Sherman E. Lee, "Janus in Limbo," CMA *Bulletin*, L (January 1963) 2-6, repr. 5, 24. M. Medley, *The Chinese Potter*, p. 183, fig. 134. Idem, *Yüan Porcelain and Stoneware*, p. 58, fig. 45b.

LITERATURE John A. Pope, *Fourteenth-Century Blue and White: A Group of Chinese Porcelains in the Topkapu Sarayi Müzesi, Istanbul*, Freer Gallery of Art Occasional Papers, vol. II, no. 1 (Washington, D.C., 1952) pp. 30, 31 (two *kuan* in above collections), pl. 40 (*kuan* in Wat Mahathat, Lamphun, Thailand). Sir Harry M. Garner, *Oriental Blue and White* (London: Faber and Faber, 1954) p. 19, pls. 20-21. John A. Pope, *Chinese Porcelains from the Ardebil Shrine* (Washington, DC: Smithsonian Institution, Freer Gallery of Art, 1956) pl. 26.

120 Bowl 64.222

Porcelain with molded and incised decoration under a copper-red glaze. H. 5.5 cm., Diam. 8 cm. China, Ching-te-chen, Chianghsi Province. Late Yüan Dynasty or Hung-wu period, ca. third or fourth quarter 14th century AD. Severance A. and Greta Millikin Collection.

Within the extremely small family of early copper-red porcelains decorated with raised cloud and dragon *shu-fu* design, some nuances can be detected with possibly slight differences in date. A bowl in the Sir Percival David Foundation, University of London, for example — with remarkable consistency in its red color, a distinctly white mouth rim and glazed base — probably dates from the Yung-lo era (1403–1424). The Sedgwick dish in the British Museum is stylistically very close to the stem cup in underglaze red-brown (outside) and indigo blue (inside) in the Nelson Gallery-Atkins Museum, Kansas City, which in turn is almost identical in color as well as in the design of the twin headed *ju-i* clouds with the well-known Hung-wu (1368–1398) fragment discovered at the Ming palace site in Nanking. The small Millikin bowl with a rather steep profile is decorated likewise with the twin-headed cloud motif at the center of its bottom very similar to the Hung-wu pieces. Its two five-clawed dragons surrounded by the "long-tailed" *ju-i* clouds in relief also share the same basic iconography but are less evenly covered and precisely defined by the glaze. The maroon glaze on the exterior is thinly and superbly applied, but the scattered white spots on the wall and underneath the lip as well as the relative mellowness of its tone suggest that there was still something to be perfected both in the technique of glazing and in the control of firing temperature. The foot is slightly splayed and shows a second cut slanting inwardly at an angle to the flat bottom of the foot, exposing the unglazed, fine grained "sandy base" with marks of the knife cutting in a concentric movement. These seem to be some of the significant and overlapping characteristics of the transition between late Yüan and Hung-wu, a period not yet fully explored and understood.

The control of temperature and reduction is extremely difficult for the unstable copper oxide. The experiment with copper-red in Ching-te-chen began with the imitation of Chün ware through the late-Yüan early-Ming underglaze red and finally achieved a total success with the brilliant "sacrificial red" of the Hsüan-te period. For various reasons, however, the production of copper-red was discontinued at the end of the fifteenth century in favor of decoration with overglaze iron red enamel, and was not resumed until the K'ang-hsi reign (1662–1722) of the Ch'ing Dynasty. WKH

EXHIBITION Cleveland, 1968: The Cleveland Museum of Art, Chinese Art Under the Mongols: The Yüan Dynasty (1279–1368), cat. by Sherman E. Lee and Wai-kam Ho, no. 165.

121 Plate *(p'an)* with Relief Dragon: Lung-ch'üan Ware 61.92

Porcelain with celadon glaze and decoration in biscuit reserve. Diam. 43.2 cm. China, Chechiang Province. Yüan Dynasty (AD 1279–1368). Purchase, John L. Severance Fund.

Under Southern Sung rule, Lung-ch'üan celadons dominated the Chechiang ceramic industry by quantity of production and inventiveness of design (see [109]). This position continued for a time during the Mongol control of China, when Yüan potters maintained a high standard of quality control and introduced new decorative devices to the celadon industry of the province. This plate — the largest of a rare type preserved in only two other known examples — sums up the high points of Yüan production. In form, its flanged lip, shallow well, and broad proportions imitate Islamic metalwork which fascinated the Yüan potter as it had his Sung predecessor. In decoration, the vessel is completely Chinese. Seventeen prunus blossoms, traditional flowers of late winter, decorate its rim. The plate's curving walls are etched with an undulating wave pattern, and on its flat interior a dragon writhes energetically amid clouds. The motifs illustrate a concept of the dragon as rain god — benevolent in nature but fearsome of form to an agricultural people dependent upon the destructive yet life-giving necessity of the late winter monsoon season.

The dragon, clouds, and prunus were stamped and cut from a thin sheet of unglazed clay and floated upon the already glazed surface of the basin. Subjected to the oxygen-reduced firing atmosphere of the kiln, the white Lung-ch'uan clay took on a reddish brown color against an olive-green glazed surface. A similar reddish color appears on the exterior base of the vessel. Evidently the sheer bulk of this and many other Yüan Lung-ch'üan vessels necessitated support in the form of a thick tubular spur which scarred the base with a ring after firing.

Rich and bold though this combination of russet and green might seem, the decorative possibilities of this firing method were short lived. In Chiangsu Province, underglaze blue patterns painted on the crisp white body clays of Ching-te-chen wares were just being perfected and eventually revolutionized the whole ceramic industry. Until the end of Ch'ing imperial rule, all future innovations would be made at Ching-te-chen, while celadon glazes would reappear intermittently as nothing more than an archaizing revival.

HJK

EX COLLECTION Tanimura Shokei, Kanagawa.

EXHIBITION Cleveland, 1968: The Cleveland Musem of Art, Chinese Art Under the Mongols: The Yüan Dynasty (1279–1368), cat. by Sherman E. Lee and Wai-kam Ho, no. 156.

PUBLICATION S. E. Lee, CMA *Bulletin*, L (January 1968) 2-6.

LITERATURE Ernst Zimmerman, *Altchinesische Porzellane im Alten Serai*, vol. II of *Meisterwerke der Türkischen Museen Zu Konstantinopel* (Berlin and Leipzig: Walter de Gruyter, 1930) pl. 19 (Topkapu Sarayi). M. Medley, *Yüan Porcelain and Stoneware*, p. 71, color pl. E (Percival David Foundation).

122 Vase *(Mei-p'ing)* 64.167

Porcelain with incised underglaze decoration *(T'ien-pai)* H. 32.1 cm., Diam. of base 12.1 cm. China, Ching-te-chen, Chianghsi Province. Ming Dynasty, reign of Yung-lo (AD 1403–1424). Severance A. and Greta Millikin Collection.

"*Nan-ch'ing pei-pai*" ("Southern celadon and Northern white") — this well-known saying is basically correct as long as it refers only to the two main monochrome traditions of the T'ang Dynasty, the Yüeh ware in the south and the recently discovered Hsing ware in the north. It was no longer true, however, after the fall of Northern Sung when the main center for white ware was shifted from Ting-chou in Hopei (see [103]) to Ching-te-chen in Chianghsi. But as a continuation of the Ting tradition, the finest white porcelains from the fourteenth century on, notably the famous *shu-fu* group, were still mostly made for the court, especially for sacrificial and ceremonial purposes. The production of such court-centered white porcelain was carried on at the beginning of the Ming Dynasty and reached a new height of splendor during the Yung-lo period. The emphasis as before was on the sacrificial wares. This is proven by the report that "white porcelain sacrificial wares with dragon and phoenix designs" were made for the imperial ancestral temple under the direction of the eunuch Chang Shan, who supervised the ceramic production at Ching-te-chen from the Hung-wu period to 1425, when he was executed for some unknown offense. Probably for economic or other reasons, in 1459 the annual production of this type of sacrificial white wares was sharply reduced.

This beautiful vase is an elegant testimony to the extremely high standards demanded for such ceremonial wares. Exquisitely potted with the utmost care paid to its shape and to the subdued dignity of its decor, it is a noble statement of the *mei-p'ing* form. The high rounded shoulder is decorated in *an-hua*, or "hidden decoration," incised under the translucent glaze, with the formal cloud-collar motif, or *yün-chien,* which is balanced at the base by equally stylized floral scrolls. In between these bands are sprays of peonies, much more freely drawn and realistically represented. The early Ming white glaze employed in Ching-te-chen was reportedly "made of a paste from Hsiao-kang-tsui mixing with the leaf ashes of the palm bamboo." This glaze has a lustre and purity unequaled in any other period; its color radiates with such a soothingly soft glow like melting snow that can be described only as *t'ien-pai* ("sweet white"). The *t'ien-pai* ware has always been considered a great achievement of the Yung-lo period. Its rarity makes it all the more precious among Ming porcelains. Its frequent association with the so-called "bodiless" or "semi-bodiless" pottings invokes a wonderful image of such delicacy and provides inspiration for such poetic exaggeration as in the following lines:

> One is afraid that it may be blown
> away by the wind,
> And worried that it will meet under the
> sunlight.

WKH

EX COLLECTION Alice Boney.

EXHIBITION New York, 1974: Asia House Gallery, The Colors of Ink, cat. by Sherman E. Lee, no. 66, repr. p. 129.

PUBLICATION S. E. LVEE, *A History of Far Eastern Art,* 4th edition, p. 419, fig. 567.

123 Blue-and-White Foliate-Rimmed Brush Washer 64.166

Porcelain decorated in underglaze blue *(ch'ing-hua)*. H. 4.5 cm., Diam. 18.1 cm. China, Ching-te-chen, Chianghsi Province. Ming Dynasty, reign of Hsüan-te (AD 1426–1435). Severance A. and Greta Millikin Collection.

There are a few early fifteenth-century Blue-and-White wares of the ten-lobed variety which are of extraordinary quality; the Millikin washer is one of the finest of them. As a new variant derived from a popular Yüan Dynasty form by the use of twin molds in its making, the foliations of the rim are carried down the fluted well to the foot ring. The flared body is divided in this way into ten lobes, each decorated with double-lined borders and a five-clawed dragon in medallion. These encircling dragons *(t'uan-lung)*, ascending and descending alternately, are vigorously repeated and enlarged as the prime motif for both the interior and exterior bottoms, a unique feature among such pieces. Two special effects characteristic of the period can be observed in this example: the "orange peel" surface texture and the so-called "heaped and piled" effects. Both are supposedly caused by the rather coarse grinding of the glaze material, and when concentrations of the blue pigments are oxidized black by letting fresh air into the kiln before they were cooled, the result is the "iron rust" beloved by the Chinese connoisseurs for the depth and undulation of the colors inimitable by later potters.

Partly based on a series of tests conducted at Oxford since 1955, it has been argued that among Chinese Blue-and-White wares of the fifteenth century, the unmarked specimens are Yung-lo (1403–1424) and the marked are of the Hsüan-te reign (1426–1435). The Millikin washer is unmarked. However, this argument must be weighed against its comparison with such marked pieces as the fluted washer formerly in the Edward Chow collection and a number of other comparably decorated pieces. Their close relationships are unmistakable. Unless the Hsüan-te mark is to be disregarded altogether, as proposed by some skeptics, a more conservative dating for the Millikin piece seems justifiable. WKH

EX COLLECTION Geoffrey Stevenson.

EXHIBITION Philadelphia, 1949: Philadelphia Museum of Art, Ming Blue and White, cat., *Philadelphia Museum Bulletin*, XLIV, no. 223 (Autumn 1949) no. 43, repr. p. 38.

LITERATURE Suzanne G. Valenstein, *Ming Porcelains: A Retrospective*, exhib. cat. (New York: China House Gallery, 1970) p. 42.

124 Blue-and-White Plate with Grape Decoration 53.127

Porcelain decorated in underglaze blue. H. 7.6 cm., Diam. 43.2 cm. China, Ching-te-chen, Chianghsi Province. Early 15th century (before AD 1435). Anonymous Gift by Exchange.

The Blue-and-White wares of the Yung-lo (1403–1424) and Hsüan-te (1426–1435) reigns are considered, by traditional Chinese and current Western standards, the zenith of the type. The brilliant lustre of the slightly greenish-white ground color combines with the resonant and deep blue decoration to produce an effect that is neither too cold and mechanical nor too informal and careless. The Chinese texts dwell lovingly on the "heaped and piled" appearance of the blue color and the "orange-peel" undulations of the covering glaze. Examples of this ware made at the imperial kilns at Ching-te-chen are now well known, reasonably numerous, and represented in most major Western collections, in the former Ardebil shrine collections of the Safavid rulers of Persia now in the Teheran Museum, in the Palace Museum, Peking, and the National Palace Museum, Taipei, as well as in other collections of mainland China and Japan. The demands of the imperial court were large and pressing, and it is amazing that they were met with compliance at the highest levels of quality.

Collectors and critics are not necessarily consistent in their use of criteria for evaluating Ming porcelains. In general, the most common criteria are "importance," quality, rarity, and condition — the first being really a combination of the last three. The large grape plates of this general type are relatively numerous and considered highly desirable. But the peculiarly rich and complex combination of features — foliate rim, wave pattern border, free and elegant drawing, and

brilliant color — are found on only two other known examples, one in the Ardebil shrine collection and the other belonging to Mrs. William H. Moore III, on loan to The Metropolitan Museum of Art in New York.

The base is unglazed and fired cream to orange in color. The lack of an imperial mark makes it impossible to assign the piece specifically to one of the Yung-lo or Hsüan-te reigns, but current opinion, if favoring Yung-lo, prefers to assign these examples to the early fifteenth century.

The grape motif was popular in the Sui (581–618) and T'ang (618–906) periods as a fresh importation from the Near East. By the late Sung and especially the Yüan and early Ming periods, the depiction of grapes was commonly used by both Ch'an Buddhist and Taoist priest-painters as a microcosm of both the mystic universe and the specific and meager elements of the daily regimen. Their appearance with the floral sprays on expensive plates for conspicuous use by the highest personages probably indicates nothing more than a sensuous enjoyment of representations of pleasurable flora contained within the waves of all-embracing waters. SEL

EXHIBITIONS Detroit, 1952: The Detroit Institute of Arts, The Arts of the Ming Dynasty, cat. introd. by Paul L. Grigaut, no. 104. Bloomington, 1966: Indiana University, East-West in Art: Patterns of Cultural and Aesthetic Relationships, cat. by Theodore Bowie et al., no. 130.

PUBLICATIONS Sir Harry M. Garner, *Oriental Blue and White*, p. 18, pl. 14. Sherman E. Lee, "Early Ming Blue and White Porcelains," CMA *Bulletin* XLII (February 1955) repr. p. 28. Fujioka Ryoichi, ed., *Gen Min* [Yüan and Ming], vol. XI of *Seikai toji zenshu* (1956) pl. 56. Idem., ed., *Gen Min-sho no sometsuki* [Blue-and-White porcelain of the Yüan and early Ming dynasties], vol. XI of *Toki zenshu* (1960) pl. 40. Mayuyama, *Chinese Ceramics in the West*, pl. 92. S. E. Lee, *A History of Far Eastern Art*, 4th edition, p. 420, fig. 568.

LITERATURE J. A. Pope, *Chinese Porcelains from the Ardebil Shrine*, pl. 37. Suzanne G. Valenstein, *A Handbook of Chinese Ceramics*, p. 129, fig. 41 (collection of Mrs. William H. Moore III).

125 Blue-and-White Bowl (*wan*) with Land of Taoist Immortals 62.260

Porcelain decorated in underglaze blue. H. 6.8 cm., Diam. 19.7 cm. China, Ching-te-chen, Chianghsi Province. Ming Dynasty, mark and reign of Hsüan-te (AD 1426–1435). Purchase, John L. Severance Fund.

While most of the early Ming Blue-and-White wares rely on floral motifs (see [124]) or mythical beasts for decoration, a few examples of bowls such as this one are decorated with figures set in an architectural and landscape setting. They recall a major type of figural decoration used during the Yüan Dynasty, but there embodying fictional or dramatic narratives rather than mythical scenes. The decoration on the Cleveland bowl, matched closely by others in major ceramic collections, represents on one side two female Taoist immortals riding in clouds on phoenixes and on the other an elaborate temple set in a sharp-peaked mountain landscape. The interior of the bowl is plain white, while the six character reign mark is placed on the glazed base within the usual double circle. SEL

EX COLLECTION Jean-Pierre Dubosc, Paris.

EXHIBITIONS Philadelphia, 1949: Philadelphia Museum of Art, Ming Blue-and-White, cat., *Philadelphia Museum Bulletin*, XLIV, no. 223 (Autumn 1949) 13, no. 52 repr. Venice, 1954: Palazzo Ducale, Mostra d'arte Cinese: Settimo centenario di Marco Polo, cat. by Jean-Pierre Dubosc, no. 52.

PUBLICATION Daisy Lion-Goldschmidt, *Ming Porcelain* (London: Thames and Hudson, 1978) p. 109, pl. 76.

126 Stem Cup *(pa-pei)* with Design of Sea Monsters — 57.60

Porcelain decorated in underglaze blue and overglaze red enamel. H. 8.9 cm., Diam. 9.8 cm. China, Ching-te-chen, Chianghsi Province. Ming Dynasty, mark and reign of Hsüan-te (AD 1426–1435). Purchase, John L. Severance Fund.

The stem cup was known in the Tang Dynasty (618–906), most notably in silver vessels, but it is exceedingly rare in genuine Sung wares. It reappears in the Yüan Dynasty, both in plain white wares and in the earliest types of porcelain with decoration in underglaze blue. From this time on its profile is changed and refined until relatively modern times, but the imperial marked stem cups of the Hsüan-te reign are thought to be the finest of the shape by Chinese and Western writers alike. The base of Hsüan-te stem cups is characteristically flat and unglazed; the reign mark is usually found inside a double circle on the bottom of the interior.

The blue is "heaped and piled," especially in the wave pattern used as a background for the mythical sea monsters. These animals were reserved in white against the blue ground and then colored in a separate firing with overglaze iron-red enamels. The type is extremely rare, only a few being known; the closest parallel is a *pa-pei* in a Japanese private collection. The rarest of all are similar cups with the animals or dragons in underglaze copper-red, with only two examples known, both in the Percival David Foundation, University of London. The National Palace Museum, Taipei, has none of this type but, oddly enough, does possess a marked stem cup with underglaze animals against an overglaze red wave background.

The bold and rich nature of the decoration represents a movement away from the austerity of plain Blue-and-White towards a more sumptuous taste characterized by an increase in the number of enamel colors used in later reigns — three in Ch'eng-hua, five in Wan-li, and even more and blended enamels in special palace wares of the Ch'ing Dynasty (see [136]). Here the simple use of red, white, and blue provides a richly textured and progressive contrast to the traditional purity of the white interior with its elegantly written mark — *Ta Ming Hsüan-te nien chih* ("Great Ming Hsüan-te period made"). It should be stressed that Chinese critics and collectors did not value size in itself. On the contrary, smaller objects of high quality suitable for the writing table, the private altar, or the collector's shelves, were prized above all others, and certainly two of the Museum's Chinese ceramics, this one and [127], are among the smallest, but most precious of all. SEL

See also color plate following page 86.

EX COLLECTIONS Probably Palace Collection, Peking; Edward Chow, Hong Kong; Men-chu Wang, San Francisco.

EXHIBITION New York, 1970: China House Gallery, Ming Porcelain, cat. by Suzanne G. Valenstein, no. 16.

PUBLICATIONS S. G. Valenstein, *A Handbook of Chinese Ceramics*, p. 137, fig. 44. D. Lion-Goldschmidt, *Ming Porcelain*, p. 97, color pl. 63. S. E. Lee, *A History of Far Eastern Art*, 4th edition, p. 420, repr. p. 425, color pl. 41 (top).

LITERATURE Margaret Medley, *Illustrated Catalogue of Chinese Porcelains Decorated in Underglaze Blue and Copper Red in the Percival David Foundation of Chinese Art*, School of Oriental and African Studies, University of London (London, 1963) no. B638, pl. XVIII; no. A635, pl. X and p. 30. Sato Masuhiko and Nakano Tetsu, *Chugoku III Gen Min* [China, part III: Yüan and Ming], vol. VII of *Toki koza* [Lectures on ceramics], ed. Fujio Koyama (Tokyo: Yuzankaku, 1973) pl. 84.

127 Wine Cup with Decoration of Children Playing 57.61

Porcelain decorated in underglaze blue and overglaze red and green enamel (*tou-t'sai*). H. 4.8 cm., Diam. 6.1 cm. China, Ching-te-chen, Chianghsi Province. Ming Dynasty, mark and reign of Ch'eng-hua (AD 1465–1487). Purchase, John L. Severance Fund.

Each generation has its favorites among the Chinese porcelains of the past, but a knowledgeable and monied consensus agrees that the colored enamel decorated porcelains of the Ch'eng-hua reign are unsurpassed in their unctuous luminosity of glaze, vibrancy of color, and the unification of these elements within the relatively few shapes of the small luxury utensils of the reign. The most famous of these are the small wine cups decorated with images of chickens, the so-called "chicken cups." The cups with figural decoration are even rarer — only two examples of the present type are known, this one and its mate in the National Palace Museum, Taipei. Each shows five children, three holding plants, one flying a three-streamer kite, and the other dancing. Rocks, clouds, and plants complete the decoration. In addition to the blue color of the underglaze brushwork, red and green enamels are added, hence the appelation *tou-ts'ai* ("fighting color" ware). The reign mark, *Ta Ming Ch'eng-hua nien chih*, is on the base within a double square enclosure.

While it may seem foolish and self-indulgent to revel in the exquisite refinement of the "oily" glaze and the violet tinge of the luminous blue, these pleasures are the essence of enjoyment and evaluation of such cabinet porcelains. Such connoisseurship has a long history in China and a strong recent one in the West. The *tou-ts'ai* cups set standards by which other porcelains are judged.

The subject of children playing is an auspicious one, implying both fecundity and well being. It ranges in complexity from the *One Hundred Children at Play* on a Sung album painting in Cleveland (CMA 61.261) to the *Family Gathering on New Year's Morning* in the tapestry woven by the Ch'ien-lung emperor's workshop as a gift for the King of France, also in this Museum (CMA 42.825).

Sun Cheng-tse's *Yen-shen-chai tsa-chi*, written about 1660 says: "colored wares were finest in Ch'eng-hua. There are cups with decoration of beautiful ladies admiring flowers by candlelight . . . with ladies playing on swings in a garden in springtime. The cups with grapes around them are most dainty and those with children and scholars life-like to the very hairs." SEL

EX COLLECTIONS Probably Palace Collection, Peking; Edward Chow, Hong Kong; Men-chu Wang, San Francisco.

EXHIBITION New York, 1970: China House Gallery, Ming Porcelain, cat. by Suzanne G. Valenstein, no. 24.

PUBLICATIONS J. G. Moore, *The Eastern Gate*, repr. p. 79 and p. 87 (color). S. E. Lee, *A History of Far Eastern Art*, 4th edition, p. 420, repr. p. 425, color pl. 41 (center).

LITERATURE *Enamelled Ware of the Ming Dynasty*, book I, vol. XV of *Porcelain of the National Palace Museum* (Hongkong: Cafa Company, 1966), pl. 11, a-c. Keng Pao-ch'ang, "A Hsüan-te red-glazed water-chestnut shaped basin and a Ch'eng-hua *tou-ts'ai* cup," in Chinese, *Wen wu*, 1980/2, color pl. I (above).

See also color plate following page 86.

128 Blue-and-White Bowl with Lily Decoration 67.64

Porcelain decorated in underglaze blue. H. 6.9 cm., Diam. 14.5 cm. China, Ching-te-chen, Chianghsi Province. Ming Dynasty, mark and reign of Ch'eng-hua (AD 1465–1487). Gift of John D. Rockefeller, III and Purchase, John L. Severance Fund.

The shape of this bowl is closely related to the earlier Yung-lo and Hsüan-te types called *lien-tzu* ("lotus form"). By the Ch'eng-hua period the last vestiges of lotus decoration were abandoned and the simple shape became the ground for other floral decoration — most notably that using lilies as the dominant motif. The imperial mark in six characters is to be found on the glazed base of the bowl.

While the colored wares of Ch'eng-hua (see [127]) were prized above all others, the Blue-and-White wares of the reign were considered to yield precedence to the wares of Hsüan-te (see [125]). Certainly the blue color is less vibrant in Ch'eng-hua, but the refinement of drawing and particularly the judicious balance of decoration against the unctuous white ground demands high praise. "Palace bowls" of this type are more numerous than the enameled types but can hardly be deemed common.

In Lan P'u's *Ching-te-chen t'ao lu* published in 1815, the author writes: "It is said that the Wan-li Emperor liked to drink from Ch'eng-hua cups which were priced at one hundred thousand cash for a pair. There were very few like them at the end of the Ming Dynasty." SEL

EX COLLECTION Herschel V. Johnson.

PUBLICATION Sir Harry M. Garner, *Oriental Blue and White*, pl. 35.

129 Yellow Monochrome Plate

Porcelain with overglaze yellow enamel. Diam. 21 cm. China, Ching-te-chen, Chianghsi Province. Ming Dynasty, mark and reign of Ch'eng-hua (AD 1465–1487). Severance A. and Greta Millikin Collection.

A rarity, this deep plate with thin sides and slightly flared rim rests on a tapering high foot ring and is enameled inside and out with an evenly applied bright yellow over a high-fired feldspathic glaze. The convex white base has a double-circled six character mark in underglaze blue, *Ta Ming Ch'eng-hua nien chih.* The pale blue of the reign mark is accentuated by dark flecks of excess cobalt which has an iridescence not unlike the so-called "hsi-kuang" on early fifteenth-century Blue-and-White ware. The high foot ring, while tapering inside and out as differentiated from the wedge-shaped type, is cut twice at the unglazed rim, showing a paste of exquisite quality. In the interior between the wall and the bottom of the well a narrow band of extremely fine crackling can be seen sparkling from reflections of some crystalline particles. These seem to be seldom found on some of the Chia-ching, Wan-li or early Ch'ing *chuang-yao* (1681–1688) examples in which the yellow enamel was applied directly to the biscuit, or to a much thinner feldspathic layer.

Among Chinese collectors, the name Hsüan-te yellow is often mentioned together with Hsüan-te red *(Hsüan-hung Hsüan-huang)* as the twin crowns of monochrome in the fifteenth century. While the high reputation of Hsüan-te copper-red never raised any serious question, yellow monochrome attributed to the same period has always been viewed with great suspicion. For practical purposes, perhaps the following reign of Ch'eng-hua should be singled out as the true beginning of a new monochrome yellow enamel produced by antimoniate of iron fluxed with lead. This brilliant new color, so much clearer and richer than the muddy low-fired alkaline glaze of the T'ang Dynasty, is called Imperial Yellow in the West because it was normally reserved for court use. The Ming potters had succeeded in creating a color sufficiently strong and pure to represent the essence of the earth — one of the five elements in Chinese cosmology — completing the foundation for later developments in polychromed porcelains. This deep plate, an extremely rare shape in Cheng-hua Imperial Yellow, epitomizes these developments. WKH

EXHIBITION Houston, Texas, 1954: Fine Arts Museum, no. 94.

PUBLICATION S. E. Lee, *A History of Far Eastern Art*, 4th edition, p. 421, color pl. 42, p. 426 left.

LITERATURE National Palace Museum, *Monochrome Ware of the Ming Dynasty* (Hong Kong: Cafa, 1968) I, 76, pl. 15 (identical plate with Ch'eng-hua reign mark). Mr. and Mrs. F. Brodie-Lodge, Arts Council of Great Britain, and OCS, *The Arts of the Ming Dynasty* (1957) no. 104, pl. 32 (identical plate with Ch'eng-hua reign mark).

130 Blue-and-White Arrow Vase *(Chien-hu)* 64.170

Porcelain decorated in underglaze blue. H. 26.1 cm., Diam. 7 cm. China, Ching-te-chen, Chianghsi Province. Ming Dynasty, reign of Cheng-te (AD 1506–1521). Severance A. and Greta Millikin Collection.

The appearance for the first time of many unusual shapes in Blue-and-White in place of the traditional round bowls and dishes is characteristic of the Cheng-te period. Generally classified either as *cho-ch'i* ("sculptured ware") or *yin-ch'i* ("piece-molded ware"), these unusual shapes were often angular which led to even bolder innovations, such as the double squares and shouldered hexagon, in the following Chia-ching, Lung-ch'ing, and Wan-li reigns. Most of the new prod-

ucts were utensils or ornaments intended for the gentleman's study. Among these the table screens and covered writing boxes were known particularly as palace pieces. Many of them were further marked by new decorations with Persian or Arabic scripts derived from the Koran, a striking feature usually attributed to the powerful influence of the Muslim eunuchs in the court. However, the imperial rule under the unpredicatable playboy Emperor Cheng-te was one of the most unconventional and bizarre in Chinese history. The Mohammaden wares were only one of the peculiar products of a time that has yet to be fully explained.

This vase of extremely fine quality in the Millikin collection is a remarkable example of this group of Blue-and-White. The faceted, quadrangular body is surmounted by a tall, tapering cylindrical neck, with double handles and six tubes surrounding the mouth, and stands on a flared conical foot. Each facet of the body and two sides of the neck are decorated with Persian inscriptions in medallions, which are surrounded by the so-called Mohammadan scrolls (*hui-hui wen*) with their evenly outlined and color-washed vines and trefoils. The inscriptions have been freely translated as: "Oh Beautiful! Oh Powerful!" and "None know the extent and limits of thy power and majesty." The potting is heavy and powerfully structured. The color is brilliant in deep cobalt blue. The glaze is thick, glossy, and oily in touch with a greenish tone typical of the period. There is a six-character mark of Cheng-te on the base.

The unusual shape of the vase is derived from *t'ou-hu*, an early type of bronze vase used in the "arrow game" originating from ceremonial archery in Confucian tradition dating back to the Spring and Autumn Period (770–480 BC). The quadrangular faceted body, however, is clearly a Cheng-te deviation from the classical form. Among the five recorded Ming manuals of the "arrow game," only one, *T'ou-hu i-chieh* ("Rituals and rules for the arrow game") by Wang T'i (preface dated 1527) has survived today. The ten popular game plays ("twin dragons entering the ocean," "three religions converged in the main stream," etc.) are illustrated in the manual with bronze contemporary arrow vases. A comparison of these bronze examples with this vase clearly demonstrates that they represent the same new shape which distinguished the early sixteenth century. WKH

131 Vase *(Mei-p'ing)* with Lotus Decoration 42.716

Porcelain with biscuit outlines and polychrome glazes in cloisonné style *(fa-hua)*. H. 37.5 cm., Diam. 19 cm. China. Ming Dynasty, late 15th century AD. Bequest of John L. Severance.

Vessels of this group are often called *san ts'ai* or "three color" wares, but this confuses the issue because the same designation describes the lead-glazed earthenware burial pottery and figurines of the T'ang Dynasty (see [97–99]). The other, older term, *fa-hua* — "enamel painting," calling to mind cloisonné techniques in Ming metalwork — seems more descriptive.

While few, if any of these wares bear reign marks, at their best they are clearly porcelains of the highest quality — bold and original. Their decoration, using such somber colors as aubergine and deep blue with yellow, and the technique of defining color boundaries with a raised thread or cloison of body clay. The results are sumptuous, but they became tawdry in the stoneware and even earthenware imitations of later date.

This example is matched by others in the Metropolitan Museum of Art, New York; the Musée Guimet, Paris; the Freer Gallery of Art, Washington, D.C.; and elsewhere. All have lotus as the major element of the decor but with varying shoulder and foot decoration. The Cleveland example retains the "cloud-collar" motif of Yüan on its shoulder and the "rising-gadroon" decoration at the foot, often found in late fifteenth-century Blue-and-White examples. SEL

PUBLICATIONS *Catalogue of the John L. Severance Collection: Bequest of John L. Severance*, 1936, no. 147, pl. XXX (lower right). Mayuyama and Igaki, *Tosetsu*, no. 41 (August 1956), p. 42, pl. 3. Mayuyama, *Chinese Ceramics in the West*, pl. 85. D. Lion-Goldschmidt, *Ming Porcelain*, color pl. 97. J. G. Moore, *The Eastern Gate*, repr. p. 78 and p. 87 (color).

LITERATURE A. le Bonheur et al., *Musée Guimet*, vol. VIII of *Oriental Ceramics: The World's Great Collections*, color pl. 30. Suzanne G. Valenstein, Julia Meech-Pekarik, and Marilyn Jenkins, *The Metropolitan Museum of Art*, vol. XII of *Oriental Ceramics: The World's Great Collections* (Tokyo: Kodansha, 1977) color pl. 35.

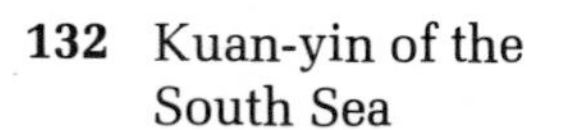

132 Kuan-yin of the South Sea 50.579

Porcelain. H. 45.1 cm., W. 21 cm. China, Te-hua, Fuchien Province. Late Ming or early Ch'ing Dynasty, 17th century AD. Gift of Mrs. R. Henry Norweb.

In Chinese Buddhism, there is no deity — not even the Buddha himself — that can compare with Kuan-yin (the Bodhisattva Avalokitesvara) for popular devotion. This is especially true since the Sung Dynasty with one particular form of his various manifestations, Kuan-yin of the South Sea (otherwise known as *Potalaka* in more formal literature, basically identical with the "Water and Moon" and "White-Robed" Kuan-yin). For centuries Buddhist scholars have been trying to theorize the actual location of Mt. Potalaka — an academic problem of absolutely no meaning to either the imperial courts or the general public. From the tenth century on, the Chinese were perfectly content to believe that there is only one sacred mountain for the Bodhisattva and that it is Mt. P'u-t'o, a small island in the Chou-chan archipelago off the coast of the Chechiang Province. According to the tradition, in 916 an auspicious image of the Kuan-yin Bodhisattva was carried by a Japanese monk from Mt. Wu-t'ai to the island and the first shrine was built under the Purple Bamboo Grove. Since then, every Sung emperor has added new temples to the island (which was considered located in the "South Sea" in relation to the Chinese northern capital). In 1214 Emperor Ning-tsung officially proclaimed Mt. P'u-t'o as the sacred abode for Kuan-yin and his worshipping attendant Zen-ts'ai (Sudana); it still attracts thousands of pilgrims to the island three times each year from all over the country.

The Cleveland Kuan-yin is identified by his extraordinarily elaborate lotus pedestal resting on the crest of surging waves. The craftsmanship and its state of preservation are both remarkable. It is believed that the kilns at Te-hua had begun production in the Sung period. During the Yüan Dynasty, its white porcelains and *ch'ing-pai* wares were exported throughout Southeast Asia, especially the Philippines and Indonesia. Marco Polo, who mentioned the town Te-hua in his book as *Tiunguy*, was so intrigued by the enormous quantity and the very low price of its ceramic production that he left a lengthy description of its manufacture. In the domestic market, however, the Te-hua ware had never been very highly regarded except for its Buddhist figures and other types of sculptural works. But so far no examples of these sculptural types have been found from the main kiln sites at Ch'ü-tou Kung in Te-hua since their discovery in 1953 or during the extensive excavations of recent years. Given little archaeological evidence, attempts to date these Buddhist figures have been highly tentative. Nonetheless, the seated Kuan-yin in Cleveland not only admirably exemplifies the technical achievement of *blanc de chine,* but also presents a rather peculiar iconography suggesting a close derivation from late Ming Buddhist prints such as the illustrations in the Wan-li *Tripitaka* (dated 1589). Further comparisons with late Ming styled Buddhist art both in China and in Korea seem to support the possibility of a date somewhere around the middle of the seventeenth century. WKH

PUBLICATIONS D. Lion-Goldschmidt, *Ming Porcelain,* p. 251, illus. no. 271. S. E. Lee, *A History of Far Eastern Art,* 4th edition, p. 423, fig. 558.

LITERATURE P. J. Donnelly, *Blanc de Chine* (London: Faber and Faber, 1969) pls. 76c, 77b.

133 Water Chestnut Shaped Vase *(Pi-ch'i ping)*: Lang Ware 44.201

Porcelain with copper glaze. H. 38.1 cm., Diam. 21.4 cm. China. Ch'ing Dynasty, reign of K'ang-hsi (AD 1662–1722). The Elisabeth Severance Prentiss Collection.

Since the appearance of the copper-red splashes on Chün wares (see [105]) in Sung Dynasty times, red glazes were much favored in China and have played a significant role in the history of Chinese ceramics, partly because red symbolizes happiness and festivity to the Chinese. This copper-red led to the development of underglaze red in Yüan wares (see [120]). Mastery of the techniques of using copper-red for monochromes and for underglaze painting was not perfected until the period of Hsüan-te. The famous Hsüan-te monochrome is called *chi-hung* ("sacrificial red" or sometimes "sky-clearing red") in Chinese literature. Further great achievements were made in Ch'ing, the most significant being the inventions of the *sang-de-boeuf* (Lang-yao) and peach-bloom *(chiang-tou-hung)* in the K'ang-hsi reign.

Sang-de-boeuf, or "ox-blood," is known as Lang-yao in China. It is not exactly clear how the term was derived. Various names have been associated with it, including the names of three members of a

Lang family who were in high favor in the K'ang-hsi court. The most frequently mentioned and perhaps the most likely candidate is Lang T'ing-chi, who was Governor of Chianghsi from 1705 to 1712 and also the supervisor of ceramic production at Ching-te-chen during the same period.

Lang-yao derives its color from copper which is reduced from a cupric oxide with the aid of iron oxide or tin. It is fired in a reducing atmosphere at the outset, but finished off with a very limited amount of oxidation. The characteristic Lang-yao is a deep blood-red or cherry-red. Unlike the "sacrificial red," the color of Lang-yao is rarely uniform. It generally flows in a downward movement, creating rich, varied tones and some streaked effects; in some cases, it gives the speckled appearance of crushed strawberries. On the finest pieces, the glaze has been skillfully controlled and stops just short of the foot. White and sometimes pale green hues appear around the rim where the glaze thins.

Contrary to what some have believed, Lang-yao glaze was applied directly to the already high-fired porcelain body and no other glaze was added on top of it. Ironically these crucial facts were already reported by Père d'Entrecolles in a letter written in 1722 (and cited by Hobson in 1915). In addition he noted that the red glaze was composed of granulated red copper and powdered stone of a reddish color, among other ingredients, and that a yellow clay was used in place of petuntse. Apparently, the yellow clay supplies the iron oxide which helps reduce the copper oxide and stabilize the red layer of colloidal copper required to give Lang-yao its red hue. The powdered "red stone" merely adds to the brilliancy and transparency of the glaze.

The Lang-yao vase in the Cleveland Museum collection is one of the finest specimens made in the K'ang-hsi period. It has a powerful and unusual shape. Its drastically compressed globular body rises to a tall, thick, and cylindrical neck, and is supported by a straight, well-proportioned, and very secure foot. The Chinese call this particular shape *pi-ch'i p'ing,* because the body of the vase is shaped like a water chestnut. The glaze of the Cleveland vase is characteristic of the finest Lang-yao. It is a bright cherry red, covered wth fine crackles and minute pin-holes caused by the bursting of the bubbles in the glaze. The shade is darker on the neck, edged with an unusually even white band around the mouth. Downward flowing streaks appear on the lighter ground of the body. The glaze stops just above the rim of the unglazed foot in a thick and uneven roll. Interior and base are covered with a white glaze shading to buff probably due to the presence of iron oxidized in the firing process. The superb craftsmanship of the K'ang-hsi potters is well demonstrated in this vase.

WCH

PUBLICATION *Catalogue of the Elisabeth Severance Prentiss Collection: Bequest of Elisabeth Severance Prentiss* (Cleveland: The Cleveland Museum of Art, 1944) no. 72, pl. XXXV.

LITERATURE R. L. Hobson, *Chinese Pottery and Porcelain* (New York: Funk and Wagnalls Co.; London: Cassell and Company, 1915) II, 122-123. A. L. Hetherington, *Chinese Ceramic Glazes* (Cambridge: Cambridge University Press, 1937). T'ung Shu-yeh and Shih Hsüeh-t'ung, *Chung-kuo tz'u-ch'i'shih lun-tsung* [Collected essays on the history of Chinese ceramics] (Shanghai: Jen-min ch'u-pan she, 1958). Soame Jenyns, *Later Chinese Porcelain: The Ch'ing Dynasty (1644–1912)* 4th edition (London: Farber and Farber, 1971). *Masterworks of Chinese Porcelain in the National Palace Museum* (Taipei: National Palace Museum, 1973) pl. 38. M. Medley, *The Chinese Potter.*

134 Peach-Bloom Lotus Petal Vase 42.669

Porcelain with copper glaze. H. 21.1 cm., Diam. 9 cm. China, Ching-te-chen, Chianghsi Province. Ch'ing Dynasty, mark and reign of K'ang-hsi (AD 1661–1722). Bequest of John L. Severance.

Peach-bloom, variously known as t'ao-hua-p'ien ("peach-bloom") or *ch'ang-tou-hung* ("bean-red") in Chinese, is one of the most striking achievements in the reign of the K'ang-hsi emperor. It ranks among the finest monochromes ever made because of its exquisite colors and unusual effects. The term *t'ao-hua-p'ien* is self explanatory; *chiang-tou-hung* refers to the resemblance of the glaze to the variegated pink and brown spots of the small Chinese kidney bean. Indeed, the color of peach-bloom is not uniform like the "sacrificial red" of early Ming, nor does it flow like Lang-yao (see [133]). Peach-bloom is a soft pink interspersed with a mottled darker tone, shading off to green occasionally. The Chinese have various names for the different effects. The rarest and perhaps the most beautiful is the exquisite pink which "flushes" with the freshness and beauty of the rosiness of peach blossoms in bloom. This is called *mei-jen-tzui,* or "drunken beauty," a term used on labels in some museums in China. The pink marked with green spots is called *t'ai-tien-lu,* or "moss-dot green," while the variant marked with areas and patches of green is called *p'ing-kuo-lu,* or "apple green."

Peach-bloom is a technical triumph. The effects are much more difficult to produce than those of Lang-yao, although the basic principle is the same in both cases. Peach-bloom is a high-fired glaze, deriving its colors from copper which is reduced from cupric oxide with the aid of iron-oxide or tin. Because of the volatile nature of copper, it is vital to apply two or three layers of "different-natured" and easily fused glazes on top of the copper glaze. Reducing atmosphere is first used, then followed by a very slight oxidizing atmosphere. Unlike Lang-yao whose copper forms into layers in the glaze, the copper of peach-bloom is not evenly distributed. Globules of copper in different sizes are scattered all through the glaze, denser in some parts, and sparser in others — creating patches of all sizes. The colors depend on how the globules of copper are dispersed. If they are close to the surface, or sparsely scattered in the glaze, they are oxidized in the latter part of the firing and turn slightly green or colorless. Should there be any iron oxide present, a yellow tint would be produced. The red owes its color to the copper globules which gather mainly but not evenly in the middle stratum of the glaze, somewhat similar to Lang-yao. The bright green is due to the concentration of the copper globules on the surface, which change to copper oxide in the oxidizing atmosphere.

The effects of peach-bloom are extremely difficult to control. Not infrequently, the glaze turns into muddy yellow, brown, or grayish color, cunningly labeled "ashes of rose" by the trade. No potter can count on producing the results desired. Even if the same glazes are used, completely different color effects can result because of the numerous factors involved, such as the position of the ware in the kiln, the flow of smoke, firing, and atmospheric conditions.

Specimens of peach-bloom are rare. It seems that the glaze was mainly reserved for small vases and objects of high quality intended for the "scholar's desk." According to Ralph M. Chait, the K'ang-hsi marked peach-blooms consist of "eight separate and distinct restricted shapes." Most of the shapes of the peach-bloom vases in this group are exceptionally beautiful. Their long, slender, and delicate bodies remind us more of the Liao Dynasty shapes than of the typical K'ang-hsi ones, the latter being known for strength and masculinity. The striking resemblance between the peach-bloom and some Liao vases suggests a strong possibility of the influence of Liao. It should be remembered that the Manchus came from Manchuria, the ancient region of the Liao Dynasty. This problem deserves further research.

The Cleveland vase is known as a "lotus petal vase," or more popularly as a "chrysanthemum vase." The name apparently is derived from the band of slender petals that encircles the base of the body just above the foot rim. The shape of the vase conveys a sense of elegance and balance. The slender, ovoid body tapers from the high, broad shoulder toward the slightly curved foot rim, forming a smooth gentle curve. This is balanced by an equally graceful tall neck which terminates with a broad, flared lip. The color effects of the vase are exceedingly exquisite, with "pinkish red petals of the peach blossoms" showing through the misty pink. The Cleveland vase is a rare and perfect example of the *mei-jen-tzui*, or "drunken beauty," described by Chinese sources. WCH

PUBLICATIONS *Catalogue of the John L. Severance Collection: Bequest of John L. Severance*, no. 179, pl. XXXIII. Ralph M. Chait, "The Eight Prescribed Peachbloom Shapes Bearing K'ang Hsi Marks," *Oriental Art*, IV, no. 3 (Winter 1957) 133, bottom. S. E. Lee, *A History of Far Eastern Art*, 4th edition, p. 465, color pl. 49.

LITERATURE A. L. Hetherington, *Chinese Ceramic Glazes*. Margaret Medley, *Illustrated Catalogue of Percival David Collection* (London: Percival David Foundation, 1953) section 6, no. 579. Miyazaki Ichisada et al., *Sei-cho hen, fu Annan, Tai* [Ch'ing Dynasty and Annamese and Thai Ceramics], vol. XII of *Sekai toji zenshu* (1956) pl. 51. Yeh Che-min, *Chung-kuo ku t'ao-tz'u ke-hsüeh ch'ien-shuo* [A brief introduction to the science of old Chinese ceramics] (Peking, 1960). Liaoning Provincial Museum, *Liao-t'zu hsüan-chi* [Selected works of Liao ceramics] (Peking: Wen-wu ch'u-pan-she, 1961) S. Valenstein, *A Handbook of Chinese Ceramics*, pl. 138 top right. M. Medley, *The Chinese Potter*.

135 *Famille Verte* Baluster Vase with *Chin-ti K'ai-kuang* Decoration 42.696

Porcelain decorated with overglaze polychrome enamels. H. 44.2 cm., Diam. 19.5 cm. China, Ching-te-chen, Chiang-hsi Province. Ch'ing Dynasty, reign of K'ang-hsi (AD 1662–1722). Bequest of John L. Severance.

Among Ch'ing ceramics, works produced during the K'ang-hsi reign are of the utmost importance. Not only are they known for their beautiful colors, original and vital shapes, and splendid decoration, but more importantly, their impact on ceramics in both the East and the West was felt for centuries to come. One very popular design, and probably the most significant one in terms of later influence, is called *chin-ti k'ai-kuang* ("brocade ground with openings"), commonly described as "panels in brocaded ground" in the West. The general idea of having an ornamental motif surrounded by a fully decorated ground can be traced back to Shang Dynasty bronzes. This type of ornamentation was later developed into "panels reserved in decorated ground" design in textiles, metalwork, lacquer, etc. Subjects for the panel decorations varied from simple designs of flowers and birds to complex topics of folk lore, history, religious legends, and landscape.

Adaptation of such an ornamental scheme to ceramics probably began with the Tz'u-chou wares during the Chin Dynasty, if not earlier. Because of the white surface provided by Tz'u-chou wares, potters were able to execute decorative ideas borrowed from other branches of Chinese art. It is worth noting that the "panels in decorated ground" design was executed in black as well as in colors, most frequently found on surfaces of ceramic pillows.

However, it was in the K'ang-hsi period that this design reached its height of splendor and refinement. While the old tradition continued, a taste for color and ornament brought forth a new mode of decoration, *chin-ti k'ai-kuang*. Exquisite, colorful brocade designs were used as the ground cover, with panels depicting birds and insects, flowers and trees, rocks and plants, and occasionally landscape as if the viewer were looking at a garden or distant scenes through windows. To make it more realistic, a moon or a sun was sometimes included. The garden scene panels apparently were inspired by Chinese gardens of the Ming and Ch'ing times. Flowers, plants, and rocks were strategically placed so as to give a poetic view akin to a Chinese painting through every artistically designed window.

This baluster vase represents one of the very best examples of its kind. Essentially decorated in the multiple-band design, its surface is completely covered with colorful decoration except for the "openings" on the bands around the body, the neck, and the shoulder, which are separated between borders of key frets, *ju-i* lappets, floral patterns, etc. A band of stylized lotus petals encircling the base serves as a kind of pedestal for the two tall rectangular panels on each side of the body — the focal points of the vase. In one, a brightly plumaged bird is depicted perching on a flowering prunus branch, eyeing the hovering insects beneath him with a wide-open mouth. A new moon is at the upper left corner; below it are bamboo and rock. In the other, another gaily colored bird perches on a barren, gnarled branch, looking attentively at the peonies below. The sun is shining at the upper left corner with butterflies and insects to balance the "one-corner design" which weighs heavily at the lower right corner. These two tall panels are accompanied by a round panel of insects and a leaf-shaped panel with a rooster on each side. The

neck band is occupied by two leaf-shaped panels, each showing a distant landscape. On the shoulder are four small lobed, lozenge-shaped panels of gold fish and sea weeds.

The brocade ground of the vase is most extraordinary. It has a rare black background. "Superimposed" on it is an exceedingly fine and delicate drawing of floral scrolls with bright green stems, green leaves of varied tones, and dainty blossoms in iron-red, yellow, aubergine, and purplish blue. There is some variation in the brocade ground of the shoulder; the "fish roe" design is used to fill in the space between the floral scrolls.

The paintings, especially those in the two rectangular panels, demonstrate superb skills. The technique of *p'ing-tu*, or "flat wash," is used, as different from *hsüan-jan*, or "graded-washes,"' of the *famille rose*. Outlines and details are mostly drawn in fine black lines except in rare cases such as the iron-red blossoms. Shading is achieved by means of dots, lines, and flat washes in darker colors, and by variation of strokes. Similar to other typical *famille verte* wares, the dominant color of this vase is green, augmented chiefly by iron-red although other colors are also used. The soft and delicate tones suggest that the vase belongs to the later K'ang-hsi period, since a change from strong colors to softer tints on *famille verte* wares took place in the latter part of the reign.

The *chin-ti k'ai-kuang* design, being extremely ornamental and appealing to the popular taste, was imitated time after time in subsequent reigns, with increasingly unfortunate effects — crowding and mechanical execution. WCH

PUBLICATIONS Edgar Gorer and J. F. Blacker, *Chinese Porcelains and Hard Stones* (London: Bernard Quaritch, 1911) I, pl. 21. Miyazaki et al., *Sei-cho hen, fu Annan, Tai*, vol. XII of *Sekai toji zenshu* (1956) pl. 29. S. E. Lee, *A History of Far Eastern Art*, 4th edition, repr. p. 462, fig. 623. Mayuyama, *Chinese Ceramics in the West*, pl. 112.

LITERATURE R. L. Hobson, *Chinese Pottery and Porcelain*, vol. II.

136 Vase (*Wen-hu:* Warming Vessel) with Decoration of Golden Pheasants 71.145

Porcelain decorated with overglaze polychrome enamels. H. 19 cm., Diam. 10.5 cm. China. Ch'ing Dynasty, mark and reign of Ch'ien-lung (AD 1736–1795). Purchase, John L. Severance Fund.

This rare and fine small vase belongs to a group of some one hundred similar wares made for the emperors of the Yung-cheng and Ch'ien-lung reigns and known by the traditional misnomer "Moon Pavilion wares" (*ku-yüeh hsüan*). They are all characterized by a brilliant opaque and chalk-white ground, small size, and carefully executed decoration in colored enamels, usually of *famille rose* type, often showing some Western influences in shading or modeling, and usually with the imperial mark executed in raised blue or more rarely rose enamels rather than the more common underglaze blue. They are uniformly almost perfect in technique and were obviously made for respectful admiration, not use. Most seem to have been made during the time the imperial kilns were under the direction of T'ang Ying between 1736 and, at the latest, 1756. All combine pictorial decoration —

See also color plate following page 86.

usually of flora and/or birds, more rarely of landscapes — with literature in the form of poems, often repeated, painted in black enamels on the white ground. They are generally accepted as the last great effort at the production of a luxury porcelain conforming to the highest standards of Chinese taste.

This particular vase is among the few with large-scale representations of birds in a flowering environment. While realistic depictions of birds have a long tradition in Chinese painting, this particular one, along with its counterparts on other *ku-yüeh hsüan* wares, is represented by rather careful modeling, shading, and blending of colors due to the influence of Western painting at the Ch'ing court in the mid-eighteenth century through the Jesuit artist, Giuseppe Castiglione, known to the Chinese as Lang Shih-ning. One persuasive theory about much *ku-yüeh hsüan* production is that the undercoated porcelains were forwarded to Peking from the kilns at Ching-te-chen in Chianghsi Province and that the overglaze enamel decoration was applied there by the court painters particularly associated with the studio of Castiglione. In any case, the style of the decorations reveals his influence, cunningly combined with the old Chinese tradition of "fur and feathers" painting. The results are technically refined and aesthetically exquisite.

The poem on the side of the vessel opposite the decoration is like that on a vase in the Percival David Foundation, University of London:

> Just as each morning light en-
> velopes the lovely moon,
> So, too, each passing year retains
> enduring Spring.

The oval seal at the beginning reads *Chia-li* ("beautiful"). The last two square seals read, *Ssu-chih* ("four seasons") and *Ch'ang-ch'un* ("enduring spring"). SEL

EX COLLECTIONS Charles Russell, London; Barbara Hutton, Honolulu.

PUBLICATION R. L. Hobson, B. Rackham, and W. King, *Chinese Ceramics in Private Collections* (London: Halton and Truscott Smith, 1931) p. 192, color pl. 28.

LITERATURE S. Jenyns, *Later Chinese Porcelain*, pl. LXXVIII, 1 and 2; pl. LXXIX, 1 (erroneously given to The Musée Guimet, but actually in the Tournet Collection, Paris). The similar bottle-vase here has decoration representing birds and a poem signed Ch'ang ch'un ("Enduring spring"). See J. P. Goidsenhoven, *La Ceramique Chinoise* (Brussells: Editions de la Connaissance, 1954) p. 183, pl. XCIV.

Korean

137 Water Ewer for Buddhist Ceremony *(Kundika)* 21.631

Stoneware with celadon glaze and incised decoration. H. 36.2 cm., Diam. 18.2 cm. Korea. Koryo Dynasty, late 11th-early 12th century AD. John L. Severance Collection.

This *kundika*, or holy water vessel, is distinguished by two spouts: a tall, pointed one for pouring or sprinkling water and a shorter, capped one with cup-shaped rim for filling the container. Appearing in India as early as the fourth century BC, it is thought to have originally functioned as a monk's drinking vessel. Altered in shape and purpose, it was introduced to China by the eighth century (as is evident from the existing examples in the collections of the Horyu-ji Temple and the Shoso-in imperial repository) and to both Korea and Japan. In these Far Eastern

countries the *kundika* became an essential element of Buddhist iconography and liturgy. Especially popular in Korea between the eleventh and fourteenth centuries, this type of vessel was fashioned from either bronze or celadon stoneware. The large number of *kundikas* remaining in Korea indicates the pervasiveness of the Buddhist faith during the Koryo Dynasty.

The three long-tailed parrots finely incised into the body of this vessel illustrate the influence of the earliest Chinese celadon, Yüeh ware (cf. [91, 92]), in the initial development of Koryo celadons. Similar bird motifs of flying phoenixes also accent the interiors of tenth-century Yüeh bowls produced in southern China in the present-day provinces of Chianghsi and Chechiang. Historic records chronicle the exchange of official envoys in 924 and 925 between this region, then known as the state of Wu-Yüeh , and the Koryo court. The refined Yüeh bowls served as gifts of state and became the models for early Korean celadons. Although the parrot-like motif is commonly found on Korean celadon bowls dating from the late eleventh and early twelfth centuries, its combination with the *kundika* shape is unique. This *kundika* was a product of the kilns located in Kangjin, the largest celadon center in southwest Korea. MW

EX COLLECTION Dr. A. I. Ludlow.

PUBLICATIONS "Korean Ceramics," *Far Eastern Ceramic Bulletin*, IX, nos. 3-4 (serial no. 38) (September-December 1957) pl. 6. Sherman E. Lee, *A History of Far Eastern Art*, 4th edition (Englewood Cliffs, NJ, and New York: Prentice-Hall and Harry N. Abrams, 1982) p. 372, fig. 500.

LITERATURE Ananda K. Coomaraswamy and Francis Stewart Kershaw, "A Chinese Buddhist Water Vessel and Its Indian Prototypes," *Artibus Asiae*, III (1928–1929) 122-141. G. St. G. M. Gompertz, *Korean Celadon and Other Wares of the Koryo Period* (London: Faber and Faber, 1963) pl. 23A. Margaret Medley, *Korean and Chinese Ceramics from the 10th to the 14th Century*, exhib. cat. (Cambridge: University Printing House, 1975) p. 32, no. 68. Byung-chang Rhee, ed., *Kankoku bijutsu shusen: Masterpieces of Korean Art* (Tokyo: Byung-chang Rhee, 1978) III, 25, pl. 24; p. 27, pl. 25; p. 119, pl. 123. *5,000 Years of Korean Art*, exhib. cat. (Seoul: Samhwa Printing Co., 1979) no. 109, XX.

138 Prunus Vase (*Maebyong*) 61.270

Stoneware with celadon glaze, underglaze iron slip, and inlaid decoration. H. 29 cm., Diam. 17.8 cm. Korea. Koryo Dynasty, 12th century AD. Purchase from the J. H. Wade Fund.

The *maebyong*, or prunus vase, is one of the most common shapes utilized in the Korean stoneware tradition. Originating in China where it is known as the *mei-p'ing* (cf. [116, 122, 131], the vase-shape is found in both Korean celadon and *punch'ong* wares and probably functioned as a wine or water vessel. The *maebyong* is the most dominant form of one particular and rare type of ware identified by a rich dark color instead of the usual celadon "blue-green" tones. Dating from the twelfth century, the vase exemplifies the wares produced at Sadang-ri, Taegu-myon, and Kangjin-gun, in Cholla-namdo Province.

The dark color of this *maebyong* is the result of an underglaze iron slip coating

the stoneware body. The black ware is related to Koryo celadons through the inlay decoration technique. The botanical sprays accenting the shoulders were first incised into the slip-covered body. After carving away the dark slip, a white slip was brushed into the shallow recess. The iron-bearing glaze with green hues, the final step in the creative process, is evident only in areas where the glaze has run forming thickened streaks and drops. MW

EX COLLECTION Gregory Henderson.

EXHIBITIONS New York, 1963: Asia House Gallery, Tea Taste in Japanese Art, cat. by Sherman E. Lee, p. 59, pl. 36. New York, 1968: Asia House Gallery, The Art of the Korean Potter, cat. by Robert P. Griffing, Jr., p. 99, pl. 76.

PUBLICATION B.-c. Rhee, ed., *Masterpieces of Korean Art,* III, 313, pl. 314.

139 Lobed Vase 44.164

Stoneware with celadon glaze and incised decoration. H. 25.4 cm., Diam. 13 cm. Korea. Koryo Dynasty, 12th-13th century AD. The Elisabeth Severance Prentiss Collection.

This twelfth-century celadon vase represents early stages of the Korean celadon tradition when Koryo Dynasty (918–1392) potters closely emulated the shapes, decorations, and potting techniques of Chinese porcelains and celadons. This particular shape with pleated foot, lobed body, and incised lotus petals surrounding the neck was probably derived from Chinese *ch'ing-pai* porcelains (cf. [107–108]). A popular export ware, *ch'ing-pai* porcelains have been found throughout the Asian countries. In Korea *ch'ing-pai* vases similar to this celadon vase were discovered near tombs located around the Koryo capital, Kaesong. Korean celadons, manufactured primarily for the imperial palace and ruling aristocracy, also served as mortuary furnishings for upper-class tombs. King Injong's (r. 1123–1146) tomb in particular yielded examples of Korean celadons dating from the early twelfth century. A vase similar to this example in the Cleveland Museum was among these wares. MW

EX COLLECTION Mrs. Francis F. Prentiss.

EXHIBITION New York, 1968: Asia House Gallery, The Art of the Korean Potter, cat. by Robert P. Griffing, Jr., p. 70, pl. 24.

PUBLICATION *Far Eastern Ceramic Bulletin,* IX, nos. 3-4 (serial no. 38) (September-December 1957) pl. 9.

LITERATURE Margaret Medley, *Oriental Ceramics; Percival David Foundation of Chinese Art* (Tokyo: Kodansha, 1976) VII, pl. 9 (Chinese *ch'ing-pai* vase). *5,000 Years of Korean Art,* pls. 111-112 (celadon wares from King Injong's tomb).

140 Placenta Jar: *Punch'ong* Ware 63.505

Stoneware with celadon glaze and inlaid and stamped decorations. H. 37.5 cm., Diam. 27 cm. Korea. Yi Dynasty, 15th century AD. Purchase, John L. Severance Fund.

Punch'ong ware was a product of the Yi Dynasty (1392–1910) kilns located throughout the central and southern part of Korea. Its dense, gray stoneware body, greenish-colored glaze, and decorative techniques demonstrate its origins in the celadon tradition of the previous Koryo Dynasty (918–1392). The decorative scheme of this particular jar reveals its affinity to both the intricate, inlaid motifs of the Koryo celadons and the more spontaneous decorative patterns of *punch'ong* ware. The jar's surface is divided into three concentric bands of decoration. Inlaid motifs of grape vines and stylized lotus leaves define the middle and lower registers. These patterns were first incised into the clay then the recessed areas were brushed with a white slip. Any excess slip was scraped away from the surface leaving only the white color in the intaglio design.

White slip, a distinguishing feature of all *punch'ong* ware, also covers the shoulders of the pot. The "rope-curtain" pattern stamped into the slip is a common design of fifteenth-century *punch'ong* ware. This combination of inlaid and stamped techniques indicates the jar was produced during the transitional period between the refined, inlaid Koryo celadons and the coarser *punch'ong* wares — the late fourteenth to early fifteenth centuries. Although uniquely decorated, this jar is very common and intrinsically related to Korean folk customs. The afterbirth of a child was buried in this type of jar to ensure its health and future prosperity. MW

EXHIBITION New York, 1968: Asia House Gallery, The Art of the Korean Potter, cat. by Robert P. Griffing, Jr., p. 103, pl. 81.

PUBLICATIONS Andre Eckardt, *Koreanische Keramik* (Bonn: H. Bouvier u. Co. Verlag, 1970) p. 142, pl. XX, fig. 62. B-c. Rhee, ed., *Masterpieces of Korean Art*, II, 7, pl. 4.

LITERATURE G. St. G. M. Gompertz, *Korean Pottery and Porcelain of the Yi Period* (New York: Frederick A. Praeger, 1968) pl. 13. B.-c. Rhee, ed., *Masterpieces of Korean Art*, II, 4, pl. 1; p. 6, pl. 3; p. 14, pls. 10, 11.

141 Wine Bottle: *Punch'ong* Ware 62.153

Stoneware with celadon glaze and incised decoration. H. 30.5 cm., Diam. 16.5 cm. Korea. Yi Dynasty, 15th century AD. Purchase, John L. Severance Fund.

Although *punch'ong* ware, a descendant of Korean celadon, is frequently described as the "folkish" pottery of the lower classes, it was also used in the palaces and homes of the aristocracy. Produced in plentiful quantities throughout the country, the stoneware is characterized by diverse decorative techniques that include carving, stamping, incising, inlaying, and painting. A white slip, applied over the gray body, is the common element of all these decorative possibilities. The presence of this slip frequently affected the glaze (containing small quantities of iron) so that it appeared gray instead of green in color.

This particular wine bottle typifies in both shape and decoration fifteenth-century *punch'ong* ware. The pear-shaped bottle with flaring mouth and tall foot was freely covered with white slip. Incised lines divide its surface into concentric bands of decoration. The incised fish, foliage, and band of stylized lotus leaves encircling the neck are common among *punch'ong* decorative schemes.

MW

EXHIBITION New York, 1968: Asia House Gallery, The Art of the Korean Potter, cat. by Robert P. Griffing, Jr., p. 104, pl. 86.

PUBLICATIONS A. Eckardt, *Koreanische Keramik*, p. 142, pl. XX, fig. 63. Korean Government Archaeological Survey, *Chosen Koseki Zufu [Pictorial album of ancient Chosen]* (Korea: Government-general, 1935) XV, 2128, pl. 6092.

LITERATURE: G. St. G. M. Gompertz, *Korean Pottery and Porcelain of the Yi Period*, pl. 22 (pear-shaped wine bottle with similar neck border). B.-c. Rhee, ed., *Masterpieces of Korean Art*, II pls. 79-81, 86 (*punch'ong* ware with incised fish motifs).

142 Jar with Relief Design of Four Characters 81.3

Porcelain with molded and incised decoration. H. 20 cm., Diam. 21.5 cm. Korea. Yi Dynasty, late 18th century AD. The Severance and Greta Millikin Purchase Fund.

Although porcelaneous wares were manufactured in Korea as early as the Koryo Dynasty, they were not fully developed until the following Yi Dynasty (1392–1910), when the ruling kings and their courts patronized the white-bodied wares. Beginning in the middle of the fifteenth century, official palace porcelains were manufactured in the area of Kwangju, Kyonggi-do. This region not only hosted an abundant supply of Kaolin-rich clay and the necessary wood for fuel but also was within close proximity to the capital, Seoul.

This melon-shaped jar dates from the late eighteenth century, the flourishing era of Korean porcelains. Its thick body, fluted form with molded symbols, and blue-tinted glaze — recalling the similarly colored glaze of Chinese *ch'ing-pai* porcelains — indicate the jar was probably a product of the Punwon-ri kilns. Its swelling shape is accented with molded floral medallions inset with the auspicious characters: *su, neung, kang, bok* (Chinese: *shou, ning, k'ang, fu*) — long life, safety, health, and happiness. The black, lacquer lid is a later Japanese addition to the jar which was used as a cold-water jar (*mizusashi*) in the tea ceremony (see [144-145]). MW

LITERATURE G. St. G. M. Gompertz, *Korean Pottery and Porcelain of the Yi Period*, pls. 59, 114A.

Japanese

143 Storage Jar: Shigaraki Ware 73.18

Stoneware with incised decoration. H. 42 cm., Diam. 39 cm. Japan, Shigaraki, Nagano district, Minami-Matsuo kilns(?). Muromachi period, ca. AD 1400. Purchase, John L. Severance Fund.

Medieval Japanese ceramics have traditionally been designated as the "Six Old Kilns," one of which is Shigaraki, a fertile agricultural valley southeast of Kyoto. During the fourteenth and fifteenth centuries kitchen wares and grain storage jars, such as this sturdy vessel, formed the bulk of ceramic production by the artisan-farmers in this area.

Constructed of four separate coiled sections, smoothed and joined together, its rugged, globular appearance is enhanced by the gritty clay body and warm surface tones. Shigaraki clay is distinguished by its high feldspathic content, visible as white, partly melted granules, and by the natural reddish-brown skin broken by linear splits and gaseous eruptions. The yellow mat surface on the upper third of the vessel body represents wood ash present in the kiln atmosphere which has adhered to the molten clay surface during firing, frequently pooling in sufficient quantity to form beads of olive-green glaze. The incised "lattice-fence" pattern on the shoulder is extremely rare for a Shigaraki vessel of this size.

Originally the everted neck possessed a rolled lip enabling the mouth to be capped more easily for sealing. In its present state it serves to enhance the jar's enduring, robust character. MRC

EXHIBITIONS Kyoto, 1963: Kyoto National Museum, Earthenware of Ancient Japan, fig. 171. Cleveland, New York, and San Francisco, 1978–1979: The Cleveland Museum of Art, Japan House Gallery, and Asian Art Museum of San Francisco, Folk Traditions in Japanese Art, cat. by Victor and Takako Hauge, no. 56, p. 237, repr. p. 91. New York, 25 March –17 May 1981: One Thousand Years of Japanese Art (650-1650), cat. by Sherman E. Lee, Michael R. Cunningham, and Ursula Korneitchouk, no. 31, pp. 60, 61.

PUBLICATIONS Daniel Rhodes, *Tamba Pottery: The Timeless Art of a Japanese Village* (Tokyo: Kodansha, 1970) p. 10. Sherman E. Lee, "Some Japanese Tea Taste Ceramics," CMA *Bulletin*, LX (November 1973) 269, fig. 1. Janet Gaylord Moore, *The Eastern Gate* (Cleveland and New York: William Collins Publishers Inc., 1979) p. 204, repr. Louise Allison Cort, *Shigaraki, Potters' Valley* (New York: Kodansha, 1979) repr. p. 100, fig. 118.

LITERATURE Katsura Matasaburo, *Jidaibetsu ko-Shigaraki meihin zuroku* [Outline history of masterpieces of Shigaraki ware] (Tokyo: Kobijutsu Kogei, 1974) pls. 31, 34. Kawahara Masahiko, *Shigaraki*, vol. XII of *Nihon toji zenshu* [Pageant of Japanese ceramics] (Tokyo: Chuokoronsha, 1977) pls. 1, 5.

144 Water Jar *(Mizusashi)*: Bizen Ware 73.17

Stoneware with iron-glaze. H. 15.4 cm., Diam. 21.2 cm. Japan, Imbe. Momoyama period, early 17th century AD. Purchase, John L. Severance Fund.

The wares of Bizen (modern Okayama prefecture) are direct descendants of the older folk wares of Heian times, typified by the old Sue wares. Most of the sixteenth- and seventeenth-century production comes from near the village of Imbe. Bizen and Imbe are more or less interchangeable designations of the products of the region. From the later Muromachi period on the kilns often catered to specific tea ceremony requirements and the humble characteristics of old Bizen ware began to show a more sophisticated adaptation to the new use. The rusty brown color of its clay and iron glazes was well suited to the new aesthetics of tea. The most notable types produced were the freshwater jars (*mizusashi*) for replenishing the water in the kettle during the tea ceremony. This example is in the form of a wooden water pail, *oni-oke* ("devil-bucket"), a type commonly found represented in numerous narrative scrolls with village scenes centered on the communal well. This origin is in keeping with the "humble" aspirations of the tea ceremony. The glaze ranging from olive to mustard is developed from an application of a thick clay slip with high iron content. Although the prototype is wooden, the thrown clay character of the shape is strong and contrasts in a subtle way with the clay adaptations of the wood binding of the base and the upright pierced handles. The ceramic *mizusashi* sits more heavily on the ground than its light wooden counterpart. The subtle allusion to a different material common to folk culture and the tension between form and medium must have been a particularly satisfying conundrum to a tea master using this container.

The dating of these Bizen wares is highly controversial and problematical since a Momoyama period date is considered preferable to an Edo period one. Good judgment and tea taste reticence suggests an early seventeenth-century date for even the most excellent examples. SEL

EXHIBITION New York, 1981: Japan Society, One Thousand Years of Japanese Art (650–1650), cat. by Sherman E. Lee, Michael R. Cunningham, and Ursula Korneitchouk, no. 40, p. 74.

PUBLICATIONS Katsura Matasaburo, *Jidaibetsu ko-Bizen meihin zuroku* [Outline history of masterpieces of Bizen pottery] (Tokyo: Kobijutsu Kogei, 1973) color pl. 85. Sherman E. Lee, CMA *Bulletin*, LX (November 1973) 274-275, fig. 6.

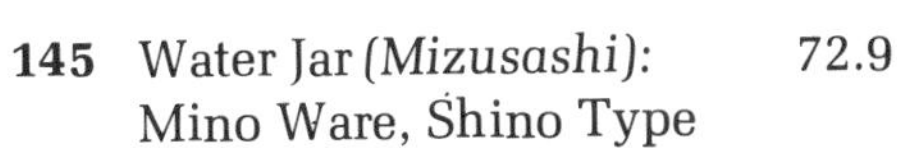

145 Water Jar *(Mizusashi)*: Mino Ware, Shino Type 72.9

Stoneware with underglaze iron slip decoration. H. 18.4 cm., Diam. 19.6 cm. Japan. Momoyama period, 16th century AD. Purchase, John L. Severance Fund.

By the last half of the sixteenth century the tea ceremony had become a fairly standardized ritual among upper-class Japanese, especially in the Kyoto-Osaka area. The recent civil wars and ensuing political unrest through mid-century had drained the country economically and caused the destruction of many cherished tea utensils, most of which were Chinese. To fill the economic void an emerging merchant class arose as financiers to Japan's new military rulers. To replace lost tea ceramics and furnish the increasing numbers of tea followers with suitable utensils, the arbiters of tea culture turned to domestic wares, especially those produced at one of Japan's "Six Old Kilns" (see [143]). These tea masters selected vessels from among the comparatively rustic wares whose appearance suggested novel, domestic virtues and whose shapes could be adapted for use in the tea ceremony. In this way they infused the practice of tea with a renewed spirit.

Initially traditional as well as some contemporary pieces were sought after. Subsequently tea taste items were made to order with the advent of changing values in social tea culture and with the increasing demand for even scarcer "certified" pieces. Consequently new kilns began to appear during the last decades of the sixteenth century, all essentially responding to the burgeoning demands from tea masters and their *aficionados* for original, sophisticated wares. Of these kilns some of the most innovative were grouped in Mino Province, present-day Gifu prefecture, not far from the important "Six Old Kilns" site of Seto. These Mino wares are differentiated as Shino (see also [146]), Yellow Seto, and Oribe (see [147]).

One of the most prized of tea ceremony objects is a Shino freshwater jar or *mizusashi*. They are characteristically the most ceramiclike of tea wares and were made for or under the close supervision of knowledgeable tea devotees. The Shino wares were traditionally named for a famous tea master, Shino Soshin, who lived in the Daiei era (1521–1527), and were made at the Mino Province kilns just north of Seto. Thus the new wares were inheritors of the tradition of the Seto kilns active from the Kamakura period onwards. Standard Shino ware was marked by a thick milky glaze with sparsely brushed decoration in iron oxide, as in this *mizusashi*.

The most famous of the Shino *mizusashi* — such as the example in the Hatakeyama Museum in Tokyo, called *Kogan* ("ancient stream bank") — display apparent weight, fluid plasticity in modeling, and rough, bold, and abbreviated decoration. The present example, one of the few early water jars outside Japan, is free and plastic in its thrown shape, while the suggested weight and the brushed fence and panel decorations are lighter and more elegant than those of the pot called *Kogan*. The square panel decoration is related to that often found on Oribe wares (see [147]). This may indicate a date slightly later than the Momoyama period.

The tea taste so well embodied in this water jar requires special study and close attention. Rough, but not too rough; natural and free but with the clear evidence of human art (manufacture), these wares have now found a sympathetic audience — the modern artist-potter. The influence of such Japanese wares has been particularly marked in recent years. SEL

EXHIBITIONS New York, 1981: Japan Society, One Thousand Years of Japanese Art (650–1650), cat. by Sherman E. Lee, Michael R. Cunningham, and Ursula Korneitchouk, p. 75, no. 41.

PUBLICATIONS Fujioka Ryoichi, "Shino to Oribe," *Nihon no bijutsu*, LI (1970) pl. 6.

LITERATURE Mitsuoka Tadanari, *Chaki* (Tea utensils), vol. VII of *Sekai toji zenshu* [Ceramic art of the world], ed. Koyama Fujio et al. (Tokyo: Kawade Shobo, 1955) pl. 129. Seattle Art Museum, *Ceramic Art of Japan*, exhib. cat. (Seattle, 1972) p. 109, no. 38. Hayashiya Seizo, *Shino*, vol. XV of *Nihon toji zenshu* (1975) pls. 63, 64.

146 Dish with Design of Ferns and Rocks: Mino Ware, Gray Shino Type 66.24

Stoneware with underglaze iron slip and incised decoration. L. 23.3 cm., W. 20 cm. Japan, Kujiri, Inkyo Nishi kiln(?). Momoyama period, ca. AD 1600. Purchase, John L. Severance Fund.

This dish was built by pressing clay into a mold designed to produce a sophisticated "rough" shape suitable for serving tea cakes. A number of other dishes were produced from the same form, differing from one another only in their incised designs and border patterns. These include plates in the Tokyo National Museum, the Seattle Art Museum, the Umezawa, and Matsuoka collections, as well as several other private Japanese and American collections.

The buff-colored body has been coated with a clay slip rich in iron-oxide through which the simple landscape design was incised. Following this the entire dish was covered with a viscous feldspathic glaze. The warm orange-brown color visible along the rim is the clay body where it has been covered by insufficient glaze. The open pores in the same area, caused by gas escaping during firing, indicate that the dish was made of two or more slabs of clay pressed into a mold. The four small indentations on the interior show where spurs were placed to separate the dishes for stacking in the kiln. Four round clay buttons applied to the bottom corners serve as feet.

The uneven character of the edges and body became desired effects of *nezumi* ("mouse gray") Shino ware during the course of its development and were only later routinely exploited to enhance the overall design. They were considered natural, technical assets of ceramic form which aesthetically complimented the primitive garden landscape drawing. These features of course epitomize tea taste in Momoyama Japan — studied, rough forms elegantly, but modestly applied. MRC

EXHIBITION Albuquerque, 1980: Albuquerque Art Museum, Katachi: Form and Spirit in Japanese Art, no. 11.

LITERATURE Matsuoka Museum, *Matsuoka Bijutsukan meihin zuroku: kaikan kinen* [Masterpieces of the Matsuoka Museum commemorating its inauguration], exhib. cat. (Tokyo: Matsuoka Museum, 1945) pl. 118. Tokyo National Museum, *Tokyo Kokuritsu Hakubutsukan zuhan mokuroku: Nihon toji-hen* [An illustrated catalog of the Japanese ceramics in the Tokyo National Museum] (Kyoto: Benrido, 1966) pls. 157, 158. Osaka Municipal Museum, *Mino koto*, exhib. cat. (Osaka, 1972) pls. 44, 45. Seattle Art Museum, *Asiatic Art in the Seattle Art Museum* (Seattle, 1973) p. 239, no. 220. Hayashiya Seizo, *Shino*, vol. XV of *Nihon toji zenshu* (1975) pls. 83, 84, 85. Setsu Gatodo, *Kiseto, Shino, Oribe*, exhib. cat. (Tokyo, 1979) pl. 12.

147 Tile: Red Oribe Ware 65.79

Stoneware with underglaze iron slip and painted decoration. 32.4 cm. sq. Japan, Kujiri district, Motoyashiki kiln(?). Momoyama period, ca. AD 1600. Anonymous Gift.

Named after the famous tea master Furuta Oribe (1544–1615), who initially provided the ceramic designs and commissions, Oribe ware typically features geometrically shaped vessels of an unusually wide variety with drawn designs and rich, green glazing. This tile is called Red Oribe due to the warm rust-red slip applied over its buff-white fabric. This clay body shows through clearly where four, offset rectangular designs of a seemingly modern aesthetic have been outlined in tripartite channels. The same potter's brush has drawn two sets of stylized plum blossoms over the red slip, applied a thin slip wash of iron-red to the white rectangular channels, and added the floral motifs on three side panels. Before firing in the kiln the heavy tile was coated with a milky, translucent glaze which has pooled in attractive configurations, much like the red slip underneath. To the Japanese these "accidental" effects of glazing and drawing enhance the character of the tile, giving it a personal touch. This is also physically apparent in the two thumb prints left intact as part of the tile design; they indicate where the tile was lifted while still wet. Comparable finger indentations can be seen along each underside edge. The bottom possesses only the dull red slip and two large spur marks showing how it rested in the kiln.

Several aspects of the tile's technique and design are in fact indebted to the Shino ware potters of the same area working slightly earlier. Indeed the rarity of this tile lies both in its being virtually unique and in its serving as a valuable link between the flowering of Shino wares (including Red Shino) ca. 1580s and the beginnings of Oribe a decade later. The Motoyashiki kiln in central Mino played an important role in production of both wares and is a likely source for this tile. Oriented with undecorated side panel away from the tea participants, it may have served as a platform for the brazier used in heating water for summer tea ceremonies. It may also have served as, or been inspired by, ceramic architectural tiles. These survive in the later seventeenth-century treasure houses at Joko-ji (Shino and Oribe) and Nishi-hongan-ji (Kakiemon) where they were used on the walls and floors. MRC

EX COLLECTION Higashi-Honganji, Kyoto.

EXHIBITIONS New York, 1963: Asia House Gallery, Tea Taste in Japanese Art, cat. by Sherman E. Lee, pl. no. 30. Dallas, 1969: Dallas Museum of Fine Arts, Masterpieces of Japanese Art, no. 37, repr. p. 16. New York, 1981: Japan Society, One Thousand Years of Japanese Art (650–1650), cat. by Sherman E. Lee, Michael R. Cunningham, and Ursula Korneitchouk, no. 43.

PUBLICATION Mayuyama Junkichi, ed., *Japanese Art in the West* (Tokyo: Mayuyama and Co., 1966) p. 359, repr. p. 291, pl. 344.

LITERATURE Mitsuoka Tadanari et al., *Nihon II: Momoyama* [Japan II: Momoyama period], vol. II of *Toki koza* [Lectures on ceramics] (Tokyo: Yuzankaku, 1972) pl. 131. Hayashiya Seizo, *Shino*, vol. XV of *Nihon toji zenshu* (1975) pls. 35-38, 53. Koyama Fujio, ed., *Shino, Oribe: Taiyo yakimono shirizu* [Shino and Oribe wares: The Sun Magazine Ceramics Series] (Tokyo: Heibonsha, 1976) pp. 76-77. Takeuchi Junichi, *Oribe*, vol. XVI of *Nihon toji zenshu* (1976) pls. 9, 29, 47-48. Fujioka Ryoichi, trans. S. C. Morse, *Shino and Oribe Ceramics* (Tokyo: Kodansha, 1977) in English, p. 120 ff.

See also color plate following page 150.

148 Large Bowl: Hagi Ware 62.211

Stoneware, with underglaze, inlaid decoration. H. 23.8 cm., L. 31.8 cm., W. 31 cm. Japan. Momoyama period, ca. AD 1615. Purchase, John L. Severance Fund.

Christianity gained a foothold in Japan with the arrival in 1549 of the Jesuit priest Francis Xavier. Like the missionaries who followed him in the later sixteenth century, he enjoyed the support of European governments seeking favorable commercial relations with Japan. In return the members of the various Christian orders served as interpreters and negotiators, performing the difficult task of representing foreign merchantmen before the government and local officials. However as the number of converts to Christianity increased dramatically and as rivalries between religious orders mounted, Japan's leaders began to suspect the intentions of merchants and priests alike. What had begun as a mutually attractive economic trade arrangement deteriorated by the end of the Momoyama era into a mounting concern for political and military security. This culminated in 1587 with an edict banning Christianity and ordering the expulsion of European priests. Although issued more as a warning to converted Japanese and foreign missionaries, by 1600 executions of Christians had taken place, and by 1625 their persecution was well underway.

As a result converts to Catholicism began to conceal their beliefs, especially in the Kyoto-Osaka area and in western Japan where many lived. The most powerful political figure in these western provinces was Mori Terumoto, a convert openly hostile to the military rulers of the time. The Mori's home province of Suo (present-day Yamaguchi) is the location of the seaside city of Hagi from which this famous ware takes its name. Typified by a high-fired stoneware with high iron content and sandy fabric, Hagi ware was first produced by kilns in the area during the late sixteenth century. Initially inspired by Korean shapes and glaze decoration of the late fifteenth–sixteenth centuries, these wares rapidly became prized among tea followers for their high-footed shapes and warm surface appearance.

This large, thick-walled bowl was made of a gray sandy grog, wheel thrown into the form of a closed keg. Known as a *tawarade* ("split bale") shape, the body was sliced lengthwise with a spatula and a high circular ring attached to the remaining wall. The principal surface designs include Christian crosses on the sides, a flower at one back end, and at the other a linear arabesque oftentimes referred to as a pattern of religious light derived from the Jesuits' insignia. All the designs have been incised into the oval body and then filled with a clay which fired white under the creamy glaze.

This glaze covers the entire vessel and has numerous trailings inside and out. The attractive crackle pattern which exposes the underlying orange-brown skin adds a light violet hue to the whole and distinguishes this bowl from a number of similar Hagi pieces. In contrast to later tea bowls made in this *tawarade* configuration with inlaid decoration, the size of this vessel suggests its original use to Japanese Christians as a baptismal font, only later being appropriated for use in the tea ceremony of the seventeenth century.

MRC

EXHIBITIONS New York, 1963: Asia House, Tea Taste in Japanese Art, cat. by Sherman E. Lee, no. 39, pl. p. 62. Albuquerque, NM, 1980: Albuquerque Art Museum, Katachi: Form and Spirit in Japanese Art, p. 23, no. 9.

PUBLICATIONS Nishimura Tei, *Kirishitan to chado* [Christians and the art of tea] (Kyoto: Zenkoku Shabo, 1948) pl. 4. Mitsuoka Tadanari, *Nihon, Momoyama* [Japanese ceramics of the Momoyama period], vol. III of *Sekai toji zenshu* (1956) p. 234, fig. 184.

LITERATURE Taibi Yoshika, *Hagi*, vol. VI of *Kara Nihon no yakimono* [Japanese ceramics in color] (Tokyo: Tankosha, 1974) pls. 4, 5. Hayashiya Seizo, *Hagi, Agano, Takatori*, vol. XVIII of *Nihon toji zenshu* (1978) pls. 44, 45. Kyoto National Museum, *Ataka collection toyo tokiten* [Oriental ceramics in the Ataka collection], exhib. cat. (Kyoto, 1978) pl. 198.

149 Tea Storage Jar: Kyoto Ware, Shigaraki Type 78.6

Stoneware with milky white glaze. H. 28.3 cm., Diam. 18.7 cm. Japan, Nonomura Ninsei (act. ca. 1645– 1685). Edo period, ca. AD 1650. Purchase from the J. H. Wade Fund.

Although the esteem for Ninsei's accomplishments has waned since the turn of the century in favor of his "spiritual" disciple Ogata Kenzan [150], it remains apparent that both artists are without peer in Edo ceramic history. Ninsei's reputation rests primarily on a number of tea-leaf and water jars elaborately decorated with overglaze gold and enamels. These innovative pieces are complimented by numerous small incense containers and a stunning group of tea bowls all bearing enameled or painted designs which place them among the most visually sophisticated ceramic forms in all Japanese ceramics.

In addition Ninsei possessed a keen eye for earlier ceramic traditions, as evidenced by his *utsushi* ("copies") of Agano, Karatsu, Seto and — as attested by this jar — Shigaraki wares (see [143]). Of these *utsushi* he produced at least three such tea storage jars, each individuated by variations in shape, glaze pattern, and body composition. Thus, each represents a studied refinement — rather than "copy" — of this honored Shigaraki utilitarian vessel type. For instance, in contrast to other Shigaraki *utsushi*, this jar contains less feldspar in the clay grog and has not had nearly as much milky-white glaze applied to its surface. Instead this Cleveland example features an understated approach with surface splits and horizontal scraping bands left virtually intact, glaze trailed in modest amounts over the shoulder area alone, and underneath a thin wood ash covering.

In all likelihood this jar emerged from Ninsei's Omuro kiln (located near Ninna-ji), active by the late 1640s. Production of wares at Omuro suitable for the flourishing tea taste market was supported in part by the tea master Kanamori Sowa (1584-1656). He also acted as an advisor to the influential Maeda family of Kaga Province from whom this vessel reportedly came. A large, characteristic "Ninsei" seal is impressed on the base.

MRC

EX COLLECTION Maeda Collection.

EXHIBITION New York, 1981: Japan Society, One Thousand Years of Japanese Art (650-1650), cat. by Sherman E. Lee, Michael R. Cunningham, and Ursula Korneitchouk, no. 44, p. 78.

PUBLICATIONS Mitsuoka Tadanari, *Edo I*, vol. VI of *Sekai toji zenshu* (1976) pl. 120. Kawahara Masahiko, *Ninsei*, vol. XXVII of *Nihon toji zenshu* (1976) pl. 15. J. G. Moore, *The Eastern Gate*, p. 204.

LITERATURE Sugahara Hisao, *Hibai yoko* [Selected catalog of the Tokiwayama Bunko] (Tokyo: Otsuka Kogeisha, 1967) p. 126, pl. 85.

See also color plate following page 150.

150 Dish with Design of Plovers over Waves: Kyoto Ware 66.365

Earthenware with underglaze, iron-brown decoration. H. 2.7 cm., L. 21.9 cm. Japan, signed by Ogata Kenzan, potter (1663-1743), and Ogata Korin, designer (1658-1716). Edo period, ca. AD 1700. Purchase from the J. H. Wade Fund.

This famous dish, formerly in the Okochi Masatoshi collection, is constructed with upright sides, square flat base, and a beveled edge where the base and sides are joined. The light eggshell colored earthenware body has been painted in iron oxide with the signature of Kenzan on the exterior base, a cloud and flower pattern on both surfaces of the sides, and a design of plovers over waves, signed by Korin, on the flat interior surface of the dish. The glaze which covers the vessel is a creamy white raku type with some discoloration along the dense network of crackle. In shape, material, and dimensions, the Cleveland dish conforms quite closely to the well-known "Poet Watching Seagulls" plate in the Tokyo National Museum, the "Kanzan-Jittoku" plates in a private collection, and the equally famous set of ten *mukozuke* ("small dishes") in the Fujita Art Museum. Although such pieces could have been used for the tea ceremony, their flat bases make them difficult to handle, and their painted decoration does not provide a harmonious surface for the presentation of food. Therefore Sato Masahiko recently suggested that Kenzan designed such dishes purely for the aesthetic enjoyment of his brother's boldly painted designs.

Korin amply rewards the viewer of the Cleveland dish with a playfully painted flock of plovers flying over a rhythmically spuming wave. In using this motif, Korin recalls the classical literary tradition of Japan: the flock of plovers flying over Shio no yama (*Kokinshu*, Chap. VII, poem no. 345). Since Korin signs the scene without the Hokkyo title he proudly used after 1701, the Cleveland dish was probably completed during the first two years of the brothers' collaboration at the Narutaki kiln. HJK

EX COLLECTION Okochi M., Tokyo.

EXHIBITION Tokyo, 1951: Tokyo National Museum, The Sotatsu-Korin School, pl. 100.

PUBLICATIONS Mitsuoka Tadanari, *Edo II*, vol. V of *Sekai toji zenshu* (1957) pl. 53. Tanaka Ichimatsu, ed., *The Art of Korin* (Tokyo: Nihon Keizai Shimbun, 1959) pl. 59. Kobayashi Taichiro, *Kenzan Kyoto-hen* (Kyoto: Zenkoku Shobo, 1959) pl. 59. *Nippon sogo bunkazai zukan* [Illustrated album of Japanese cultural properties] (Tokyo: Miyako Shimbunsha, 1959) repr. p. 50. *Sekai bijutsu zenshu* [Survey of world art] (Tokyo: Kadokawa Shoten, 1961) repr. no. 59, p. 180. Bernard Leach, *Kenzan and His Tradition* (London: Faber and Faber, 1966) pl. 39.

151 Plate with Design of Pine, Prunus, and Bird: Old Kutani Ware 69.253

Porcelain decorated with overglaze polychrome enamels. H. 8.3 cm., Diam. 37.5 cm. Japan, Kaga Province. Edo period, late 17th century AD. Gift of Mrs. Terrence O. Kennedy in memory of her husband, Terrence O. Kennedy.

This large plate, broken across the middle but with no appreciable losses, is one of a substantial number of similar plates decorated with overglaze enamels — in this case mustard yellow, green, blue, and aubergine — in designs of remarkable breadth, strength, and large scale. They are distinctive in their boldness and stand apart from the more delicate and refined wares from the Arita area (cf. [154–162]). They are traditionally and still largely described as *Ko-Kutani* (Old Kutani) and as coming from Old Kaga Province, present-day Ishikawa, on the Sea of Japan side of Honshu, directly north of Nagoya. Many pieces, including this one, have a roughly drawn seal mark in enamel reading *fuko* ("longevity") on the base. Bold borders of fret designs, medallions, or scrolls, as in this plate, are also characteristic of the type which is clearly influenced by the Swatow export porcelains from south China of late Ming date.

Modern scholarship has reached no firm conclusions based on documents or excavations, beyond establishing the presence of kilns before 1660 at Kutani village, eighteenth- and nineteenth-century kilns at other Kaga sites, and the patronage of the powerful and wealthy Maeda clan, lords of Kaga Province. What one cannot deny is the existence of Old Kutani as a major aesthetic presence in the world of Edo ceramics. Whether the dishes were made and fired at Kutani and then enameled at some other center, such as Kanazawa, is unclear and aesthetically unimportant especially when confronted with the only Edo porcelains expressing the energetic and masculine qualities of Edo society in the outlying feudal regions.

It should be noted that the painter Kusumi Morikage (ca. 1620–1690), a pupil of Kano Tan'yu, has traditionally been associated with some of the landscape designs on Old Kutani ware. Comparison of some details from the Museum's screen by Morikage (CMA 68.105) with the pine tree on this plate provides some visual confirmation of this tradition. SEL

LITERATURE Kawasaki Yoshitaro, *Choshunkaku kansho* [Masterpieces of Far Eastern art from Baron Kawasaki's collection] (Tokyo: Kokka-sha, 1913) VI, pl. 18. Tanaka Sakutaro, *Edo II*, vol. VI of *Sekai toji zenshu* (1957) color pl. 15, pl. 52. Yamashita, *Ko-Imari to ko-Kutani* [Old Imari and Old Kutani wares] (Tokyo: Yuzankaku, 1968) fig. 138, nos. 160, 182. Nakagawa, trans. F. J. Bester, *Kutani Ware* (Tokyo: Kodansha, 1979).

152 Plate with Fan Design: Old Kutani Ware

Porcelain decorated with overglaze enamels. Diam. 21.2 cm. Japan. Edo period, late 17th or early 18th century AD. Severance A. and Greta Millikin Collection.

While this predominantly green enameled type of Kutani ware is customarily called *Aode-Kutani* (Green Kutani) and variously assigned to the late seventeenth or the early eighteenth century, most of the Green Kutani has a less homogeneous body material fired at a lower temperature than the true porcelains of Old Kutani. This striking plate, with a bold and original design of fans related to the Sotatsu-Korin tradition of decorative painting and the ceramics influenced by that tradition, is a high-fired porcelain with a relatively compact body — hence our tentative assignment of the plate to the Old Kutani category. SEL

EXHIBITION Cleveland, 1961: The Cleveland Museum of Art, Japanese Decorative Style, cat. by Sherman E. Lee, no. 166.

LITERATURE Tanaka, *Edo II*, vol. VI of *Sekai toji zenshu* (1957) pl. 85. *Japanese Ceramics from the Collection of Captain and Mrs. Roger Gerry* (Brooklyn Museum, 1961) no. 68, pl. 19. Yamashita, *Ko-Imari to ko-Kutani*, fig. 183.

153 Plate: Green (*Aode*) Ware 60.224

Porcelain decorated with overglaze polychrome enamels. H. 7.8 cm., Diam. 37.7 cm. Japan. Edo period, ca. AD 1823–1831. Purchase from the J. H. Wade Fund.

Among Japanese overglaze decorated wares Old Kutani porcelains are among the most problematic historically. Ceramic tradition maintains they were produced in Kaga Province, northeast of Kyoto, beginning in the late seventeenth century, but excavations have yet to confirm this satisfactorily. The issue is further clouded by the many numbers of "Kutani" produced in the early nineteenth century when the area kilns experienced a brief revival. At that time classic enameled Old Kutani as well as Green Kutani — the most distinctive development in the ware reappeared — although somewhat modified.

This large Green Kutani plate possesses a sandy brown, rather grainy body fabric over which a design of peonies set against a field of pine needles has been drawn. In keeping with classic *Aode* ware the principal design is boldly rendered against a single color base glaze (pale yellow) and the other colors are limited to two — in this case the green of the peony leaves and the aubergine of the flowers.

These have been quite freely and thickly applied in keeping with the spirit of the overall design and brushwork, which, as is evident on the underside scrolls, is rather crude. The unglazed lip gives an idea of body thickness and its considerable weight compared to earlier wares. The base is also substantial, glazed, and has a curious raised spiral surface and arabesque design without seal. The milky underglaze has trailed frequently on the underside and fired to a dull finish, in marked contrast to the clear upper glaze which so enhances the lustrous green and purple colors.

The subject of peonies is a favorite one in Japanese art and among ceramic wares is particularly associated with Kutani. Two well-known plates in the Umezawa collection and another in the Tokyo National Museum depict the theme, including butterflies, set against a white reserve. Thus this plate invokes and consolidates the thematic tradition as well as earlier examples of the ware, although within the special bold manner of Green Kutani. It possesses that artless charm and striking conception of pattern reminiscent of screen painting and textile design in Momoyama (1573–1615) Japan. Yet it dates considerably later, representing instead one of the fine *Aode* compositions which issued from the Yoshidaya kiln during its brief existence in the early nineteenth century.

MRC

EXHIBITIONS St. Louis, 1970: City Art Museum of St. Louis, 200 Years of Japanese Porcelain, cat. by Richard S. Cleveland, p. 161, repr. pl. 55, p. 70. Cleveland, 1961: Cleveland Museum of Art, Japanese Decorative Style, cat. by Sherman E. Lee, no. 161.

PUBLICATION Mayuyama, ed., *Japanese Art in the West*, p. 360, repr. p. 303, pl. 365.

158 Standing Figure of a Beauty.
Arita Ware, Kakiemon Type.
Japan. Edo period, ca. 1690.

147 Tile. Red Oribe Ware. Japan, Kujiri district, Motoyashiki kiln (?). Momoyama period, ca. 1600.

149 Tea Storage Jar. Kyoto Ware, Shigaraki Type. Japan, Nonomura Ninsei. Edo period, ca. 1650.

159 Bottle with *Namban* Designs.
Arita Ware, Imari Type. Japan.
Edo period, ca. 1700.

154 Dish: Arita Ware, Nabeshima Type 64.258

Porcelain decorated in underglaze blue and with overglaze polychrome enamels. H. 5.5 cm., Diam. 20.5 cm. Japan. Edo period, ca. AD 1700. Severance A. and Greta Millikin Collection.

Nabeshima, in contrast to the other major porcelain wares of Imari (see [159]), Old Kutani (see [151–152]), and Kakiemon (see [157–158, 160–162]), exhibits an extremely uniform degree of quality in body fabric and overglaze decoration. This is principally due to its status as the official ware of the Nabeshima clan who closely supervised its production and limited its use exclusively to their needs. Consequently the technical refinement of Nabeshima was accomplished away from the exigencies of the highly competitive market in contemporary porcelains for export.

Most of the pieces emanating from the single authorized Nageshima kiln included objects for display, presentation gifts, and dinner ware such as this plate. Sets of these shallow dishes in standardized sizes were made using calipers and templates for accuracy of reproduction, whereupon an approved design was precisely transformed from a prepared drawing to the dish surface. It is above all these striking design effects together with the ware's technical perfection which have made Nabeshima so prized in the last century. At first indebted to illustrations derived from Chinese-style painting manuals and to textile pattern books, these design motifs soon developed a distinctly Japanese decorative style and thematic content peculiar to Nabeshima.

This plate reflects the kind of ware which emanated from the official Okawachi kiln during the Genroku era (1688–1703). The potting is relatively heavy and the high foot bears the familiar comb pattern. The plate surface is composed of three linked medallions between which are triangular areas decorated in a squared textile box-pattern. Each medallion contains identical designs of a central lotus leaf and flower surrounded by leaf clusters. The lotus leaf is painted in carefully graded tones of the underglaze blue which outlines the other design elements. This creates a particularly effective tonal contrast with the translucent overglaze enamels in yellow and blue-green, and the dull red texture of the lotus bud. The yellow tone of the clear glaze evident in the central reserve and immediately under the interior lip is characteristic of contemporary wares, as is the loose red enameling in the box-patterns and the tri-partite peony theme with scrolling in blue wash on the underside. The same motif occurs on several other well-known Nabeshima pieces, but only a plate in the Hamburg Museum of Arts and Crafts has a nearly identical interior design. MRC

EXHIBITION Cleveland, 1961: The Cleveland Museum of Art, Japanese Decorative Style, cat. by Sherman E. Lee, no. 152.

LITERATURE Mayuyama, ed., *Japanese Art in the West*, pl. 376. Sister Johanna Becker, "A Group of Nabeshima Porcelain," *The University of Michigan Museum of Art Bulletin*, III (1968) 18-28, figs. 5, 9. Yabe Yoshiaki, *Nabeshima*, vol. XXV of *Nihon toji zenshu* (1976) pls. 4, 5, 11-13, 41, 65, 66. Kurita Museum, *Imari-Nabeshima* [Collection of the Imari and Nabeshima wares in the Kurita Museum] (1979) pls. 127-130.

155 Plate with Patterned Medallion Decoration: Arita Ware, Nabeshima Type 64.252

Porcelain, decorated in underglaze blue and with overglaze enamel. Diam. 15.2 cm. Japan. Edo period, late 17th century AD. Severance A. and Greta Millikin Collection.

This dish, another fine example of Nabeshima ware, is one of a set, perhaps originally five in number, owing much to silk brocade for its overall patterning. The deep red enamel is particularly characteristic of early classic Nabeshima ware and does recall the resonant enamel colors of early Chinese Ming porcelain though no clear connection can be demonstrated. As is common in almost all Nabeshima wares, the exterior decoration is only in underglaze blue with a comb pattern on the lower foot-rim and "bow-

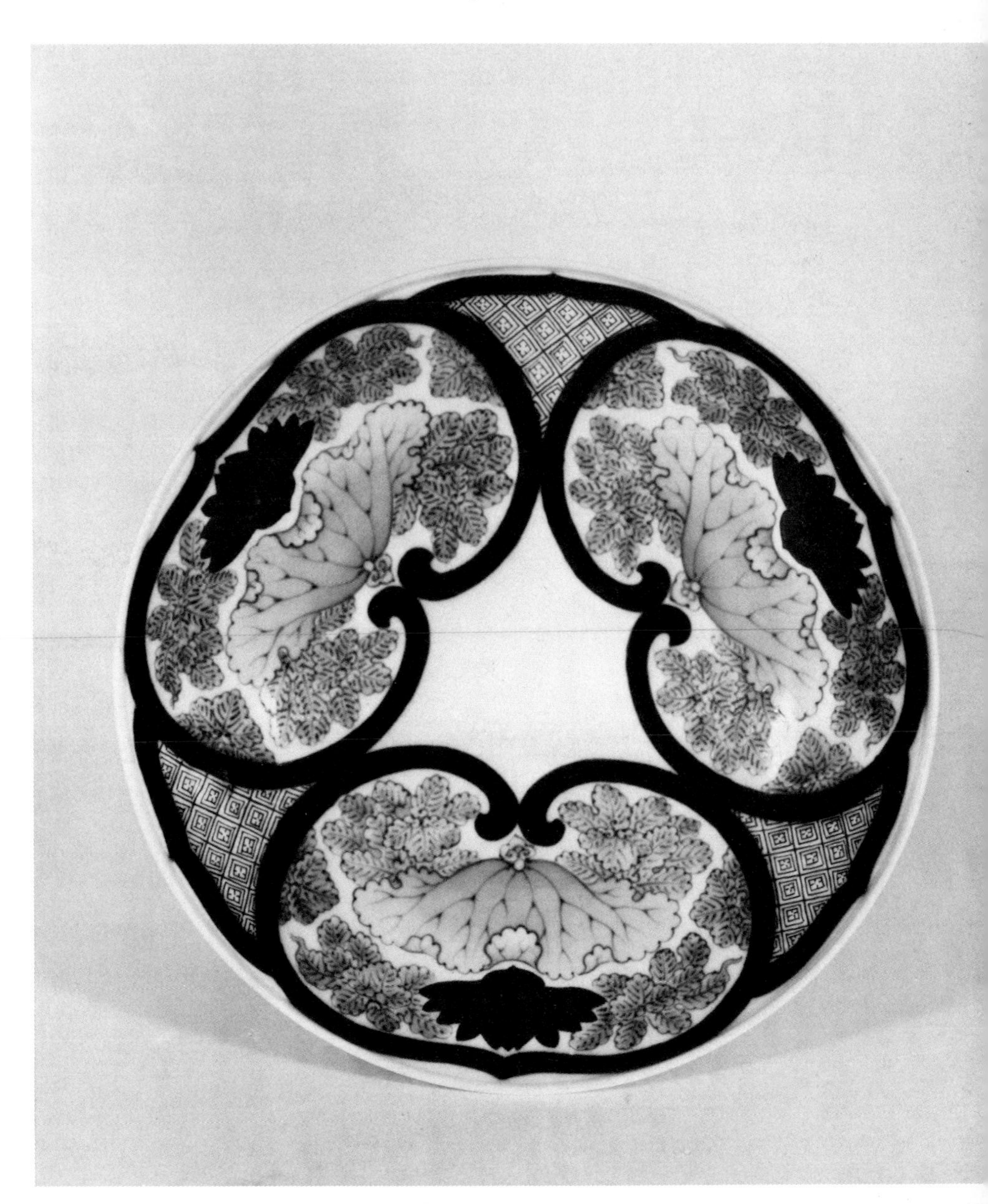

knots" on the underside of the dish. The precision of the design and the control of the materials go beyond all other contemporary Japanese ceramics. The cold bluish-white color of the ground is in marked contrast to the warm milky white of Kakiemon and the egg-shell white of Arita ware. The maintenance of these characteristics is testimony to the rigid controls over the kilns exercised by the lords of Nabeshima. SEL

PUBLICATION S. E. Lee, *A History of Far Eastern Art*, 4th ed., p. 503, fig. 672.

LITERATURE Nabeshima Hanyo Chosa Iinkai [Nabeshima House Kiln Research Committee], *Nabeshima hanyo no kenkyu* [The study of the Nabeshima house ceramic ware factory] (Kyoto: Heiando, 1954) fig. 84. T. Nagatake, *Zusetsu Kyushu ko-toki* [Ancient ceramics of Kyushu] (Tokyo: Toko Shoin, 1963) fig. 176. Mitsuoka, ed., *Edo III*, vol. VIII of *Sekai toji zenshu* (1976) pt. 3, pl. 209. J. A. Pope, *The Freer Gallery of Art*, vol. X of *Oriental Ceramics: The World's Great Collections* (Tokyo: Kodansha, 1976) fig. 182. Imaizumi Motosuke, *Nabeshima* (Tokyo: Kodansha 1981) pl. 14.

156 Incense Burner (*Koro*) with Hibiscus Scroll Decoration: Arita Ware, Nabeshima Type 64.270

Porcelain, decorated in underglaze blue and with overglaze polychrome enamels. H. 6 cm., Diam. 7.7 cm. Japan. Edo period, late 17th century AD. Severance A. and Greta Millikin Collection.

A very few small incense burners remain from the production of the early classic Nabeshima kilns, all but this one being cylindrical in shape. Its oblate spherical shape is, to date, unique. The paste, glaze color, underglaze blue, and enamels are identical with early Nabeshima plates and the few extant incense burners. The tight precision and brilliant color seem particularly appropriate to this miniature with its gold cover. Like the wine cups of Ming Ch'eng-hua porcelain or the cabinet pieces of the Ch'ien-lung emperor, this Nabeshima *koro* represents an extremely self-conscious state of aesthetic appreciation. SEL

LITERATURE Asahi Shimbun, ed., *Iro-Nabeshima* (Tokyo: Asahi Shimbunsha, 1965) pl. 51. Mitsuoka, ed., *Edo III*, vol. VIII of *Sekai toji zenshu* (1976) pls. 80, 81.

157 Large Plate: Arita Ware, Kakiemon Type 64.246

Porcelain decorated with overglaze polychrome enamels. H. 5.4 cm., Diam. 31.2 cm. Japan. Edo period, last quarter 17th century AD. Severance A. and Greta Millikin Collection.

Traditionally the early seventeenth-century discovery of porcelain on the southern island of Kyushu is linked to a Korean potter seeking to produce the underglaze blue and white ware characteristic of Yi Dynasty (1392–1910) ceramics. As a result of his success and the expanding export and domestic markets for these new white wares, porcelain technology in Japan advanced rapidly among the many kilns in the Arita area. While initially dependent upon continental models for shape types and decorative ideas, by the late seventeenth century, the wares we now call Imari (see [159]), Nabeshima (see [154–156]), Kutani (see [151–153]), and Kakiemon drew increasingly upon native inspiration for their success.

Kakiemon takes its name from a group of enamel artists working in the Arita area beginning about 1680. They produced large numbers of pieces of varying quality, due both to the vessels they received from the Arita kilns to paint and to the quality of the pigments available for use in the decoration. Early Arita porcelains make it clear that several enameling workshops and independent kilns existed by mid-century, but that the Kakiemon group joined potters and enamelists, producing increasingly sophisticated shapes bearing carefully rendered designs. This large plate was made for export and typifies in design and palette the Kakiemon wares produced in the later seventeenth century, during its early development. Such wares later became highly influential at the Meissen factory in Germany.

The design of ladies pleasure-boating and collecting lotuses, while a solitary seated figure watches from across a pond, is Chinese. Such compositions derive from late Ming and early Ch'ing wares done in five-color enamels emanating from Ching-ti-chen and from painting manuals. The distinctive orange-red enamel present in the wave patterns and scudding clouds and the sketchily outlined landscape forms help indicate the plate's age. In fact, the compositional scheme, figure type, and enameling brushwork place it among an identifiable group of plates that must have been produced by a particular Kakiemon group slightly before the square sake bottle [161]. Another, almost identical plate is known suggesting that the subject was a popular one.

The body is thinly potted with a shallow foot and is not as refined as the later *nigoshide* fabric (see [162]). Nevertheless its whiteness and clear glaze, together with its delightful, airy design, mark it as one of the fine early Kakiemon pieces which established the preeminence of Kakiemon among export wares in the later seventeenth century. MRC

EXHIBITION Cleveland, 1961: The Cleveland Museum of Art, Japanese Decorative Style, cat. by Sherman E. Lee, pp. 151, 152.

PUBLICATION S. E. Lee, *A History of Far Eastern Art*, 4th edition, p. 502, fig. 670.

LITERATURE Yamanaka Sadajiro, *Kutani, Nabeshima, Kakiemon meihinshu* [Masterpieces of Kutani, Nabeshima, and Kakiemon] (Kyoto: Benrido, 1934) pl. 97. Nagatake Takeshi, *Nihon III, Edo* [Japan III, early Edo ceramics], vol. III of *Toki koza* [Lectures on Japanese ceramics] (Tokyo: Yuzankaku, 1972) p. 315, fig. 171. Nishida Hiroko, *Kakiemon*, vol. XXIV of *Nihon toji zenshu* (1977).

158 Standing Figure of a Beauty: Arita Ware, Kakiemon Type 64.366

Porcelain decorated with overglaze polychrome enamels. H. 38 cm., W. 14 cm. Japan. Edo period, ca. AD 1690. Purchase, John L. Severance Fund.

Such figures as this beauty of the Genroku era (1688–1703) were mass-produced at Arita area kilns for a considerable export trade, rather than for the domestic market. Constructed from piece molds whose joins were carefully concealed with clay slip, these standing figures differ from one another primarily in garment designs and in enamel quality and workmanship. In this example the textile pattern of the *uchikake* ("outer garment") displays a cascade of weeping cherry blossoms alternating in pale red and yellow enamels of superb clarity. The inner garment's interlocking network, known as *shippo tsunagi,* contrasts dramatically in its iron-red color tone and density.

These major decorative elements are joined by the dark lustrous black enamels of the narrow *obi* and elaborate topknot, a coiffure of the Kanbun era (1661–1672). These serve to focus attention on the figure's fresh facial expression and gay deportment. Such personalities are of course known through the rather plump revelers in early *ukiyo-e* painting and prints, as well as in Matabei's (1578–1650) *oeuvre.*

The porcelain body is thinly molded and is glazed with a white slip which trails into the interior. The base retains impressions of the cloth used in the molding process between clay and form. The hands, seen in other figures with identical gestures, were added and modeled separately from the sleeves. The head too has been adjusted slightly upward so as to enhance the forthright attitude of the lady. The open, smiling expression of the mouth adds a buoyant note and served as a gas vent during firing. MRC

EXHIBITION St. Louis, 1970: City Art Museum, 200 Years of Japanese Porcelain, cat. by Richard S. Cleveland, p. 170, repr. pp. 96, 97, pl. 83.

PUBLICATION Mayuyama, ed., *Japanese Art in the West,* p. 361, repr. p. 317, pl. 398.

LITERATURE Soame Jenyns, *Japanese Porcelain* (London: Faber and Faber, 1965) pl. 63B. Tokugawa Art Museum, *Kinsei shoki fuzokuga-ten* [Japanese genre painting of the early modern periods], exhib. cat. (Nagoya, 1969). Asahi Shimbun, *Kakiemon meihin-ten: Nihon jiki aka-e no seika* [Exhibition of mas-

See also color plate following page 150.

terpieces of Kakiemon ware: The essence of Japanese *aka-e* porcelain], exhib. cat. (Fukuoka, 1976) pp. 22-23. Nishida, *Kakiemon*, vol. XXIV of *Nihon toji zenshu* (1977) pls. 35-41.

159 Bottle with *Namban* ("foreigners") Designs: Arita Ware, Imari Type — *19.837*

Porcelain decorated with overglaze polychrome enamels and gold, incised. H. 55 cm., Diam. 23.5 cm., Diam. of foot 15 cm. Japan. Edo period, ca. AD 1700. Gift of Ralph King.

This large, double gourd bottle is designed to be viewed from two positions: on one side is a group of standing Dutchmen, on the other an imposing sailing ship. Above each are smaller, finely painted flower designs centered on the upper gourd and featuring what may be a tulip and *nadeshiko* (dianthus) respectively. The accompanying foliate forms and floral sprays of the borders and reserves portray European imagery painted freely with extraordinary deftness.

Although the shape and imagery of the base are uncommon, this particular arrangement appears to be unique despite an obvious formality in composition. The grouping of the Dutchmen, for instance, and their particular physical appearances surely derives from printed manuals or wood block illustrations of the time. Conversely, the unusual bird design encircling the ship cartouche may be a kind of stylized hybrid combining features of the Japanese *hoho* ("Phoenix") with a European heraldic emblem.

Thus, it is likely that this vessel was specifically commissioned from an Arita area kiln for a Dutch merchantman seeking a good-sized Oriental ceramic to grace a foyer or living room. Perhaps the most revealing aspect of the painted design and the one which illuminates the relationship between foreign merchant and Japanese artist is also the most furtive: the base design. Hidden underneath is a floral compositon of two peonies drawn according to Western illusionistic techniques. The petals are shaded in black enamel and are ridden with insect holes, much as if they were copied from a Bosschaert (1573–1645) still life. MRC

EXHIBITIONS Cleveland, 1961: The Cleveland Museum of Art, Japanese Decorative Style, cat. by Sherman E. Lee, no. 148, repr. p. 124. St. Louis, 1970: City Art Museum, 200 Years of Japanese Porcelain, cat. by Richard S. Cleveland, repr. p. 85, fig. 58.

See also color plate following page 150.

PUBLICATIONS Martin Feddersen, *Japanese Decorative Art* (London: Faber and Faber, 1962) repr. p. 84, fig. 58. Mikami Tsugio, *The Art of Japanese Ceramics* (Tokyo: Weatherhill, 1972) pl. 21, fig. 181, p. 168. Nagatake Takeshi, *Imari*, vol. XIX of *Toji taikei* [Ceramics of Asia] (Tokyo: Heibonsha, 1973) 106, fig. 35. S. E. Lee, *A History of Far Eastern Art*, 4th ed., p. 503, fig. 671.

LITERATURE Okuda Seiichi, Koyama Fujio, and Hayashiya Seizo, *Japanese Ceramics* (Tokyo: Toto Bunka Co., 1954) p. 106, pls. 257, 258. Keiichi Nonogami, *Oranda-e Imari* [Dutch Imari] (Tokyo: Gohachipuresu, 1973).

160 Sake Bottle: Arita Ware 64.272

Porcelain decorated with overglaze polychrome enamels and gold. H. 27.2 cm., Diam. 14.3 cm. Japan. Edo period, ca. AD 1700. Severance A. and Greta Millikin Collection.

Sake bottles constituted a major proportion of the production at the Arita kilns, being popular in export and domestic markets alike. This vessel, in contrast to the square Kakiemon flask [161], was made for the Japanese market judging from its spare design of three figures evenly spaced across the white surface. The shape does, however, suggest a European or even Chinese model that appealed to the Arita potter.

The body is somewhat heavy but refined to a degree comparable to the Kakiemon figurine [158]. Dark iron spots as well as small coagulations can be seen in the glaze surface where gasses were expelled during firing from the clay fabric underneath. The low swelling body rests on a shallow foot to which remnants of sand still adhere. The tall neck was formed by joining a finger-length cylinder to the existing column, thus producing the slight bending of that shape. The stopper is original, a rare occurrence among such pieces.

Certainly the most compelling feature of the sake bottle is the surface design of three exquisitely drawn figures: a young man, a *bijin* ("beauty" or courtesan), and a priest. Their features are precisely outlined with a fine-haired brush, and then delicately toned. The striking garment patterns are painted in enamels whose color and clarity indicate the participation of one of the most talented enamelists working at the turn of the century. Greens and lustrous blacks predominate, with highlights in a dull iron-red and light gold.

Kambun era (1661–1673) figures in small groups or large party scenes are not uncommonly found on large Imari jars and a smaller number of sake flasks. In shape, figure and dress style, and technical mastery this bottle represents one of the finest achievements of that special collaboration which occurred between an Arita studio potter of the Imari persuasion and a Kakiemon enamelist at the beginning of the eighteenth century. MRC

LITERATURE Nagatake, *Nihon III, Edo zenki*, vol. III of *Toki koza* (1972) pl. 94, 96, 102. Yamashita Sakuro, *Shoki no Imari* [Early Imari wares] (Tokyo: Tokuma, 1972). Nagatake, *Imari*, vol. XIX of *Toji taikei* (1973) pls. 20, 78, 81. Nishida Hiroko, *Ko Imari*, vol. XXIII of *Nihon toji zenshu*, pls. 68-70.

161 Sake Bottle: Arita Ware, Kakiemon Type 64.261

Porcelain decorated wtih overglaze polychrome enamels. H. 21.8 cm., W. at top 8.3 cm. Japan. Edo period, late 17th century AD. Severance A. and Greta Millikin Collection.

This unusual vessel is a sake bottle whose shape derives from a European prototype, in all likelihood a Dutch decanter. Holland alone was permitted to maintain commercial ties with Japan after the country isolated itself about 1640. The enterprising Dutch East India Company became instrumental in placing orders for porcelains with Arita area kilns following the political disturbances in Ming China which made trade with the continent precarious, but spurred the development in Japan of porcelain and enamel technology. The first large orders were exported in the late 1650s and met with much commercial success in Europe, resulting in the introduction into Japan of novel decorative motifs and vessel shapes specifically aimed towards the foreign market. Square-shaped flasks, for example, must have been introduced rather early since Ko Imari examples dating from the Kambun era are known.

This bottle tapers slightly towards a square unglazed base which reveals a refined body fabric almost comparable to *nigoshide* (see [162]), but significantly heavier. The flask is capped with a fluted top which has been slip-joined to the molded sides. The spout has been attached in the same manner. The white body has a decided blue cast, especially noticeable on the top surface and along the upper ridges, due to thick glaze pooling. Over this an extraordinarily conceived design of a squirrel and hanging grape vines has been drawn. Appropriately, a single vine stem emanates from the bottle spout sending branches in two directions. One cascades down the two faces adjoining at the spout corner. Here, as well as on the top surface, two large grape leaves colored in brilliant green and blue enamels represent the principal design element. They are shown with delicately brushed vine branchings and small, jewel-like grape clusters rendered in pale yellow and flat red enamels. Black outlining strengthens the design and accentuates its lyrical effect.

The opposing side designs feature the extension of the main vine stem with long trailing tendrils and a curious, leaping squirrel painted in yellow enamel over detailed brushwork. The subject derives from Chinese Ming or Korean Yi Dynasty Blue-and-White wares and is particularly well-known in Japan through the often published large, Ko Imari Blue-and-White bowl in a private collection. It also appears on the later set of Kakiemon food dishes in the Tanakamaru collection. This bottle design represents an especially felicitous portrayal of the theme and is compatible with the spare compositions set against white background so emblematic of the highest quality Kakiemon wares of the later seventeenth century. MRC

EXHIBITION Cleveland, 1961: The Cleveland Museum of Art, Japanese Decorative Style, exhib. cat. by Sherman E. Lee, no. 143.

LITERATURE Kurita Museum, *Imari-Nabeshima*, pls. 11,24. Seattle Art Museum, *Ceramic Art of Japan*, pl. 58. Metropolitan Museum of Art, *Japanaese Ceramics from the Tanakamaru Collection*, exhib. cat. (New York, 1980) no. 32. Tanaka, *Edo I*, vol. IV of *Sekai toji zenshu* (1956) 230, pl. 107, fig. 149.

162 Covered Bowl: Arita Ware, Kakiemon Type 61.42

Porcelain with molded and incised designs and overglaze polychrome enamel and gold decoration. H. 14.5 cm., Diam. 21 cm. Japan. Edo period, ca. AD 1780. James Parmelee Fund (and various donors by exchange).

A small number of molded Kakiemon bowls like this Cleveland example have survived in Japan and the West although unfortunately several no longer possess the domed lid so integral to the vessel's appearance. Each sits on a rather high straight foot which supports the taut, swelling bowl shell. Its fabric is composed of a particularly fine porcelain mixed with white clay to produce the milky white body known as *nigoshide*, a development of the late seventeenth century which is found in superior export wares.

The principal design motif of the tureen and lid consists of molded wave patterns augmented by incised lines. Interspersed among the waves in reserved areas are floating chrysanthemum leaves, pods, and flower clusters, and flying plovers painted in brilliant translucent enamels and gold. The same motifs extend over the lid, capped by the European-inspired strap handle. Inside, the bowl contains an elaborately conceived design of two encircling phoenixes surrounding a pair of flaming jewels. The painting is a *tour de force* of the enameler's art, which may also be seen in the simple plum twig on the lid interior.

These designs should be viewed in relation to the exterior, for the molded waves have captured extra portions of the clear underglaze, creating a slight blue cast in the design. This not only enhances the ceramic sophistication of the bowl and the integrity of its component parts, but adds another, lyrical dimension to the theme of plovers cavorting over dancing waves. This subject originates in Heian court poetry and enjoyed another sumptuous revival during the Momoyama era, both periods of extraordinary refinement in Japan. Devotees of *ukiyo-e*, the "floating world" of Japanese prints, will be reminded of the theme's appearance in the kimonos of the Kaigetsudo School courtesans about 1700. MRC

EXHIBITION Cleveland, 1961: The Cleveland Museum of Art, Japanese Decorative Style, cat. by Sherman E. Lee, no. 147, repr. p. 124. Dallas, 1969: Dallas Museum of Fine Arts, Masterpieces of Japanese Art, no. 64. City Art Museum of St. Louis, 1970: 200 Years of Japanese Porcelain, cat. by Richard S. Cleveland, p. 174, repr. pp. 104, 105, pl. 92. Los Angeles, 1976: University of California, Frederick S. Wight Art Gallery, Birds, Beasts, Blossoms and Bugs, The Nature of Japan, cat. by Harold P. Stern, no. 37.

PUBLICATION Mayuyama, ed., *Japanese Art in the West*, p. 361, repr. p. 312, pl. 388.

LITERATURE Nishida, *Kakiemon*, vol. XXIV of *Nihon toji zenshu* (1977) pl. 60. Nagatake, *Edo III*, vol. VIII of *Sekai toji zenshu* (1978) pls. 40, 41.

163 Basket Dish: Kyoto Ware

Porcelain decorated with overglaze polychrome enamels. H. 10.8 cm., L. at base: 19.9 cm., W. at base: 11.2 cm. Japan, signed by Okuda Eisen (AD 1753–1811). Edo period. Severance A. and Greta Millikin Collection.

Among Okuda Eisen's *oeuvre* the pieces which derive from his study of the late sixteenth–early seventeenth-century Chinese Swatow wares are his most characteristic. Produced at kilns on the South China coast, large numbers of this ware in a variety of shapes were imported into Japan where they were called *gosu akae* ("red enameled" *gosu*). In Japan they caught the attention of seventeenth-century tea enthusiasts who used them as tea utensils when appropriately shaped. Later it appears that some *gosu akae* ware was produced specifically for the tea culture in Japan which appreciated its rough, but warm appearance.

Okuda Eisen was a man of tea, having learned its customs as well as Chinese literary studies at the renowned Zen monastery Kennin-ji in Kyoto. It was there that Eisen became interested as a young amateur in ceramics, setting out eventually to learn the actual potting techniques of Seto, Shigaraki, and Imari. In Kyoto Eisen established a kiln and studio where he began making *gosu akae*, blue and white ware, and the colorful *cochi* ware, a type that emulated Southeast Asian ceramics. By the time he was thirty, Eisen mastered the production of *gosu akae*, thereby introducing a porcelain ware into Kyoto which, in turn, stimulated activity at local kilns.

This dish was made for use in the *kaiseki* meal served in the tea ceremony (see also [146]). The clay body is buff white with an iron and feldspathic content visible on the base that is reminiscent of Shigaraki clay (see [143]). The dish is coated with a thick blue-green glaze that has coagulated in places to reveal the body, a desirable feature of Swatow and some domestic wares. Similarly the overglaze enamel design of phoenix, chrysanthemum, floral spray, and cloud scrolls invoke their Chinese prototypes, but with an infectious spontaneity and coarseness particularly evident in the placement of the pools of emerald-green enamels.

The Phoenix motif appears in several of Eisen's large vessels as well as in the many smaller tea ceremony wares he was clearly fond of making for his own use and as pieces for friends. This basket dish however is uncommon in joining together elements of such divergent ceramic traditions as Shigaraki ("clay"), Oribe ("shape"), and Swatow ("decoration") in one of the few signed tea pieces of his limited production. As such it represents his early work, the kind which almost single-handedly revived the ceramic industry in Kyoto in the late eighteenth century, and inspired the renown careers of the potters Mokubei (1767–1833), Dohachi (1783–1855), and Hozen (1795–1854). MRC

LITERATURE Kawahara Masahiko, *Eisen-Mokubei*, vol. XXIX of *Nihon toji zenshu* (1978) pls. 12, 13, 28, 31.

Annamese

164 Storage Jar: Blue-and-White Ware 72.40

Porcelain with underglaze blue decoration. H. 25.5 cm., Diam. 24.9 cm. Annam (Vietnam). 15th century AD. The Norman O. Stone and Ella A. Stone Memorial Fund.

Yung-lo, the third emperor of the Ming Dynasty (r. 1403–1423), possessed an expansionist vision of the role which a newly unified China should play throughout Asia. Not content to rule merely the lands bequeathed by his father, he attempted also to control Chinese maritime trade by sending out commercial flotillas that sailed as far as the Persian Gulf and the Indian and African coasts. Closer to home, he annexed the port of Haiphong — the great harbor of the Annamese kingdom. While northern Vietnam had experienced Chinese occupation during the Han and T'ang periods, in 1407 Yung-lo used the Vietnamese wars of imperial succession as a pretext for invasion. The Ming militia was finally routed from the capital city of Hanoi by the Vietnamese hero Le Loi in 1428.

During the Chinese occupation, the Vietnamese ceramic industry literally flowered with the introduction of underglaze cobalt decoration from China. This storage jar is a splendid example of how well the Vietnamese mastered the technique. Overlapping around its lip, clouds scudding across its shoulder, and scrolling peony and lotus lappets with flaming jewels surrounding its body are all decorative devices first encountered in the robustly painted Chinese Blue-and-White wares of the fourteenth century (see [118, 119]). Actually early fifteenth-century Chinese wares — whose cobalt blue decoration was smaller in scale, revealing more of the white porcelain ground (cf. [123, 124]) — were the immediate source of inspiration. The Vietnamese painter of this vessel was even more sparing with the cobalt pigment than his Chinese contemporaries. He has practically eliminated all areas of blue wash and concentrated instead on repeating a uniformly thin line throughout the various decorative registers of the jar. This simplified linear concept of decoration unites it with a famous vase preserved in the Topakapu Serai Museum, Istanbul, inscribed with the date 1450. Further distinguishing the Vietnamese from the Chinese tradition are the diminutive loop handles on the shoulder of the Cleveland jar — utilitarian devices in the local ceramic industry, predating the Ming occupation. Finally, the potter applied a brown wash to the base of the jar, while still allowing the unglazed foot rim to exhibit the ivory-toned local clay from which the jar was potted. This "chocolate" base remained a feature of Vietnamese ceramics for centuries. HJK

LITERATURE Dean F. Frasché, *Southeast Asian Ceramics: Ninth Through Seventeenth Centuries*, exhib. cat. (New York: The Asia Society, 1976) no. 73 (Mr. and Mrs. Robert P. Griffing, Jr. collection). Adrian M. Joseph, *Chinese and Annamese Ceramics Found in the Philippines and Indonesia* (London: Hugh Moss Ltd., 1977) pp. 186-187, pl. 115, (Ian Wasserman collection). Roxana M. Brown, *The Ceramics of South-East Asia: Their Dating and Identification* (Kuala Lumpur: Oxford University Press, 1977) color pl. E (bottle vase with similar decoration, dated AD 1450, Topkapu Sarayi, Istanbul).

East Indian

165 Mother Goddess 73.24

Terracotta. H. 11.5 cm., W. 5.2 cm.
India. Sunga Period, 2nd century BC.
Gift of Mr. and Mrs. Morris Everett in memory of Flora Morris Everett.

The delight that a sculptor takes in depicting female beauty and charm is universal. In India it is even more apparent than in other cultures since the artist's motivations are deeper than the pleasures derived from the portrayal of physical beauty. There, woman symbolizes the maternal energy of nature and is looked upon as the Mother Goddess of all creation. Although she appears under different disguises in various religious creeds (Devi in Hinduism, Tara in Buddhism, or secondary deities such as *yakshi* ["nature spirit"], *nagini* ["water spirit"], and *salabhanjiki* ["tree spirit"], the idea of seeing her as a symbol of fertility never changes. Therefore, her feminine aspect is greatly emphasized: she is shown with large breasts, broad hips, and a narrow waist and is adorned with little clothing and many jewels. In addition she has a finely featured face with almond-shaped eyes, straight nose, and full lips. Literary sources refer to her "fair complexion" as another requirement of feminine beauty.

This terracotta displays all of these characteristics. In addition, a point that deserves special attention is the depth of relief which in comparison with other, rather flat, Sunga terracottas creates the impression of three dimensionality and voluptuousness. There is also great attention paid to details which in combination with an easy, relaxed posture give the sculpture a quality of grace and perfection rarely achieved in other terracottas of that period. SC

LITERATURE Satish Chandra Kala, *Terracotta Figures from Kausambi* (Allahabad: The Municipal Museum, 1950) p. 81, pl. IV. Paresh Chandra Das Gupta, "Early Terracottas from Chandraketugarh," *Lalit Kala*, no. 6 (1959) pp. 45-52, pl. XIII figs. 3, 4, pl. XV fig. 16. Charu Chandru Das Gupta, *Origin and Evolution of Indian Clay Sculpture* (Calcutta: Calcutta University, 1969) figs. 88, 89. Parmesvari Lal Gupta, *Gangetic Valley Terracotta Art* (Varanasi: Prithivi Prakashan, 1972) figs. 109, 110. M. K. Dhavalikar, *Masterpieces of Indian Terracottas* (Bombay: Taraporevala, 1977) pls. 28, 29.

166 Mithuna: Amorous Couple 71.133

Terracotta. H. 38.5 cm., W. 37 cm. India, probably Ahichchhatra, Uttar Pradesh. Gupta Period, Late 5th–early 6th century AD. Purchase from the J. H. Wade Fund.

Terracotta plaques in high relief, such as this one, abundantly decorated the walls of structural brick temples during the Gupta Period. There are various temple sites in the present state of Uttar Pradesh that revealed them: Bhitargaon in Kunpur District and Ahichchhatra in Bareilly District representing two better known groups.

The Cleveland Museum tile, with its arched top, depicts an amorous couple (*mithuna*), one of the favorite subjects of the Indian sculptor. They are shown in a relaxed posture which implies the intimacy of their relationship. The woman affectionately touches her companion's thigh, while he rests his elbow on her shoulder. It is apparent that the couple is involved in conversation. The deep modeling of the figures, which almost project over the frame of the tile, is characteristic of the Gupta style, as is the composition which conveys movement through the use of various angles of the figures' arms and legs. The fleshy facial features, with high foreheads and incised eyebrows and pupils, are the trademarks of the Ahichchhatra terracottas. A very closely related piece, probably also from Ahichchhatra, is in the Pan Asian Collection. Other known tiles of similar type, such as the one at Asia Society or the tile in a private Los Angeles collection, illustrate the *Ramayana* epic and represent a somewhat softer modeling that seems to indicate another provenance, likely that of Bhitargaon, as suggested by Pratapaditya Pal. SC

EXHIBITION New York, 1978: Asia House Gallery, The Ideal Image, the Gupta Sculptural Tradition and Its Influence, cat. by Pratapaditya Pal, no. 30, p. 82.

LITERATURE V. S. Agrawala, "Terracotta Figurines of Ahichchhatra, District Bareilly, U. P.," *Ancient India*, no. 4 (1947–1948) pp. 104-179. Pratapaditya Pal, *The Sensuous Immortals* (Los Angeles: Los Angeles County Museum, 1978). Mohammad Zaheer, *The Temple of Bhitargaon* (Delhi: Agam Kala Prakasham, 1981).

167 Piggy Bank 80.16

Terracotta. H. 24.2 cm., L. 35.5 cm. Java. Majapahit Dynasty, 14th–15th centuries AD. Purchase, John L. Severance Fund.

Pottery money boxes, as found in various cultures, are not a modern invention. Their origin goes back to Roman times, The fact that they cannot be opened except by breaking them explains why so few ancient examples survive today.

This bank, representing a well-fed hog, successfully captures the nature of the animal in a humorous yet sympathetic manner. It was made under the auspices of the Majapahit Dynasty, which established itself in Java after Kublai Khan's invasion in 1292 and ruled there during the course of the fourteenth and fifteenth centuries. Money boxes are quite common among the terracotta objects which have survived from that period. Most frequently they are in animal form through occasionally they take on a human or vessel shape. It is significant that the word for "piggy-bank" in Eastern Java is *tjèlèngan* which means "wild boar."

Around its neck this hog wears a heavy chain with a Chinese-type padlock. Both are very appropriate considering the function of the object and the fact that most of the coinage in use during the Majapahit Dynasty in Java was Chinese. The export of Chinese copper coins to Java became so extensive that the Chinese tried, unsuccessfully, to combat it. The fragments of a very similar object remain in the Princesshof Museum in Leeuwarden.

Finally, one should stress the technical production of this vessel. It is made of fine, well-polished, red terracotta with very thin walls. The firing of an object of this size and fragility requires great professional accomplishment. SC

LITERATURE M. V. Jones, *Country Life*, 1 December 1960, p. 1299. H. R. A. Muller, *Javanese Terra cottas*, (Lochem: Uitgeversmaatschappij De Tijdstroom 1978) pp. 28, 30-31, 41.

Suggestions for Further Reading

General

Bernard H. Charles, *Pottery and Porcelain: A Dictionary of Terms* (London: David and Charles, 1974).

Frank Hamer, *The Potter's Dictionary of Materials and Techniques* (London: Pitman Publishing, 1975).

Masterpieces of Western and Near Eastern Ceramics, Robert J. Charleston, general editor, vols. I–VIII (Tokyo: Kodansha Ltd., 1978–1980).

Glenn C. Nelson, *Ceramics: A Potter's Handbook*, 4th edition (New York: Holt, Rinehart and Winston, 1978).

Daniel Rhodes, *Clay and Glazes for the Potter*, rev. edition (Philadelphia: Chilton Book Co., 1973).

George Savage and Harold Newman, *An Illustrated Dictionary of Ceramics* (London: Thames and Hudson, 1974).

Egyptian

A. L. Kelley, *The Pottery of Ancient Egypt: Dynasty I to Roman Times* (Toronto, 1976).

Elizabeth Riefstahl, *Ancient Egyptian Glass and Glazes in the Brooklyn Museum* (Brooklyn, 1968).

Greek

John Boardman, *Athenian Black Figure Vases* (New York: Oxford University Press, 1974).

———, *Athenian Red Figure Vases: The Archaic Period* (London: Thames and Hudson, 1975).

R. M. Cook, *Greek Painted Pottery*, 2nd rev. edition (London: Methuen and Co., 1972).

Joseph Veach Noble, *The Techniques of Painted Attic Pottery* (New York: Watson-Guptill Publications, 1965).

European

Alice Wilson Frothingham, *Lustreware of Spain* (New York: The Hispanic Society of America, 1951).

William Bowyer Honey, *European Ceramic Art from the End of the Middle Ages to about 1815*, 2 vols. (London: Faber and Faber, 1949–1952).

———, *French Porcelain of the 18th Century*, 2nd edition (London: Faber and Faber, 1972).

Arthur Lane, *French Faience*, 2nd edition (London: Faber and Faber, 1970).

Bernard Rackham, *Italian Maiolica* (London: Faber and Faber, 1952).

Islamic

Esin Atil, *Fifteenth Anniversary Exhibition, Ceramics from the World of Islam* (Washington: Smithsonian Institution, Freer Gallery, 1973).

Arthur Lane, *Early Islamic Pottery* (London: Faber and Faber, 1947).

———, *Later Islamic Pottery* (London: Faber and Faber, 1971).

A. U. Pope and P. Ackerman, eds., *A Survey of Persian Art*, vol. IV: *The Ceramic Arts, Calligraphy and Epigraphy;* vol. X: *Pottery and Faience* (London and New York: Oxford University Press, 1964–1965).

Pre-Columbian

George Kubler, *The Art and Architecture of Ancient America* (Harmondsworth, Middlesex: Penguin Books, 1975).

Henry Lehmann, *Pre-Columbian Ceramics* (New York: Viking Press, 1962).

American Indian

Larry Frank and Francis H. Harlow, *Historic Pottery of the Pueblo Indian 1600–1880* (Boston: New York Graphic Society, 1974).

Francis H. Harlow, *Modern Pueblo Pottery 1880–1960* (Flagstaff: Northland Press, 1977).

Chinese

Sir Harry Garner, *Oriental Blue and White* (London: Faber and Faber, 1954).

G. St. G. M. Gompertz, *Chinese Celadon Wares*, 2nd edition rev. (London: Faber and Faber, 1980).

A. L. Hetherington, *Chinese Ceramic Glazes*, 2nd edition rev. (London: Cambridge University Press, 1948).

Soame Jenyns, *Later Chinese Porcelain: The Ch'ing Dynasty (1644–1912)* (London: Faber and Faber, 1971).

Margaret Medley, *The Chinese Potter: A Practical History of Chinese Ceramics* (Oxford: Phaidon Press, 1976).

———, *T'ang Pottery and Porcelain* (London: Faber and Faber, 1981).

———, *Yüan Porcelain and Stoneware* (London: Faber and Faber, 1974).

Yutaka Mino and Patricia Wilson, *An Index to Chinese Ceramic Kiln Sites from the Six Dynasties to the Present* (Toronto: Royal Ontario Museum, 1969).

Masahiko Sato, *Chinese Ceramics: A Short History* (New York and Tokyo: Weatherhill/Heibonsha, 1981). Originally published in Japanese under the title *Chugoku toshoji* [History of Chinese ceramics].

Ezekiel Schloss, *Ancient Chinese Ceramic Sculpture from Han through T'ang* (Stamford, CT: Castle Publishing Co., 1977).

Suzanne G. Valenstein, *A Handbook of Chinese Ceramics* (New York: The Metropolitan Museum of Art, 1975).

Korean

G. St. G. M. Gompertz, *Korean Celadon and Other Wares of the Koryo Period* (London: Faber and Faber, 1963).

———, *Korean Pottery and Porcelain of the Yi Period* (New York: Frederick A. Praeger, 1968).

Chaewon Kim, *Arts of Korea* (Tokyo: Kodansha International, 1974).

Japanese

Rand Castile, *The Way of Tea* (Tokyo and New York: Weatherhill, 1971).

Fujioka Ryoichi, trans. Samuel C. Morse, *Shino and Oribe Ceramics* (Tokyo: Kodansha, 1977).

Soame Jenyns, *Japanese Porcelain* (London: Faber and Faber, 1965).

———, *Japanese Pottery* (London: Faber and Faber, 1971).

Koyama Fujio, trans. Sir John Figgess, *The Heritage of Japanese Ceramics* (New York: Weatherhill, 1973).

Mikami Tsugio, trans. Ann Herring, *The Art of Japanese Ceramics* (New York: Weatherhill, 1972).

Nakagawa Sensaku, trans. F. John Bester, *Kutani Ware* (Tokyo: Kodansha, 1979).

Andrew Pekarik, *Japanese Ceramics*, exhib. cat. (Southhampton, NY: The Parrish Art Museum, 1978).

Seattle Art Museum, *Ceramic Art of Japan*, exhib. cat. (Seattle, 1972).

East Indian

Charuchandra Dasgupta, *Origin and Evolution of Indian Clay Sculpture* (Calcutta: University of Calcutta, 1961).

M. K. Dhavalikar, *Masterpieces of Indian Terracottas* (Bombay: Taraporevala, 1977).

Glossary

Ash an ingredient added to STONEWARE glazes to serve as the principle FLUX. The color and texture of the GLAZE varies with the source of the ash (usually wood, straw, or leaves). Bone ash is used as a flux in the body of bone china to give it the whiteness and translucency of Chinese PORCELAIN. [71]

Biscuit unglazed EARTHENWARE or PORCELAIN that has been fired only once. [72]

Black-figure a decorative style of Greek pottery (primarily sixth century BC). The decoration, painted in SLIP on the red ground of the vase, turned black in the reducing atmosphere of the kiln. Details were rendered by colors (white and purple) painted over the slip and incision, which cut through the slip to the red ground. [12–14]

Blanc de Chine an eighteenth-century French term which describes the highly translucent white Chinese PORCELAIN made at Te-hua from the latter part of the Ming Dynasty. The color varies from ivory to chalk-white, while the GLAZE is thick and unctuous. [132]

Blue-and-White white PORCELAIN decorated with cobalt-blue UNDERGLAZE. In China the blue color was painted on the unfired ware, then covered with a feldspathic GLAZE and fired once. In Europe in the eighteenth century SOFT-PASTE porcelains were fired to BISCUIT, painted, covered with a clear LEAD GLAZE, and then refired. [60, 118, 119, 123–125, 128, 130]

Burnished a smooth, semi-lustrous surface achieved by rubbing a clay vessel when leather hard with an object like a pebble or metal tool. [2, 88]

Celadon a gray-green STONEWARE GLAZE. Derived from iron and ranging in color from putty to sea-green, it is applied before firing in a reducing atmosphere. Principally found on Chinese wares (e.g., Yüeh [91, 92, 100] and Lung-ch'üan [109, 121]), it was also used in Korea [137–141] and Japan.

Champlevé a decorative technique in which large areas of SLIP are carved away to produce broad patterns. Both the technique and the French term are derived from enamelwork. [30]

Crackle a deliberate CRAZING of a GLAZE to produce a decorative effect. It is caused by the different rates of contraction of the glaze and the body, and was developed in China during the Sung Dynasty (960–1280) in *kuan* ware [110, 111]. The cracks vary from the large "crab claw" variety to those reminiscent of fish scales. [106]

Crazing a GLAZE defect characterized by a network of fine cracks. Crazing usually occurs upon coating when the glaze has a tendency to contract more than the body. [93, 97]

Earthenware an opaque, non-vitreous, low-fired (below 1100° C) pottery. Fired clay is porous unless sealed by a covering GLAZE. [1–4, 6, 11–28, 35–50, 76–78, 80–89, 96–99]

Enamel See OVERGLAZE ENAMEL.

Faience a term which refers to two different types of ceramics. One is a TIN-GLAZED EARTHENWARE, usually that made in France, Germany, and Scandinavia. The French term is derived from the Italian town of Faenza, which produced popular wares of the same technique in the sixteenth century. [59, 65] Cf. MAIOLICA. For a description of the other type of faience produced in the ancient Near East and Egypt, see [5, 7–10].

Flux an additive used to reduce the melting point of other ingredients in GLAZES. Common fluxes are ASH and SALT. They can also be added to the clay body or to the ENAMEL decoration.

Glaze a mixture largely of oxides used to coat the surface of ceramics which fuses with the clay body when fired. The glaze serves both a practical function in sealing porous bodies, especially EARTHENWARE, and an aesthetic one in providing color and texture.

Grog filler made from pulverized fired pottery. It is blended with clays to add texture, to reduce shrinkage, or to minimize warping in the completed vessel. [148]

Hard-paste high-fired (over 1450° C.) PORCELAIN. Also called true porcelain as opposed to SOFT-PASTE porcelain. [67, 68, 74, 75, 101, 103, 107–111, 118–136, 142, 151–164]

Impasto a technique of decorating EARTHENWARE in which a thick coat of SLIP is applied to the extent that a low relief is built up. Examples of impasto include the blue of early Florentine MAIOLICA [40] or Armenian red of Isnik wares [34].

Kaolin pure clay, containing very little iron impurity and therefore white. An essential ingredient of PORCELAIN, it is also called "China clay."

Lead glaze a transparent GLAZE in which lead oxide is used as the principal FLUX. [23, 24, 30, 35, 36, 52–54, 97–99]

Lustre a metallic decoration applied over the glazed surface of pottery. [25–28, 38, 39, 49, 76]

Maiolica TIN-GLAZED EARTHENWARE made in Italy. The term (also majolica) is derived from the island of Majorca which lay on the trade route between Italy and Spain, the source of many imported lustrewares. [40–50, 58]

Overglaze enamel color derived from metallic oxides which is applied over the GLAZE on a vessel which is then refired at a relatively low temperature. Enamels have a much wider range of color than UNDERGLAZE decoration. [126, 127, 136, 151–163]

Pâte-sur-pâte a technique of relief decoration on PORCELAIN resulting from the successive application of layers of white SLIP. Details in the delicate low relief are often carved. [75]

Peach-bloom a reduced copper GLAZE of pink mottled with deeper red, with occasional flecks of green or brown. It was developed in China during the reign of K'ang Hsi (1662–1722). [134]

Petuntse a feldspathic rock, which along with KAOLIN is an essential ingredient of PORCELAIN. A fusible rock, petuntse gives porcelain its hardness and translucency. The term is a gallicized form of the Chinese *pai-tun-tzu* ("white-bricks").

Porcelain a high-fired (1450°C) ceramic ware composed of a refractory white clay (KAOLIN) and a feldspathic rock (PETUNTSE), which becomes very hard, vitreous, and translucent after firing.

Raku a form of LEAD-GLAZED EARTHENWARE originating in Japan (ca. AD 1525). The spontaneity of the technique makes raku ware unusual. The prefired BISCUIT is glazed and placed in the red-hot kiln where the GLAZE matures in a very short time, resulting in accidental flaws and imperfections which are highly prized. [150]

Red-figure a decorative style of Greek pottery invented in 530 BC. The opposite of BLACK-FIGURE, the decoration is left in reserve, while the background is covered with SLIP which becomes shiny black in the firing process. Interior details such as musculature are drawn with thin lines of slip. [15, 17–19]

Salt-glaze a method of glazing STONEWARE in which common salt is thrown into the kiln when the temperature reaches 1000°C. The sodium combines with the silicates of the body of the ware to form a thin glassy glaze. [55, 56]

Sagger (or seggar) a box of fired clay used to protect wares during firing from the direct action of the flame or kiln atmosphere. [100, 103, 106]

Sang-de-boeuf a brilliant red GLAZE colored by copper oxide which is fired in a reducing atmosphere. Also known as "oxblood." [133]

Sgraffito an Italian term (also *sgraffiato*) describing decoration made by scratching or incising through the SLIP to reveal the contrasting body color underneath. [35, 36]

Slip clay mixed with water to a creamy consistency, used as a decorative medium. [11–22, 115]

Soft-paste a low-fired (1200°C) form of PORCELAIN. Also called artificial porcelain. [51, 60–64, 66, 69, 70, 73]

Stoneware a type of pottery made from clay mixed with a pulverized fusible stone which vitrifies into a coating during firing. This vitrification makes stoneware impervious to liquids rendering a GLAZE unnecessary, although the surface is often given a SALT or LEAD GLAZE to enhance its appearance. In terms of firing temperature (1200–1300° C) stoneware lies midway between EARTHENWARE and PORCELAIN. [55–57, 90–95, 105, 106, 112–117, 143–149]

Tea ceremony a traditional Japanese ceremony related to the drinking of tea for which special wares are used. It is presided over by a Tea Master who selects the appropriate utensils on the basis of tradition and subtle aesthetic considerations. [144–147, 149]

Temmoku a Japanese term (also *tenmoku*) applied to the deep, rich black-glazed STONEWARES made in China during the Sung Dynasty (960–1280). The cups and bowls were sought by the Japanese for use in their TEA CEREMONY. The GLAZE has a characteristic tendency to shade into a brownish rust where it thins, and hence is called "hare's fur." [112, 113]

Terracotta a fired, but usually unglazed, EARTHENWARE. Terracotta is often used by sculptors to form or mold figurines and reliefs. [79, 165–167]

Tin-glaze a GLAZE made opaque and white by the addition of tin oxide. It is usually applied to EARTHENWARE, namely FAIENCE and MAIOLICA, where it forms the white background. [40–50, 59]

Underglaze decoration or marking of any kind applied to the body of a ceramic ware before glazing. The decorated ware is usually subsequently covered with a transparent GLAZE. The range of underglaze colors is restricted to those able to withstand the firing temperature of the glaze and so is more limited than OVERGLAZE ENAMEL. [51, 59, 60, 101–103, 122–128, 150, 154–155, 164]

White-ground a decorative style of Greek pottery in which the body of the vase is covered with a white SLIP over which the decoration is painted. [16]